SLOW T

Norfolk

Local, characterful guides to Britain's special places

Laurence Mitchell

EDITION 3

Bradt Guides Ltd, UK
The Globe Pequot Press Inc, USA

Third edition published March 2023
First published March 2014
Bradt Guides Ltd
31a High Street, Chesham, Buckinghamshire, HP5 1BW, England
www.bradtguides.com
Print edition published in the USA by The Globe Pequot Press Inc,
PO Box 480, Guilford, Connecticut 06437-0480

Text copyright © 2023 Bradt Guides Ltd
Maps copyright © 2023 Bradt Guides Ltd; includes map data © OpenStreetMap contributors
Photographs copyright © 2023 Individual photographers (see below)
Project Manager: Emma Gibbs
Cover research: Pepi Bluck

ISBN: 9781804690116

British Library Cataloguing in Publication Data
A catalogue record for this book is available from the British Library

Photographs
© individual photographers credited beside images & also those from picture libraries
credited as follows: Alamy.com (A); Shutterstock.com (S); Superstock.com (SS)

Front cover St Benet's, Norfolk Broads (Tom Mackie/AWL)
Back cover The village of Blakeney (Helen Hotson/S)
Title page Holme Dunes (Richard Osbourne)

Maps David McCutcheon FBCart.S
Typeset by Pepi Bluck, Perfect Picture
Production managed by Zenith Media; printed in the UK
Digital conversion by www.dataworks.co.in

AUTHOR

Laurence Mitchell has at various times worked as an English teacher in Sudan, surveyed farm buildings in Norfolk, pushed a pen in a local government office and taught geography in a rural secondary school. Having finally settled for the uncertain life of a freelance travel writer and photographer, he specialises in places firmly off the beaten track like the Balkans and Central Asia when not wandering  around his home patch of East Anglia. As well as writing walking guides and several travel guides for Bradt, his work has appeared in publications like *Geographical*, *Walk*, *Discover Britain*, *Wild Travel* and *hidden europe*. Laurence is a member of the Outdoor Writers and Photographers Guild. He is also the author of *Westering*, a lyrical account of a slow coast-to-coast walk between East Anglia and Wales. His blog can be found at ⌀ eastofelveden.wordpress.com.

ACKNOWLEDGEMENTS

My sincere thanks go to all the team at Bradt, in particular, Anna Moores, Sue Cooper, Emma Gibbs, Claire Strange and Jennifer Wildman. Thanks are due to those who contributed boxes – Penny Edwards, Donald Greig, Poppy Mathews and Andrew Paxton. My gratitude also goes to those individuals who made suggestions, provided food for thought or were good enough to answer my questions – Annie Bird, Jason Borthwick, John Hiskett, Danielle Howard, Sheila Rattray, Caroline Davison and David Vince. Thanks go too to Wendy Ellis of Boydell & Brewer for permission to quote from John Seymour's *Companion Guide to East Anglia*, and to Henry Head at Norfolk Lavender. For this third edition I would also like to thank Sara Hollowell and Graham Curtis for further feedback. As always, I also owe gratitude to my wife Jackie for her unstinting support throughout.

CONTENTS

SUGGESTED PLACES TO BASE YOURSELF

These bases make ideal starting points for exploring localities the Slow way.

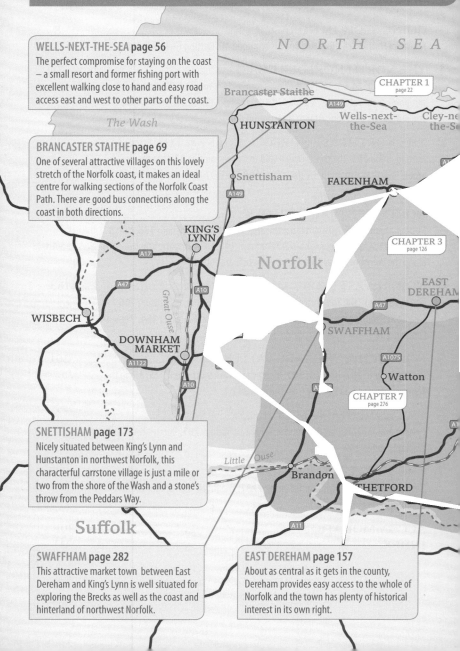

WELLS-NEXT-THE-SEA page 56
The perfect compromise for staying on the coast – a small resort and former fishing port with excellent walking close to hand and easy road access east and west to other parts of the coast.

BRANCASTER STAITHE page 69
One of several attractive villages on this lovely stretch of the Norfolk coast, it makes an ideal centre for walking sections of the Norfolk Coast Path. There are good bus connections along the coast in both directions.

SNETTISHAM page 173
Nicely situated between King's Lynn and Hunstanton in northwest Norfolk, this characterful carrstone village is just a mile or two from the shore of the Wash and a stone's throw from the Peddars Way.

SWAFFHAM page 282
This attractive market town between East Dereham and King's Lynn is well situated for exploring the Brecks as well as the coast and hinterland of northwest Norfolk.

EAST DEREHAM page 157
About as central as it gets in the county, Dereham provides easy access to the whole of Norfolk and the town has plenty of historical interest in its own right.

NORTH SEA

The Wash

Brancaster Staithe

Wells-next-the-Sea

Cley-ne the-Se

HUNSTANTON

CHAPTER 1
page 22

Snettisham

FAKENHAM

KING'S LYNN

Norfolk

CHAPTER 3
page 126

EAST DEREHAM

WISBECH

Great Ouse

SWAFFHAM

Watton

DOWNHAM MARKET

A1075

CHAPTER 7
page 276

Little Ouse

Brandon

THETFORD

Suffolk

A149

A17

A47

A10

A1122

A10

A11

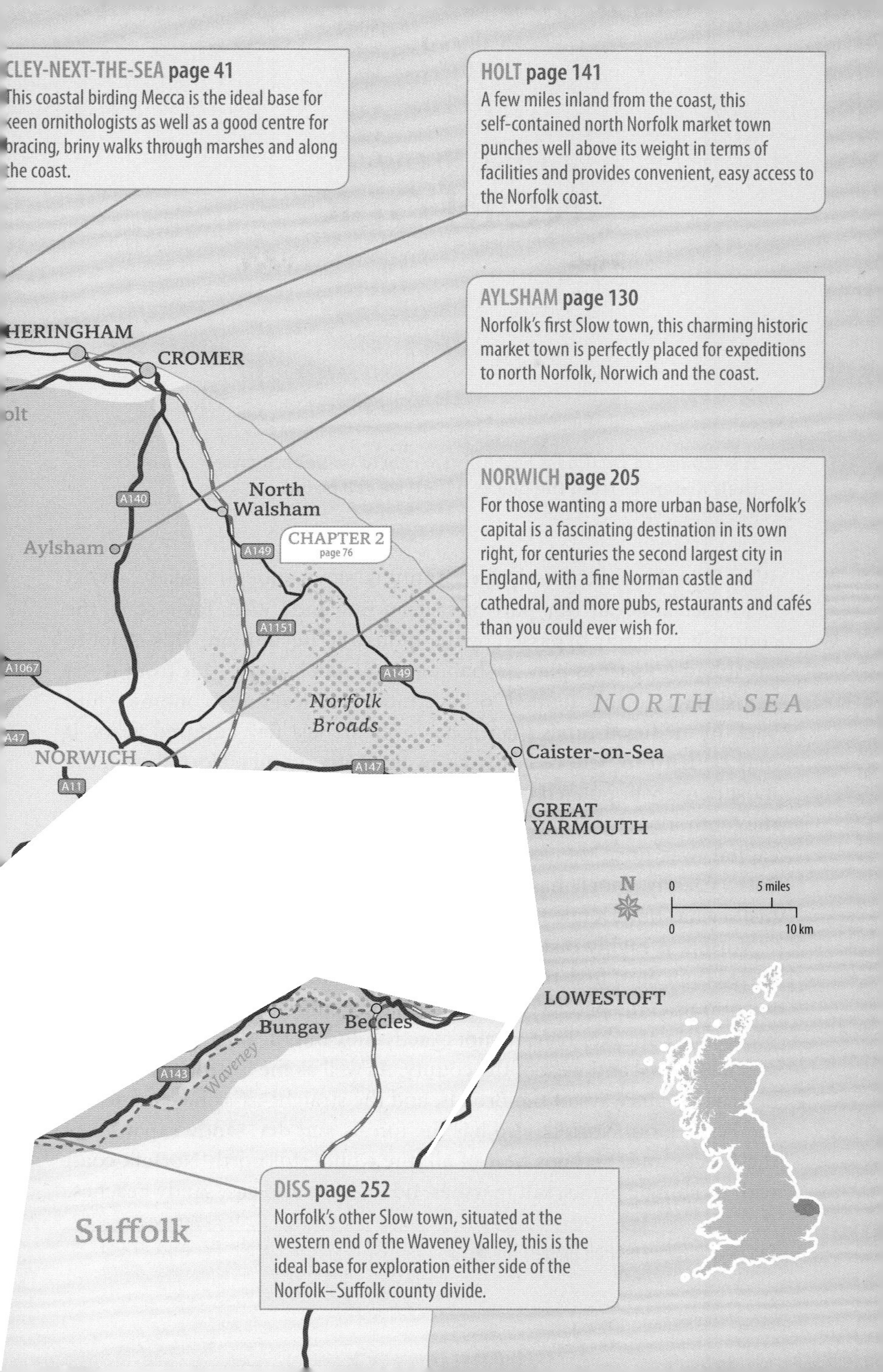

HERINGHAM
CROMER
olt
A140
North Walsham
CHAPTER 2
page 76
Aylsham
A149
A1151
A1067
A149
Norfolk Broads
NORTH SEA
A47
NORWICH
A147
A11
Caister-on-Sea
GREAT YARMOUTH
N
0
5 miles
0
10 km
LOWESTOFT
Bungay
Beccles
A143
Waveney
Suffolk

CLEY-NEXT-THE-SEA page 41
This coastal birding Mecca is the ideal base for keen ornithologists as well as a good centre for bracing, briny walks through marshes and along the coast.

HOLT page 141
A few miles inland from the coast, this self-contained north Norfolk market town punches well above its weight in terms of facilities and provides convenient, easy access to the Norfolk coast.

AYLSHAM page 130
Norfolk's first Slow town, this charming historic market town is perfectly placed for expeditions to north Norfolk, Norwich and the coast.

NORWICH page 205
For those wanting a more urban base, Norfolk's capital is a fascinating destination in its own right, for centuries the second largest city in England, with a fine Norman castle and cathedral, and more pubs, restaurants and cafés than you could ever wish for.

DISS page 252
Norfolk's other Slow town, situated at the western end of the Waveney Valley, this is the ideal base for exploration either side of the Norfolk–Suffolk county divide.

NORFOLK

It is a piece of weakness and folly merely to value things because of
their distances from the places where we call home.
Martin Martin, 1697

Why Slow Norfolk? Surely the county is 'slow' enough already? What
is so special about this part of eastern England? Well, for a start, the
county was largely bypassed by the Industrial Revolution. This is not to
say it had no part to play in shaping England's history – far from it – it
is just that Norfolk tended to have more political and economic clout
back in medieval times than it has over the last few hundred years. It
may be hard to believe but back in the 16th century Norfolk was the
most densely populated county in all Britain; nowadays, the county has
the tenth lowest population density in the country. Norwich, Norfolk's
capital, was once the second largest city in England; now it ranks as
26th. Clearly, much has changed since medieval times but Norfolk's
history has quite a tale to tell.

Norfolk is highly distinguished in terms of geography, too, and more
varied than most first-time visitors imagine it to be. In fact, there is much
to contradict the perceived wisdom that the entire county is as flat as the
proverbial pancake. True, it's not exactly hilly but the only truly flat areas
are the far east and west of the county. As well as the lustrous lakes, reed
beds and waterways of the Broads, and the straight-as-a-die channels of
the Fen region, Norfolk also has the forests and dry, sandy expanses of
the Brecks and, perhaps best of all, the wonderful north Norfolk coast
with its shingle banks, salt marshes, tidal creeks and vast sandy beaches.

The *Electric Eel* water trail (page 110). ▶

Connecting these disparate landscapes is a countryside filled with rolling farmland, tracts of ancient woodland, meandering rivers and hundreds of villages, each with its church. It may be a wealth of villages that make the county what it is, each a self-contained microcosm of rural life. As Reginald Pound, the author of *Scott of the Antarctic*, wrote, '(Norfolk) is littered with villages but uncluttered by towns'. But there are towns too, and by and large they are also handsome and distinctive.

As a rule, the built landscape reflects that which is found immediately beneath the surface: in the east of the county, thatch roofs and flint walls prevail; in the west, carrstone and chalk. Similarly, land use also depends on the soil and drainage of the area: the fertile black soil in the Fens of the west, the arable crops that thrive on the light land of north Norfolk, the sheep and cattle that predominate on the heavy clays of the south, and swathes of conifer forestry in the Brecks where sheep ranges and rabbit warrens once used to abound.

There is a common contention that Norfolk is forever a step behind the rest of the country; that it lies out on a limb at the end of a road to nowhere. And there is still sometimes a slightly sneering metropolitan view that the county is nice enough to visit but 'you wouldn't want to live there'. As for the people who do live here, 'Normal for Norfolk' remains a common jibe. It's good to see this expression being deconstructed and adopted in a non-pejorative sense as a slogan by World Class Norfolk, an enterprise that promotes business investment in the county. Of course, the fact that Norfolk remains one of just a few English counties without a motorway leading to it may be seen as an obstacle to progress by some. Others, though, see this as a virtue. Motorways and 'Slow' are not generally ideal partners.

I first came to Norfolk over four decades ago to attend university. I went away for a year or two but I have pretty well based myself here since then, mostly in Norwich but also for a few years in south Norfolk. It has been a slow burn of appreciation. To be honest, it took a while for the subtle charms of the region to grow on me. Birdwatching on the north Norfolk coast and in the Broads got me out and about in the region, as did a bit of cycling around my own patch in Norwich and south Norfolk. Then, in the mid 1980s, I got a job as team leader on a project that was carrying out an extensive survey of farm buildings and agricultural practices in Norfolk. This got me interested in vernacular architecture and the way that the rural landscape had been shaped by

THE SLOW MINDSET

Hilary Bradt, Founder, Bradt Travel Guides

**We shall not cease from exploration
And the end of all our exploring
Will be to arrive where we started
And know the place for the first time.**

T S Eliot, 'Little Gidding', *Four Quartets*

This series evolved, slowly, from a Bradt editorial meeting when we started to explore ideas for guides to our favourite part of the world – Great Britain. We wanted to get away from the usual 'top sights' formula and encourage our authors to bring out the nuances and local differences that make up a sense of place – such things as food, building styles, nature, geology or local people and what makes them tick. Our aim was to create a series that celebrates the present, focusing on sustainable tourism, rather than taking a nostalgic wallow in the past.

So without our realising it at the time, we had defined 'Slow Travel', or at least our concept of it. For the beauty of the Slow Movement is that there is no fixed definition; we adapt the philosophy to fit our individual needs and aspirations. Thus Carl Honoré, author of *In Praise of Slow*, writes: 'The Slow Movement is a cultural revolution against the notion that faster is always better. It's not about doing everything at a snail's pace, it's about seeking to do everything at the right speed. Savouring the hours and minutes rather than just counting them. Doing everything as well as possible, instead of as fast as possible. It's about quality over quantity in everything from work to food to parenting.' And travel.

So take time to explore. Don't rush it, get to know an area – and the people who live there – and you'll be as delighted as the authors by what you find.

farming and feudalism. I interviewed many north Norfolk farmers as part of this work and some of these were just old enough to remember working with horses.

Even just 35 years ago, things were different. Large-scale agribusiness had not taken such a firm hold and the majority of the farms were family-run, 200-acre affairs that, besides mechanisation, were not managed all that differently from the way they had been in the inter-war period. Memories of many of the farms I visited have blurred with the passing of time but I vividly recall one small and rather old-fashioned place near North Walsham, more of a large smallholding than anything else, which was lovingly farmed by a wonderful old couple. After I had

looked around, the farmer gave me a mug of tea and took me to one side, 'Some people might cart right across the world looking for beautiful scenery but we are blessed, we've got it right here.' He gazed across a dung-covered farmyard alive with feeding swallows, past a rickety old barn to the fields beyond. 'Have a look at that view, will you? Have you ever seen anything better than that? Me and the missus never go on holiday and we've never been abroad either. What's the point when you've got all this on your doorstep?' I didn't have the slightest doubt about his sincerity – and he was absolutely right, it was a lovely view in a bucolic, John Constable sort of way. He was a wise and happy man, this old farmer; perhaps the perfect ambassador of what the Slow outlook is all about.

Hamish Fulton, whose art results from the experience of walking, once staged an exhibition entitled *An Object Cannot Compete with an Experience*. It's a mantra that stands me in good stead. The Slow movement is all about savouring the moment. A good meal taken slowly is an experience, so is a long walk with never-to-be forgotten views. So is a conversation that gives you an insight into someone else's life and celebrates a shared humanity. It's about a sense of being where you are, what makes it special, what makes it unique.

While I was researching the first edition of this book, I was fortunate to attend a talk by the writer Richard Mabey who was discussing the paintings of Mary Newcomb, a recently deceased local artist whose works were on display in a special exhibition at Norwich Castle Museum. Mary Newcomb's gloriously naive, almost Zen-like, paintings, along with Richard Mabey's insightful appraisal, helped me realise that an appreciation of the subtle beauty of rural East Anglia depends on having an eye for detail and a fondness for the drama of small events. Perhaps that is what the essence of Slow is: finding the extraordinary in the commonplace – that which makes a place distinctive, the unique patina of time and custom that makes somewhere special. Everywhere has these qualities to some extent; it is just that, in terms of distinctiveness, Norfolk probably has more than its fair share. Let's not get carried away, there are places here as humdrum as anywhere else but the thing to do is to scrape away the veneer a little and see what is beneath.

◀ 1 The Weavers' Way. 2 Canoeing on the River Waveney. 3 Wise advice on a local sign.
4 The North Norfolk Heritage Railway at Holt.

People who have close contact with the land generally know this. The Northamptonshire shepherd poet John Clare, who modestly and perhaps disingenuously claimed, 'I found the poems in the fields, and only wrote them down', extolled the spirit of Slow when he wrote:

O who can pass such lovely spots
Without a wish to stray
And leave life's cares a while forgot
To muse an hour away?

I hope this book will help to inspire some happy musing.

A TASTE OF NORFOLK

With something like 90 miles of North Sea coastline it is hardly surprising that Norfolk has a wealth of seafood to savour. Probably the most highly regarded are the Cromer crabs (page 28) that are caught just off the north Norfolk coast. There are plenty of lobsters and shellfish too, the most famous being 'Stewkey Blues' (page 53) – a type of cockle – and tasty fresh mussels from Brancaster. The wet fish options are also excellent; cod and haddock especially, and herring too, a nutritious and plentiful fish for which the port of Great Yarmouth was once world-famous (page 239). Several smokehouses around the coast, like the one at Cley-next-the-Sea (page 47), make good use of such provenance and produce all manner of delicious goods like kippers and smoked mackerel.

To complement your seafood you may wish to try a seasonal favourite, marsh samphire (page 52), a salty delicacy that grows in abundance in the saltmarshes of north Norfolk in the summer months.

For committed carnivores Norfolk meat is a treat too, especially that which comes from some of the county's rare breed varieties, like beef from Red Poll cattle. Many Norfolk restaurants make use of locally reared meat on their menus, but the county also has a large number of farm shops and farmers' markets where such products can be purchased for home consumption.

---

1 The Fur and Feathers pub, in Woodbastwick. 2 Seafood for sale in Blakeney.
3 Local produce on sale, Cley-next-the-Sea. ▶

VISITNORFOLK.CO.UK

NICHOLAS SIMON JACKSON/S

With a relatively dry climate and a tendency towards arable, Norfolk is not really much of a place for dairy farming, but the county does produce a number of cheeses with a distinctive local flavour. Probably the best known are those made by Mrs Temple's Cheeses at Wighton in north Norfolk, especially Binham Blue, which is made with vegetarian rennet and milk from British Holstein cows.

Vegetarians are well provided for as a rule: the county has a wealth of fresh vegetables and there are a number of organic providers, too. A decent number of restaurants also specialise in, or serve only, vegetarian food. This is particularly true of Norwich, the county capital. Asparagus is one of the county's specialities, abundant in early summer, especially in those areas that have light, sandy soil.

NORFOLK TIPPLES

Contrary to expectation, Norfolk actually has a few vineyards – some of the most northerly in the country – one of which has produced prize-winning wines (page 226). Overall, however, it is probably fair to say that the county is better celebrated for its beer. Norfolk has a plethora of small-scale real ale breweries scattered around the county – Woodforde's (page 117) from Woodbastwick, Lacons from Great Yarmouth, Wolf from Besthorpe, Yetman's from Holt and Humpty Dumpty from Reedham, to name just a few. If these are not enough to quench your thirst then there are always Adnams, Green Jack or St Peter's Brewery ales from over the Suffolk border.

Surprisingly, perhaps, the county is also a whisky producer, with the St George's Distillery (page 293) distilling a range of hand-crafted whiskies conjured from Norfolk barley and deep aquifer water at its base in Roudham in the Brecks.

HOW THIS BOOK IS ARRANGED

This book divides Norfolk into seven fairly distinct geographical areas starting with the north Norfolk coast and ending with the Brecks in the southwest of the county. *Chapter 1* covers the north Norfolk coast and its immediate hinterland between Cromer in the east and Holme-next-the-Sea in the west. This coincides to a large extent with the boundary of the Norfolk Coast Area of Outstanding Natural Beauty. *Chapter 2* deals with the northeast coast between Overstrand and Caister-on-Sea as well as the Norfolk Broads that lies inland. *Chapter 3* (North Central Norfolk) covers the area south of the north Norfolk coast and west of the Broads as far as the Fakenham area to the west and East Dereham to the south. *Chapter 4* includes the rest of the Norfolk coast that faces west across the Wash as well as the borderland Fen region, while *Chapter 5* covers the River Yare valley from west of Norwich to the coast and includes both the county capital and Norfolk's second largest settlement, Great Yarmouth. *Chapter 6* covers that part of south Norfolk that lies close to the border with Suffolk along the course of the River Waveney, while *Chapter 7* includes Thetford and the area west and north of it as far as Swaffham. Both of the last two chapters make occasional short forays across the border into Suffolk.

MAPS

Each chapter begins with a map with **numbered stopping points** that correspond to numbered headings in the text. The featured walks have maps accompanying them.

Norfolk is a large county and requires a total of seven 1:50,000, Landranger OS maps to cover it fully. One very useful map to have is the double-sided 1:25,000, scale OS Explorer OL40 The Broads map, which shows much interesting detail and has plenty of walker- and cyclist-friendly information. Similarly, the three 1:25,000 OS Explorer maps of the Norfolk coast (West 250, Central 251 and East 252) are a boon to walkers or anyone with an interest in exploring the geographical and historical features of the area.

FOOD & DRINK

I've listed some of my favourite pubs, cafés, tea rooms and places to eat, favouring those places that serve local produce or are worth a visit for some other reason, such as appealing quirkiness or distinctive character.

ACCOMMODATION

Accommodation has been recommended on the basis of location and because it embraces a Slow approach either in its 'green' ethos or its overall feel. Hotels and B&Bs are indicated by the symbol 🏠 after town and village headings, self-catering options by 🏠 and campsites by ▲, with a cross-reference to the full listing under Accommodation, page 308. For full descriptions of these listings, visit 🖉 bradtguides.com/norfolksleeps.

GETTING THERE & AROUND

Cycling and walking are the ideal methods of Slow travel. I'd like to encourage people to **visit without a car** but I appreciate that this can be difficult in some parts of Norfolk, particularly in those areas of the county that lie well away from the primary routes. Details of how best to get around are given in each chapter. Below is a brief overview and suggestions of how to reach Norfolk from other parts of the country.

A useful website for **planning journeys by bus or train**, or a combination of the two, is ⊘ traveline.info.

TRAINS

There are regular rail services between Norwich and Great Yarmouth, Norwich and Cromer, and Norwich and Cambridge via Thetford. Norwich is connected to London by direct trains from Liverpool Street station and to the Midlands and North by means of a change at Peterborough or Ely. Direct trains that stop at Manchester, Sheffield, Derby and Nottingham also run between Norwich and Liverpool. King's Lynn can be reached by direct trains from London via Cambridge and Ely. Within Norfolk, there are also short preserved **heritage railways** like the Mid-Norfolk Railway between Wymondham and East Dereham, and the North Norfolk Railway between Sheringham and Holt, as well as narrow gauge lines that connect Wells with Walsingham and Wroxham with Aylsham.

BUS & COACH

Norwich has regular long-distance coach services with National Express that connect the city with London, the major airports and other cities around the country. Several bus companies provide routes within the county, most notably First Eastern Counties, Konectbus, Lynx, Stagecoach, BorderBus, Simonds and Sanders Coaches. Bus travel details for a locality are given at the beginning of each chapter.

WALKING

Norfolk abounds with walking potential, from linear coastal strolls to circular walks through forest and open farmland. As well as walking suggestions made at the beginning of each chapter a number of personal favourites are offered throughout the book together with a sketch map and directions for the walk. Walking in Norfolk is rarely very demanding thanks to the reasonably flat topography. The going is mostly easy and so walkers just need to decide how far they are prepared to walk if attempting a route. Any obstacles, such as they are, are limited to nuisances like overgrown nettles, hungry mosquitoes, obstructing herds of cows or the occasional recalcitrant bull. Otherwise, it's ideal, especially when a walk takes in a country pub and/or an interesting village church to explore en route.

Several notable **long-distance paths** run through the county. The best known of these is the **Peddars Way** between Knettishall Heath near Thetford and Holme-next-the-Sea close to Hunstanton. This route connects with the **Norfolk Coast Path** to continue to Cromer and along Norfolk's northeast coast to Hopton-on-Sea. Cromer is also the start of the **Weavers' Way**, which meanders through the Broads to finish at Great Yarmouth, where another route, the **Angles Way**, leads back to Thetford using paths on both sides of the River Waveney and the Norfolk–Suffolk border. As well as these routes that combine together to effectively circumambulate the county there is another succession of routes – **Wherryman's Way**, **Marriott's Way**, **Wensum Way** and **Nar Valley Way** – that connect together to pass through the middle of Norfolk linking Great Yarmouth with King's Lynn. Lesser routes in the county include the **Tas Valley Way**, **Boudicca Way** and **Kett's Country**, all in south Norfolk, and the **Paston Way** in the Broads. For a useful overview of the various walking options in Norfolk on offer, consult the Norfolk Trails website at ⊘ norfolk.gov.uk/out-and-about-in-norfolk/norfolk-trails.

FEEDBACK REQUEST

At Bradt Guides we're aware that guidebooks start to go out of date on the day they're published – and that you, our readers, are out there in the field doing research of your own. You'll find out before us when a fine new family-run hotel opens or a favourite restaurant changes hands and goes downhill. So why not tell us about your experiences? Contact us on ✆ 01753 893444 or ✉ info@bradtguides.com. We will forward emails to the author who may post updates on the Bradt website at ⊘ bradtguides.com/updates. Alternatively, you can add a review of the book to Amazon, or share your adventures with us on social:

🖪 BradtGuides 🗩 BradtGuides 🖸 BradtGuides & eastofelveden

CYCLING

Norfolk has plenty to offer cyclists, from quiet country lanes and disused railway lines to off-road routes that follow bridleways and forest tracks. Details of suggested routes and areas with good potential for cycling are outlined at the start of each chapter, as are local outlets for cycle hire. The website ✐ cycle-route.com has many good suggestions for routes in the county. For off-road cycling probably the best part of the county to head for is the Brecks, where a large number of routes criss-cross Thetford Forest.

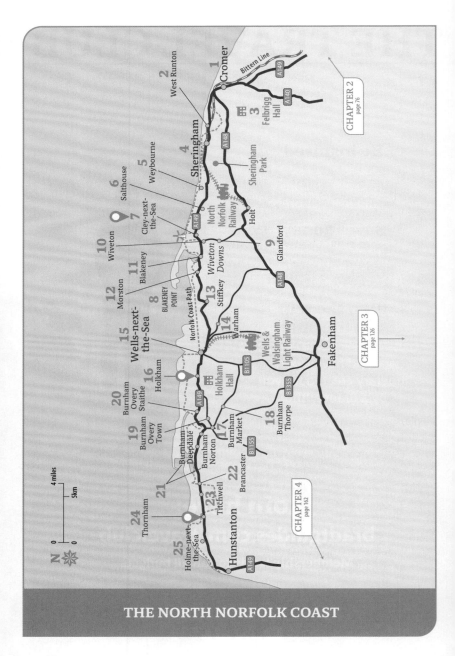

THE NORTH NORFOLK COAST

1
THE NORTH NORFOLK COAST

From the slightly faded Victorian resort of **Cromer** to the village of **Holme-next-the-Sea**, the north Norfolk coast stretches resplendently east to west (which is how this chapter is ordered): a classic landscape of wide beaches, salt marshes, offshore sandbanks, muddy tidal inlets and all-too-rare harbours. This is the Norfolk that most city-dwellers hanker after: big skies, golden beaches and neat pebble-built cottages; mewing gulls and fishing boats beached in the mud. This stretch of coastline is quite unlike any other place in the United Kingdom, and has been designated an AONB (Area of Outstanding Natural Beauty). The icing on the cake is that there are even some modest hills here, with Beacon Hill near Cromer – 345ft high – marking the highest point of the ridge where the southbound glaciations of the last Ice Age finally gave up the ghost as they deposited chunks of Scandinavia and North Sea seabed on Norfolk soil.

In spring, the road verges are emerald green with alexanders, a plant related to celery (of which it tastes strongly) that is particularly abundant at the coast and was recently considered for selection as the county flower of Norfolk. Predictably, the powers that be chose the poppy instead – a safe, if less representative, choice. In summer, the saltings glow purple with large swathes of sea lavender, and, with bright blue skies, the coastal marshes become an Impressionist painting of sea, sand and sky. Autumn brings waves of migrating birds, and the bushes twitch with freshly landed migrants at this time of year, as do the salt marshes where exotic waders feed cheek by jowl much to the delight of birdwatchers. In winter, the sky is often alive with noisy flocks of geese in their thousands. In fact, if you can put up with onshore wind that seems to hail directly from the Arctic, a bright, crisp winter's day is hard to beat for a bracing walk along the seashore followed by lunch in a cosy pub.

With a range of distinct habitats for wildlife that include salt marshes, sand dunes, pebble banks, reed beds and woodland, it is hardly surprising that birds – even some rarities – are found everywhere, and that conservation bodies like the RSPB and NWT (Norfolk Wildlife Trust) have several reserves along this coast, as does the National Trust. In fact, **Cley-next-the-Sea**, a village with the vast **NWT Cley Marshes Nature Reserve** of salt marshes and reed beds, has long been considered one of the best sites for birding in the entire UK. Seals are easy to see too, and a boat trip out among them is invariably a hit with visitors of all ages.

This coast is largely a place of small fishing villages that have turned, in part at least, to tourism. Flint and pebble rules supreme, with whole villages – houses, pubs, churches, even bus shelters – constructed out of these plentiful beach materials. It's almost a surprise that public phone boxes aren't made out of them – since public conveniences generally are.

GETTING AROUND
PUBLIC TRANSPORT

This is better than you might think – far better than the dire situation a few decades ago when travelling along the coast required either a car or a willingness to hitchhike. Thankfully, the excellent and convenient **Bittern Line** (∂ bitternline.com) links Norwich with Cromer and Sheringham on the coast. A **Bittern Ranger ticket** entitles unlimited travel at weekends and any time after 08.15 Mondays to Fridays, and for a small supplement, unlimited travel on the Coasthopper bus service between Mundesley and Wells and the Coastliner 36 service between Wells and Hunstanton. Trains run more or less hourly during the daytime and evenings Monday to Saturday, with a slightly reduced service on Sundays.

The Bittern Line connects with the useful **Coasthopper** bus service that runs hourly between Cromer, Sheringham and Wells. This connects with the Coastliner 36 that runs along the coast road between Wells and King's Lynn. Both services call at each village along the way as well as stopping on request – very useful indeed for walks along the coast. Easy connections can be made between King's Lynn, and Cambridge by rail. King's Lynn is not connected to Norwich by rail but there is a direct X1 bus service via Swaffham, which takes a couple of hours.

Coasthopper and Coastliner drivers are generally excellent ambassadors for the north Norfolk coast and are courteous and helpful in the extreme, so if you are unsure as to where to get off, just ask.

As well as the Bittern Line, there are a couple of short-distance, privately owned heritage railway lines that, while tourist-oriented, can sometimes come in useful for getting about. The **North Norfolk Railway** (✆ 01263 820800 ⌂ nnrailway.co.uk; page 38), also known as the '**Poppy Line**', runs between Sheringham and Holt and the **Wells and Walsingham Light Railway** (✆ 01328 711630 ⌂ wwlr.co.uk) plies the eight miles between Wells-next-the Sea and Little Walsingham.

WALKING

Exploring on foot can be sublime along this stretch of coast. It's flat certainly, but here you'll find some of the best marsh and coast walking anywhere in the country. And away from the coast, three magnificent estates have free year-round access for walkers, with lots to look at: **Felbrigg**, **Holkham** and **Sheringham Park**.

The **Norfolk Coast Path**, which links to the **Peddars Way** at Holme-next-the-Sea before meandering 44 miles eastwards to Cromer, takes in nearly all of the best bits: the whole thing, known rather clumsily as the Peddars Way & Norfolk Coast Path, is a National Trail, with the route shown with acorn markers. Since 2016 the coast path has been extended to follow the northeast Norfolk coast as far as Hopton-on-Sea at the Suffolk border south of Great Yarmouth. Quite a lot of the coastal portion leads along grassy sea walls that zigzag between drained grazing land (much of it drained by Coke of Holkham, the agricultural pioneer) and vast expanses of seemingly impenetrable salt marsh cut by countless creeks and gulleys. Sections of the Peddars Way and Norfolk Coast Path make for excellent day walks, although circular walks will sometimes entail a stretch along the busy A149 coast road, which is

NORTH NORFOLK COAST WALKING HIGHLIGHTS

- **Cromer to Sheringham**, following the Norfolk Coast Path, which ventures inland to take in some modest hills and Norfolk's highest point. Returning from Sheringham, you can either take the train or bus back or walk along the beach beneath the cliff.
- **Blakeney to Cley-next-the-Sea**, following the North Coast Path, taking the dyke out through the marshes to Cley Channel before heading inland towards Cley village along the bank of the River Glaven.
- **Cley-next-the-Sea to Salthouse**, alternating between the beach and sea wall.
- **Burnham Overy Staithe to Holkham Gap**, walking along the dyke and beach, then returning by bus. You can extend the walk through the Holkham Estate, across fields to Burnham Overy Town, and back.
- **Burnham Deepdale to Burnham Overy Staithe**, along the dyke, returning by bus.
- **Holme-next-the-Sea to Thornham**, following the North Coast Path along the beach and dykes, perhaps having a drink at the Lifeboat on the way back.

tolerable but not really that much fun. With the exception of the paths through the Holkham Estate and the sandy heaths behind Cromer and Sheringham, the walking is not nearly so good away from the coast anyway, even if you do manage to avoid the awful coast road. This is where the Coasthopper and Coastliner bus services really come into their own: walk in one direction along a stretch of coast and take the bus back – the ideal solution. Those expecting stereotypical Norfolk flatness may be surprised when they venture a little way inland from the coast, but ropes and climbing gear are not required.

CYCLING

Along the coast itself the prospects are not as good for two wheels as they are for two legs. The Norfolk Coast Path is a footpath, not a bridleway, and so it's out of bounds to cyclists (and horses). In summer, the A149 has far too much motor traffic along it to be enjoyable for most cyclists, and inattentive holiday drivers rubber-necking the scenery are an additional hazard.

A better bet is to make use of the **Norfolk Coast Cycleway**, a 59-mile route just inland from the coast that links King's Lynn with Cromer (and Great Yarmouth), using National Cycle Network Route 1 between King's Lynn and Wighton (southeast of Wells-next-the-Sea) and Regional

Route 30 on to Cromer and Great Yarmouth. Felbrigg and Sheringham Park estates also have some very family-friendly traffic-free cycle routes.

The **Norfolk Coast Partnership** (✆ 01263 513811) publishes a map of the entire Norfolk Coast Cycleway (£3.50 from tourist information centres or direct by post from them for £5.00). Ten Explorer tours of between six and 40 miles are also offered as circular day routes. These appear on the reverse of the map but can also be downloaded free from ⌀ norfolkcoastaonb.org.uk.

CYCLE HIRE

Deepdale Cycle Hire Deepdale Backpackers, Burnham Deepdale ✆ 01485 210614 ⌀ deepdalebackpackers.co.uk/bike-hire. Provides bikes for hire complete with lock, pump, repair kit and helmet. They can also offer cyclists free route planning and advice.

Holkham Cycle Hire Holkham Hall, Wells-next-the-Sea ✆ 01328 713071 ⌀ holkham. co.uk. Adjacent to the car park in Holkham Park, with cycles and e-bikes for hire between April and October. Can suggest routes around the estate.

Holt Overland Cycles 34 Norwich Rd, Holt ✆ 01263 713293 or 01252 837937. This cycle shop has a variety of bikes – mountain bikes, tandems, etc – for hire. Helmets and panniers provided free.

On Yer Bike Cycle Hire Nutwood Farm, Wighton ✆ 01328 820719 or 07584 308120 ⌀ norfolkcyclehire.co.uk. Situated on Norfolk Coast Cycleway Route 30, they have bikes for hire that may be collected from their Wighton base, or delivered to holiday accommodation along the coast.

Wells Bike Hire 7 Southgate Cl, Wells-next-the-Sea ✆ 07920 016405 ⌀ wellsbikehire. co.uk. Year-round bike hire, servicing & repairs.

THE END OF THE LINE: CROMER & SHERINGHAM

Cromer and Sheringham, the last places on the Bittern Line, are a long way from any notion of wild, remote Norfolk. With origins as modest fishing ports, they were both developed as resorts during the late Victorian period. They were fashionable once but nowadays are often dismissed as old-fashioned or faded. I still have a soft spot for them both, though – especially Cromer, and especially out of season when winter wind whips up the sea and rattles the pier. At such times, it is plain to see that there's nothing between here and the North Pole, other than a few wind turbines.

1 CROMER

🏠 **Gunton Arms** Thorpe Market, near Cromer (page 308)

'I am not enjoying myself very much,' a young, homesick Winston Churchill once wrote home to his mother regarding his stay in Cromer. For some reason – hurt pride, perhaps – Cromer's town council have seen fit to commit this to posterity and Churchill's youthful words are now engraved in the town's seafront promenade just in front of the pier entrance. As they say, there is no such thing as bad publicity. Cromer became popular as a family resort in the late 19th century when the railway link to Norwich and London was established and those who could afford it would escape the capital's infernal smog and come here to grab a healthy lungful of north Norfolk air. Cromer's first railway station came into service in 1877, somewhat inconveniently located at the town's outskirts, but ten years later 'Cromer Beach' station was opened right in the centre of town.

Even before the steam age, city dwellers had come to Cromer to breathe its bracing salt air. Daniel Defoe came here in the 1720s and Jane Austen visited in the early 19th century and later wrote of it in *Emma*: 'Perry was a week at Cromer once, and he holds it to be the best

CROMER CRABS

Cromer crabs may be a little on the small side but they are universally loved for their plump, sweet meat. The best come from the waters just offshore from Cromer and Sheringham. The crabs are *Cancer pagaraus*, exactly the same species as other British edible crabs, so it is hard to tell what it is that makes them so special and distinctive in taste. It may be that they are especially slow growing and so fill their shells with meat more plentifully, or that they contain sweeter white meat than their counterparts do. Alternatively, it may be that the seabed here has less mud than other parts of coastal UK and this influences the flavour. Whatever it is, their reputation has ensured a decent living for Cromer and Sheringham's

small crabbing community over the years. Not that long ago, around 50 crab boats used regularly to put out to sea from Cromer's beach, but these days just a handful remain.

Crabbing technique involves the setting of long lines of baited pots called 'shanks' in the rocky offshore waters. These are marked with buoys and left overnight, to be hauled in again the next day and re-baited with white fish once the catch has been removed. Men work in pairs to haul in the lines, remove the crabs and re-bait the pots. Sorting takes place at sea and a good four-fifths are returned to the water simply because they are too small.

The crabbing season usually begins in March when crabs can be found relatively close to of all the sea-bathing places.' Although popular in the Victorian period with the families of Norfolk's banking aristocracy like the Gurneys, it took a prince – and a railway – to really put it on the map. The future King Edward VII did just that when he started coming here to play golf at the end of the 19th century (probably one of the more innocent activities that the prince got up to whilst gallivanting in Norfolk away from the watchful gaze of his mother and wife). Around the same time, the journalist, Clement Scott, started to write about the resort in the London papers and inevitably, with its easy access by train, and prior royal approval, it soon became a popular holiday resort with the late-Victorian chattering classes. The German Kaiser, Oscar Wilde and the aforementioned Winston Churchill all subsequently came to see for themselves.

These days, Cromer is probably best known for two things: crabs and its pier. **Crabs** are still caught here and are as sweet and delicious as ever. The pier, however, has had a rather troubled life over the past half-century or so. It was badly damaged by storms in 1953 and 1989, and in 1993 suffered the ignominy of being sliced in half by a storm-tossed drilling rig that had broken adrift. Currently it is in rude health

shore – they tend to retreat further out to sea to deeper waters during the colder months.

The season lasts until the autumn, although there is a lull in high summer when the crabs breed and grow new shells and sensibly tuck themselves away from the reach of preying lobsters that might attack them.

Because it is on a relatively small scale, crabbing is also reassuringly sustainable, but in recent years, there has been concern about dwindling stocks, probably the consequence of offshore dredging and rising seawater temperatures caused by global warming disrupting breeding patterns. There may also be competition for food and habitat from velvet crabs, which are usually found in the southwest but have been moving north thanks to warmer sea temperatures.

The crabber's secret, of course, is to know exactly where to lay their pots, and when to check them: the sort of thing that can only be learned by hard experience. Some Cromer crab dynasties like the Davies family have been catching and selling crabs – and staffing the lifeboat – for generations. Cromer has a number of marvellous fish shops and the same families that catch the crabs often run these – Bob Davies' excellent fish shop is a case in point. Whether boiled or dressed, the important thing is freshness, so buying and eating one here is about as close as it gets to crustacean perfection.

and one of the few places in the country where you can still take in a genuine end-of-the-pier show of the likes of a summer variety show or a Neil Diamond tribute act, or the annual **Folk on the Pier** weekend held in May (⌀ folkonthepier.co.uk); these take place at the **Pavilion Theatre** (✆ 01263 512495 ⌀ cromerpier.co.uk). Otherwise just do what everybody else does and take a stroll along it. Looking back towards land from its end you can admire Cromer's grand neo-Gothic hotels along the clifftop beach road with their towers, turrets and elegant picture windows.

"This is Cromer's 'crab central', where small, clinkerbuilt boats are launched from the beach."

Sadly, with British seaside holidays spiralling out of favour over recent decades, some of Cromer's hotels have gone the way of those in other resorts and struggle for business. Directly facing the pier, the **Hotel de Paris** manages to maintain an air of slightly faded elegance. Very much a Cromer institution, this may not be the most up-to-date of hotels but it is hard to imagine a better view of the pier and North Sea than that provided by one of its upper sea-view rooms. TV polymath Stephen Fry claims to have worked here as a waiter in his youth.

The true heart of Cromer is not in the narrow streets of the railway-age resort that stretch behind the main promenade, pleasant though they are, but in the far older fishing community that lies immediately east of the pier. This is Cromer's 'crab central', where small, clinker-built boats are launched from the beach, and where Cromer's inshore lifeboat, *George & Muriel*, dedicated in June 2011, is housed (the offshore lifeboat station is, of course, at the end of the pier). The indisputable hero of the Cromer Lifeboat tradition is Henry Blogg (1876–1954), who remains the most decorated of any lifeboatman in the United Kingdom. Cromer's central church of St Peter & St Paul has a stained-glass window commemorating the man (and another lovely window by Burne-Jones) as well as the tallest church tower in the county. The Burne-Jones window was damaged in a 1942 air raid but has since been fully restored. The **RNLI Henry Blogg Lifeboat Museum** (✆ 01263 511294 ⌀ rnli.org/henryblogg) is dedicated to the history of the

---

1 Cromer beach and pier. **2** Felbrigg Hall. **3** Cromer crabs for sale. **4** The Mo – Sheringham Museum. **5** The North Norfolk Railway near Sheringham. ▶

1

3

4

5

Cromer Lifeboat and, naturally enough, Henry Blogg also figures prominently. There is a life-size figure of the former coxwain with his dog here, as well as the *H F Bailey*, a rescue vessel that came into service in 1935 and saved over 500 lives during its tenure as the town's lifeboat. The **Cromer Museum** (✆ 01263 513543 ⬧ museums.norfolk.gov. uk ⊙ Apr–Oct) also has some absorbing exhibits, mostly concerned with the Victorian 'bygone days'. These include old photos of Cromer folk of yore, including a fisherman with the unfortunate sobriquet of 'Belcher'. Its geology gallery features a few bones from the famous West Runton Elephant, whose skeleton was found propping up the cliffs just west of here (see opposite). The museum also has a permanent display that features the work of Olive Edis, a pioneering local woman who photographed the full spectrum of British society at the beginning of the 20th century, from royalty to fishermen.

If you are in Cromer on New Year's Day, you can witness one of the best firework displays you are ever likely to see. The pyrotechnics, which take place over the North Sea from the end of the pier and usually coincide with a town fun run, are impressive enough to temporarily scatter the local gulls and probably send Cromer's offshore crab population scurrying to safety along the sea bed towards Dogger Bank. Be sure to come early for a good viewing position on the promenade.

¶¶ FOOD & DRINK

Cromer is not a place for fancy dining, rather it's somewhere for fish and chips on the promenade or afternoon scones in a tea shop. Having said that, **No. 1 Cromer** (1 New St ✆ 01263 515983 ⬧ no1cromer.com) is definitely a cut above, with a fish and chip restaurant and take-away downstairs and a smarter, more expensive dining area upstairs that has a great view of the pier and offers a wider variety of dishes, along with a good selection of wines and beers.

Of the other fish and chip shops, **Mary Janes Fish Bar & Restaurant** (27–29 Garden St ✆ 01263 511208) is considered by many to be the best. Not surprisingly, the town is also a good place to buy wet fish and especially crabs. **Davies' Fish Shop** (7 Garden St ✆ 01263 512727) is claimed by many to be the best place to buy freshly boiled or dressed crabs. The Davies family have been catching and cooking them for generations. Lobsters and wet fish are also available. For a meal or snack with a sea view, the **Rocket Café** at The Gangway (✆ 01263 519126 ⬧ rockethousecafe.co.uk) is a bright, modern café and restaurant conveniently situated directly above the Lifeboat Museum. Here you can have your coffee outside on the balcony and watch the crab boats go about their business.

Crabs are central to the Cromer psyche. In late May, Cromer is gastronomically linked to its fishy neighbour Sheringham by the annual **Crab & Lobster Festival** (crabandlobsterfestival.co.uk), which since its launch in 2009 has celebrated the fine crustacean produce of these two resorts. It's all great fun – there's a restaurant trail, cookery destinations, taster sessions, street theatre and lots of free events to raise money for charity. (The festival was cancelled in 2022 because of a shortage of organisers but is expected to return in 2023.)

2 WEST RUNTON

The A149 coast road runs west through East Runton and West Runton to Sheringham, along manicured green cliff tops that are home to regimented caravan sites and golf courses. Arriving by train on the Bittern Line gives a slightly different perspective, and you may notice that West Runton station with its pretty garden has won several awards for 'Best Unstaffed Station of the Year' and 'Best Small Station'. There is even a small 'wildlife area' to attract butterflies and the like. The West Runton station adopters, who are responsible for the floral flamboyance on display, are so enthusiastic about their station that for many years they held an annual tea party on August Bank Holiday weekend – with all proceeds going to the upkeep of the station garden. In 2022, West Runton, together with three other stations in Norfolk, received 'Wildlife Friendly' accreditation from the Norfolk Wildlife Trust in recognition of its work to improve biodiversity and support nature.

A choicer but slower route to Sheringham is – tide permitting – on foot along the **beach**. Here you'll find chalky rock pools and soft crumbling cliffs that are home to fulmars and the odd fossilised mammoth. When the tide is out this is a great place to see *paramoudra* on the exposed chalk of the beach. *Paramoudra*, sometimes known as 'pot stones', are large, curious-looking flint nodules with a hollow centre that resemble giant donuts or vertebrae. They are the sort of thing that might look perfect adorning a rockery but please leave them where they are. This is also a good place to find fossils, especially bullet-shaped belemnites and echinoid sea urchins. The best times to look are after a high tide and/or heavy rain. The so-called **West Runton Elephant** was discovered in the cliffs here by two locals back in 1990. The 'elephant' was, in fact, a steppe mammoth and turned out to be the largest, near-complete *Mammuthus trogotheni* skeleton ever found. The 600,000-year-old beast, which would have stood 13ft-tall and weighed around ten tons, twice the weight of an African elephant, was not fully excavated until 1995. Because of its weight and size, it is not possible to see the animal in its full, reconstructed glory but a few selected bones may be viewed in the Cromer and Norwich Castle museums.

Elephants aside, West Runton's other taste of fame comes from once being home to the **West Runton Pavilion**, a venue that was used back in the 1970s and early 1980s by big-name rock bands wishing to begin national tours in a no-pressure, rural location. The Clash, Joy Division, Slade and, most famously, the Sex Pistols all played here in their heyday – not bad for a village of 1,600 with a rather elderly demographic. The venue was demolished in 1986 but is commemorated by a blue plaque on the wall of the Village Inn today.

West Runton is also the base of the **Norfolk Shire Horse Sanctuary** (✆ 01603 736200 🖎 hillside.org.uk ☉ Apr–Oct), which operates under the auspices of the Hillside Animal Sanctuary at Frettenham near Norwich. The centre, close to the railway station, has five breeds of heavy horse – Shire, Punch, Clydesdale, Percheron and Ardenne – as well as a collection of old farming machinery. Ploughing demonstrations are held each day and special blacksmith days and sheepdog events are organised from time to time. Shire horses are magnificent creatures and farmers used to form strong bonds with their beasts of burden. Horse ploughing was a common practice right up until the 1950s in some parts of Norfolk. I can remember talking to some older farmers back in the 1980s who spoke fondly of their working horses: the unquestioning companionship that these gentle giants offered ('gentle giant' may well be a dreadful cliché but here it is wholly appropriate), and the magic of the farmyard at dusk when the horses settled down for the night, snorting with satisfaction at the prospect of fresh hay and a warm stable.

West Runton parish is home to Norfolk's highest point – **Beacon Hill** – which rises behind the southern reaches of West Runton as part of Cromer Ridge, the terminal moraine deposited by the ice sheet at the end of the last glacial period, which stretches for nine miles along the north Norfolk coast. The views from here, as you might expect, are good, as 344ft of elevation counts for quite a lot in vertically challenged East Anglia. **Roman Camp**, just to the west, belongs to the National Trust and, despite the name, is not Roman at all but a set of Saxon and medieval iron workings. The Norfolk Coastal Path doesn't follow the coast hereabouts but instead passes just south of the camp en route to Cromer.

FOOD & DRINK

Rocky Bottoms Cromer Rd 07848 045607 rockybottoms.net Mar–Nov. A family-run seafood restaurant in a lovely setting serving freshly caught local fare like lobsters, mackerel, crab and oysters.

3 FELBRIGG HALL

Felbrigg NR11 8PR 01263 837444 house Sat & Sun while undergoing restoration (check website for updates); National Trust

This 17th-century Jacobean country house is a magnificent National Trust property, just south of the A149 coast road and the rolling, rather un-Norfolk-like slopes of the hall's 380-acre Great Wood. Felbrigg's construction straddled the period of the English Civil War and the house's elegant Jacobean architecture is beautifully complemented by its sumptuous Georgian interior and Gothic-style library. Outside are a nicely restored, and still productive, walled garden and a splendid 18th-century dovecote that stands centrepiece to a kitchen garden with potagers. Extensive orchards are filled with traditional 19th-century fruit varieties, a fine collection of camellias, an 18th-century orangery and a Victorian pleasure garden. The gardens contain a number of native North American specimens like red oaks and cedars. The 5,200 acres of parkland, lakes and mature woodland have a number of waymarked trails allowing free access for walking and cycling in daylight hours and, with reasonably priced parking at the hall, make a worthwhile destination in their own right.

EINSTEIN ON THE HEATH

A couple of miles southeast of Felbrigg Hall is the village of Roughton on the Norwich to Cromer road. Although the village is unremarkable, Roughton Heath just to the north was the unlikely residence of Albert Einstein for a few weeks in 1933.

The celebrated German physicist was brought here under tight security to live in a small hut on the heath after fleeing Nazi Germany. While living in his modest hut, Einstein continued with important work that would later be put to use developing the world's first atomic bomb. The scientist also found time to pose for a sculpture by Jacob Epstein. It was this brief episode by the Norfolk coast that provided inspiration for Philip Glass's opera *Einstein on the Beach*.

A blue plaque commemorating Einstein's short-lived residence on the heath adorns the wall of the New Inn in Roughton village, although the precise former location of the hut itself is not known.

4 SHERINGHAM

🏠 **Cliff Cottage** (page 308) ⛺ **Bumblebarn** (page 308)

As with Cromer, Sheringham is a crab- and lobster-fishing centre that became a resort with the arrival of the railway. Like supporters of rival teams at a local football derby, the Cromer and Sheringham crabbing communities were historically antagonistic towards each other until the realities of modern life required them to co-operate.

Although Sheringham has its neon-bright amusement arcades and might seem a bit old-fashioned in feel, it is a nice enough place for gentle pursuits like walks on the beach and afternoon tea, and does have tangible civic pride. 'Twixt sea and pine' was the slogan chosen for the post-war British Railways travel poster and in fairness Sheringham today does not look so very different from the scene on the poster during its 1950s heyday – just fewer fishing boats on the beach and more flesh showing on the holiday makers. The same evocative slogan now adorns the sea wall along with murals detailing the town's fishing history. There is also a mural of Einstein (page 35) to look out for among all the nautical themed stuff. In many ways the town is like a smaller version of Cromer, but without the pier and the large seafront hotels. Plaques outside the Poppy Line station boast that Sheringham has won numerous Anglia in Bloom awards and, in season, the town has more bedding plants than you can shake a trowel at. For entertainment beyond pubs and strolls, the **Sheringham Little Theatre** (✆ 01263 822347 🖰 sheringhamlittletheatre.com) in Station Road is just that: a 170-seat regional theatre that manages to survive by putting on a mixture of repertory plays, blockbuster Hollywood films and live screenings. Sheringham's museum (🖰 sheringhammuseum.co.uk ◷ Mar–Oct), known as '**The Mo**', has interesting displays on the town's fishing and lifeboat history. There are good views to be had too, of the North Sea and the town's narrow streets, from The Mo's viewing tower.

"In fairness Sheringham today does not look so very different from the scene on the poster during its 1950s heyday."

August sees the **Sheringham Carnival**, and July the **Lobster Potty Festival** with enthusiastic Morris dancing in the traditional Norfolk style. Late May has the **Crab and Lobster Festival**, which the town shares with Cromer (page 33). The town also boasts its very own sea shanty choir, the **Sheringham Shantymen**, who perform frequently in the north Norfolk area as well as further afield. The choir does plenty of fundraising work for the RNLI; a proud claim is that they are the only organisation, other than RNLI branches, that is allowed to wear the RNLI badge on their uniform – there's even a lifeboat named *The Sheringham Shantymen* in their honour in Wicklow, Ireland. Mick Holford, their treasurer, told me that they also had close connections with Fisherman's Friends, the well-known shanty choir from Port Isaac, Cornwall, who are probably about as famous as it gets in the contemporary sea shanty world. 'We got invited to a sea shanty festival in Cornwall once that was co-sponsored by a brewery and a Cornish pasty company. Imagine, free beer and pies for three days – just perfect.'

Sheringham Park

Upper Sheringham NR26 8TL ☏ 01263 820550 ⊙ year-round dawn–dusk; visitor centre mid-Mar–Sep daily, Oct–mid-Mar Sat & Sun; National Trust

West of Sheringham, south of the coast road, lies Sheringham Park, landscaped by Humphry Repton in 1812 and with a dazzling purple display of rhododendrons in early summer. It is often considered to be Repton's finest work – he described it himself as his 'favourite and darling child in Norfolk'. There's an exhibition of the landscape architect's life and work at the Wood Farm Barn visitor centre at the southern edge of the park. The park surrounds Sheringham Hall,

MYSTERIOUS SOUNDS AT KELLING HEATH

Andrew Paxton

We were camping at Kelling Heath at the beginning of July and had been having a bit of a snooze before popping down to the pub. It was just turning dusk when I became aware of a sort of raspy, mechanical noise that rose and fell, and then stopped for a few minutes before starting again. Initially I thought that it was some kind of pump in one of the nearby campervans and was becoming mildly irritated at this intrusion on an otherwise peaceful evening. Then I realised that the noise was coming from several directions at once, so unless it was pumps communicating with each other, it must be something else.

On the way to the pub we could hear the same mysterious noise all about us as we walked through the heath although we couldn't spot anything.

Later, I read that the area was noted for nightjars and so when I got home, I checked out the song on the RSPB website. Yes, definitely nightjars – unmistakable, unforgettable, and no longer irritating!

which is privately owned and not open to the public, but high above the hall there's a hilltop gazebo worth the climb for its views along the coast and the wooded country behind it. As well as numerous waymarked walks through the extensive woodland at the south of the park, there's a Tree Trail taking you past some rare and unusual trees.

North Norfolk Railway
🖉 01263 820800 🖳 nnrailway.co.uk
🛆 **Kelling Heath Holiday Park** (page 308)

Right next to Sheringham's main railway station, the terminus of the Bittern Line from Norwich, is the privately run Poppy Line station of the North Norfolk Railway that runs between Sheringham and Holt, with an intermediate station at Weybourne and a request stop at Kelling Heath. The station at Holt is a little way out of the town but a free bus shuttle service is provided. Both diesel and steam trains ply this route regularly in summer and there are special events like steam galas and family days held throughout the year. Weybourne station is convenient for Sheringham Park (a one-mile walk to the entrance), while the request stop at Kelling allows for strolls among the heather and gorse bushes of Kelling Heath, which has a nature trail and offers a reasonable chance of witnessing nightjars whirring around at dusk in high summer, an extraordinary noise (page 37). Other specialist heathland birds like stonechat, woodlark, turtle dove and Dartford warbler can sometimes be seen here too.

‖ FOOD & DRINK

Station Road has a selection of cafés, fish and chip shops and pubs scattered along its route down to the sea.

The Lobster 13 High St 🖉 01263 822716 🖳 thelobsterinn.co.uk. This family pub just off the seafront has decent pub grub, a good range of beers and sometimes live music in its courtyard in summer.

Whelk Coppers Tea Rooms 25 The Driftway 🖉 01263 825771 🖳 whelkcoppers.com. In an interesting pebble-built building (actually three former fishermen's cottages built in 1630, restored 1934) overlooking the beach, this is the place for tea and cakes with a great sea view from the outside terrace. Inside, there's an open fire in a wood-panelled room during winter. The interior teak panelling originates from a 1820 Royal Navy frigate built in Calcutta. The wrought iron gates were reputably designed by Walt Disney.

5 WEYBOURNE

Weybourne is a pretty, leafy village with a windmill on the twisting coast road just west of Sheringham. Weybourne's North Norfolk Railway station lies a mile or so from the village. The station's greatest claim to fame is its use as a location for an episode of *Dad's Army* ('The Royal Train'). Norfolk featured quite prominently as a backdrop for this classic TV series (page 299).

The shingle beach at **Weybourne Hope** lies just north of the village past the ruins of an Augustinian priory founded in 1200. The beach is sloped steeply here, with relatively deep water offshore, enough to allow invading Danes to bring their boats right up to the shoreline in the 9th and 10th centuries. Such vulnerability was well-noted and, in keeping with an old saying that claims, 'He who would all England win, should at Weybourne Hope begin', defences were built in the 16th century to prevent possible attack by the Spanish Armada. The Spaniards never came but smugglers did, bringing 'tax-free' gin and tobacco to shore here, taking advantage of the ideal natural facilities of the beach and, indeed, all the coast between Sheringham and Weybourne. This strategic nervousness continued into the 20th century, when World War II anti-invasion measures included pillboxes, barbed wire and landmines. The garrison here, Weybourne Camp, became a top-secret military site

DEEP HISTORY COAST

North Norfolk's Deep History Coast is the 22-mile stretch of coastline between Weybourne and Cart Gap, just south of Happisburgh in northeast Norfolk. It is a stretch of coastline where there have been several spectacular archaeological and geological finds in recent years. While discoveries at Happisburgh have made this the oldest archaeological site in northern Europe (page 91), the discovery of an 'elephant' in the cliffs at West Runton revealed what has turned out to be the largest fossilised mammoth ever found in the UK. Such findings provide a focus for understanding the area of land that was once Doggerland (page 48), the low-lying territory that connected the British mainland to Europe during the last Ice Age.

North Norfolk District Council has brought this coast to life by means of a number of initiatives that include an 11-point Discovery Trail between Weybourne and Cart Gap, and by the inclusion of a Deep History Coast discovery centre at the North Norfolk Information Centre at Cromer. A free Augmented Reality mobile app (⊘ visitnorthnorfolk.com/deep-history-coast/app) has also been created to bring the deep past alive along the trail.

during World War II and a training ground for anti-aircraft gunners. The camp continued with fresh intakes of national servicemen until it closed in 1959, a year before conscription was abolished.

SALT MARSHES & SAMPHIRE: FROM SALTHOUSE TO STIFFKEY

West of Kelling, the north Norfolk coast starts to take on the character that brings delight to so many: glistening silver channels snaking through salt marshes, marram-tufted sand dunes and shingle banks. And, then there are the birds, of course – mewing, piping, quacking and warbling – everywhere, birds.

6 SALTHOUSE

Salthouse is a typical north Norfolk coastal flint village with an impressive church for such a small place. Its name actually does derive from 'salt' as salt-panning was a viable industry in medieval times all along England's east coast. Being this close to Cley-next-the-Sea, this is superb birding territory and the Norfolk Wildlife Trust owns the salt marshes behind

A BEGINNER'S GUIDE TO NORFOLK BIRDERS

So what differentiates a birder from a twitcher? If you are visiting Cley for the first time then it is better that you know. Simply put, a common or garden **birder** is someone who is knowledgeable about birds, likes them, wants to protect them and goes out of his (and increasingly *her*) way to seek them out in their natural habitat. A **twitcher** is all of the above, but with the extra dimension of being preoccupied with listing new and rare species. Of course, the really rare species are in anything but their natural habitat – they are supposed to be in a North American forest or the Siberian taiga rather than stranded in a lonely north Norfolk marsh with no ticket home. The defining characteristic of a twitcher is his (and rarely *her*) 'list', or rather, lists: UK list, Norfolk list, year list, life list, etc. Some twitchers will also extend their lists to other life forms such as butterflies or dragonflies (or more personally, to real ales sampled). It is a man thing: try not to judge them too harshly. Occasionally, the live theatre of a 'twitch' can be seen being played out at Cley or its environs. It is an easy phenomenon to identify: a murmuring green-camouflage army, brandishing telescopes like bazookas, will remain motionless and silent for some considerable time before a sudden flurry of activity occurs and there is a mass movement to a fresh viewpoint. The simple explanation: the elusive and rare bird that had fled from view some time ago has just been 'relocated'.

the shingle bank. In winter, large flocks of Brent geese cloud the sky here, and a variety of slender waders probe the marshes for food. Even more exotic, Arctic species like snow buntings and shore larks can be found on the beach at this time of year. Other migrants often turn up in the marshes and dunes on passage. As with all this coastline, the quietest time of year in avian terms just happens to coincide with that which is busiest for human activity – August.

FOOD & DRINK

Cookie's Crab Shop The Green ✆ 01263 740352 ⌂ salthouse.org.uk. Cookie's is well known locally as a place to buy shellfish and order seafood platters, sandwiches and salads. Many people travel some distance to sample the good-value seafood here, so it can be hard to find a table at weekends (a lot of customers simply take their platters out on the green and sit on the grass outside). Cookie's is nothing fancy but it does offer very good value and wholesome locally sourced food. Although the premises are not licensed, customers are welcome to bring their own drinks.

Dun Cow Purdy St ✆ 01263 740467 ⌂ salthouseduncow.com. On the other side of the green, slightly elevated from the coast road, this long-serving and very popular institution is borderline 'gastro pub'. The speciality is seafood but there is a decent variety of snacks, small and large dishes made mostly using locally sourced ingredients. The best thing about it is probably the view over the marshes from the beer garden – there cannot be many places where, with luck, you can watch marsh harriers quartering the reeds while you eat your lunch.

7 CLEY-NEXT-THE-SEA

🏠 **Cley Windmill** (page 308) 🏠 **Little Orchard** (page 308)

As anyone with even a passing interest in birds will tell you, Cley is the birding Mecca. All of the north Norfolk coast is good, of course, but Cley-next-the-Sea has that bit extra, those few essential ingredients: a wide range of natural habitats for breeding and feeding, a prime position on bird migration routes, sensible and long-established farming practices and, above all, plenty of goodwill towards feathered creatures. At peak times of spring and autumn migration, Cley can get very busy, with cars nose-to-tail on the A149 and the NWT car park filled to bursting. Usually, it is perfectly manageable though; the reserve is a big place and, with wonderful walks across the marshes and along the pebble bank and out to Blakeney Point, there is something for everyone here, even those who don't quite know their dunnocks from their dunlins.

The state-of-the-art, eco-friendly NWT visitor centre and car park are on the A149 just east of the village, with the entrance to the reserve and access to some of the hides just across the road. You'll find a very decent range of bird books and birding paraphernalia at the visitor centre, while the café has a choice view over the reserve's marshes. You can peruse the bird log at reception.

With birders in abundance, most of the colour on show in the Cley area is green – ex-military camouflage clothing, green binoculars (preferably Zeiss) and probably a 'scope and tripod. It must be said that the total value of the 'optics' (for that is what birders call their 'bins' and telescopes) on display here at any given time probably exceeds the GNP of a small country.

This is birding nirvana. There cannot be many places where you can savour a Danish pastry and cappuccino while enjoying the spectacle of dense flocks of Brent geese rising above the marshes, avocets tirelessly scything the mud or even the rare public appearance of a bittern.

A walk to the sea & back from Cley

✤ OS Explorer 24 or Landranger 133; start: NWT visitor centre car park, ♀ TG054440; 3.5 miles; easy

A recommended walk from Cley is to follow the footpath across the nature reserve from the pond (Snipes Marsh) on the main road, about half a mile east of the NWT visitor centre, which is worth visiting in its own right for its cafe with views over the marshes and reed beds. To reach Snipes Marsh, cross the road and turn right from the visitor centre and follow the footpath that runs parallel to the coast road east. Just before the shingle bank is a large shallow pond called Arnold's Marsh, which is often full of wading birds. Climb up the shingle bank and admire the view back over the marshes to the low hills behind the village then follow the bank west to the beach car park.

The nature reserve is spread out beneath you as you walk, scrunching gravel to the low background roar of the seas. In summer, there will be yellow horned poppies emerging improbably out of the shingle, seemingly existing on nothing other than stones and salt; in winter, you are likely to see small flocks of snow buntings flittering about like sparrows dipped in icing sugar. The onshore wind can be pretty keen in winter, vicious even, but it is my favourite time to be here when the elements seem to be at their most primordial. Even then, it is never completely deserted – this is Cley and birders are a tough breed.

If this is not enough you can always peruse the bookshelves and fantasise about the exotic birdlife of southeast Asia, where kingfisher species run to dozens.

Cley-next-the-Sea has far more than just birds, of course. It is a charming flint and pebble village with wonderful walking potential right at its doorstep. You could easily enjoy a stay here without having the remotest interest in birdlife.

Cley Mill, the windmill here, is a north Norfolk landmark, featuring in innumerable guidebooks and articles about the county. It is, indeed, rather beautiful, and, serving as a B&B (page 308), a wonderful place to stay. Otherwise, just stand back, admire, and take your own souvenir photograph. The mill dates from the 18th century and first went up for sale in 1819. It changed hands frequently over the next hundred years, eventually falling into disrepair after World War I. In 1921, the mill was converted into a holiday home by Sarah Maria Wilson, who later passed it on to her grandson Hubert Blount in 1934. Although the 1953 floods

At the beach car park, a road follows the course of a dyke back into Cley, where, just before the village, a footpath (part of the Norfolk Coast Path) veers off to the right to skirt the windmill before returning to the High Street. You'll then need to follow the coast road east back to the visitor centre. You might well prefer to avoid the A149 as much as possible — it is, after all, a busy road. One alternative might be to skip the detour to the windmill and instead return directly to the A149 by the beach car park road, cross over the coast road and take the road left that runs parallel to it. This will bring you back to the A149 just before the visitor centre at the junction with the curiously named Old Woman's Lane.

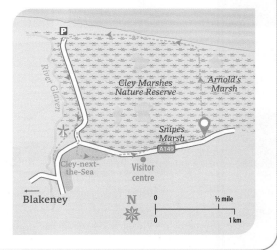

CLEY SMOKEHOUSE

CLEY SMOKEHOUSE

damaged the building, it managed to survive and, in 1979, Charles and Jane Blount, parents of the army officer turned singer-songwriter James Blunt, took over the running of the place. It passed into its present ownership in 2005.

Cley's High Street has some lovely buildings and a handful of quaint shops that include an excellent **smokehouse** and **delicatessen** (page 47). There is quite a diversity of building styles: a mixture of flint and brick, with some pebble-dash and the odd Dutch gable. The terrace next to the George pub even has an interesting art deco front to the street. The so-called **Whalebone House** on the High Street, which used to be the post office and

"It is Cley's unsung nooks and crannies that make it such a pleasure to wander around."

later a tea room and restaurant, really does have bones set among its elegantly knapped flints – in the cornice and in a pattern around the windows. These are not, in fact, whale bones at all but the vertebrae of sheep and horses, a reminder of the bonemeal fertiliser industry that once thrived in these parts.

It is Cley's unsung nooks and crannies that make it such a pleasure to wander around. There is a heavily weathered stone arch on the High Street – the entrance to two cottages – that has a framed poem on the wall inside: *The Hardest Heart* by Anne Clark. Elsewhere, charming little alleyways lead down to the mill and marshes from the High Street. If you head down the one that lies opposite Crabpot Books, turn around after passing under the archway to see the panel of St George and the Dragon set in the wall above.

Strictly speaking, Cley (usually pronounced 'Cly' by the way, not 'Clay', although there are even some locals who might differ) is no longer 'next-the-Sea', but it once stood at the mouth of the River Glaven. Although it is hard to believe looking at it today, in the Middle Ages the river was navigable for even quite large boats as far as Glandford. Cley subsequently became a prosperous port exporting wool, grain and fish to the Low Countries until it began to silt up in the 17th century, mainly the result of unsuccessful land reclamation work carried out by Sir Henry Calthorpe.

◀ **1** A view towards Salthouse. **2** Huge flocks of Brent geese can be seen at Cley Marshes during the winter months. **3** The smokehouse at Cley-next-the-Sea. **4** Cley Mill.

St Margaret's Church

A little way along the Holt road stands St Margaret's Church, the largest in the Glaven Valley, overlooking the village green with the Three Swallows pub (see opposite) – the perfect name for bird-mad Cley. Appropriate too, as swallows – usually far in excess of three – tend to gather on the telegraph wires above the green, taking turns to swoop down for flies.

Back in the days when Cley served as a port the church would have looked straight down on the harbour. Silting up has left this magnificent building high and dry, and it is sobering to think that it would have been even larger and more impressive had work not ceased when the Black Death devastated the village in 1349. The church has a bright, unusually cheerful interior, with graves among the flagstones and secondhand paperbacks for sale. In July both this and the churchyard are used as an exhibition space for contemporary artists. Its porch, stained glass and carved bench ends are all of interest but some might find themselves more drawn to the display that documents the arrival of an American white-crowned sparrow to the nearby garden of retired vicar, the Reverend Richard Bending, in January 2008. Naturally, the arrival of this extremely rare bird, which looks rather like an ordinary sparrow wearing a cycle helmet, heralded a vast influx of birders eager to tick it off their lists. The sparrow was amenable enough to hang around until March of that year, although there was much nervousness as to whether a local cat, 'Hooligan', might end up making a meal of it. The rare visitor is now immortalised in a stained-glass pane of the church's west window – a token of gratitude for the £6,400 the bird inadvertently brought to the church coffers in donations from twitchers.

I came across a local man in the church who had taken on the responsibility of managing the church's resident bat population. 'The bats are a real nuisance', he told me. 'There are two sorts – one that flies straight out after waking up, and another that needs to have a good old fly around before it leaves the church. We've got both sorts here and it's my job to clear up their mess.' The guano-removal man was eager to show me around, pointing out a wooden boss in the porch that depicts a country woman seeing off a fox attacking her goose – a charming vignette of no religious significance whatsoever. He took me back inside to show me the roof. 'It looks as if the walls are twisting outwards doesn't it? They're not of course – it's just an optical illusion.

When they rebuilt the roof, some of the resin soaked into the masonry so they skimmed it and that created the effect of the walls falling outwards.' He went on to demonstrate the church's remarkable acoustics, which had not been lost on me anyway, as an acoustic guitarist had been using the church as a practice space since I had first arrived. As I made my move to leave, the bat-man chimed, 'It's a wonderful church, don't you think? So full of light.' He was quite right: the high clerestory windows seem to gather light of such quality that you can sense you are close to the coast without even stepping outside. Besides, a church that has resident bats and acoustic guitarists can do no wrong in my book.

> "A church that has resident bats and acoustic guitarists can do no wrong in my book."

¶¶ FOOD & DRINK

Cley Smokehouse High St ✆ 01263 740282. This excellent Cley institution has a wide range of quality smoked goods like kippers, bloaters and kiln-roasted salmon, all handcrafted on the premises.

Picnic Fayre The Old Forge ✆ 01263 740587 ⬦ picnic-fayre.co.uk. This delicatessen, established in 1984, is the place where north Norfolk's foodies come for their cheese, wine and speciality breads. It also has a good selection of organic vegetables and sumptuous take-away pastries.

Three Swallows Newgate Green ✆ 01263 740526 ⬦ thethreeswallows.co.uk. Facing the green by the church, this pub has become a little more refined in recent years and serves what might be described as sophisticated pub grub, wood-fired pizzas and real ales. There is a pleasant garden out the back for fine-weather dining, while inside it's all dark leather and wood panelling. The ornate wooden bar here comes from a recycled ship's cabin.

8 BLAKENEY POINT

Blakeney Point is one of several spits along this coastline, the result of drifting sand and pebbles being deposited by offshore currents. The 'point' is a curious place that starts out as a narrow strip close to Cley beach car park before widening out to where marram-grass-covered dunes rise on its landward side opposite Blakeney harbour.

As Norfolk's most northerly point (admittedly, inaccessible Scolt Head Island does just have the edge, but we're talking yards here) this is the Ultima Thule of East Anglia – a genuinely wild place, with nothing but open sea between here and the Arctic.

DOGGERLAND

Although now an archipelago of islands, most of Britain was connected to mainland Europe not so very long ago. From the last Ice Age until about 8,000 years ago, a large land mass stood where the southern North Sea now lies. Slowly it became flooded by rising sea levels until Britain (that is England, Wales and mainland Scotland) became an island separate from the rest of Europe.

In recent years an increasing amount of evidence has shown that this former land mass, coined 'Doggerland' by archaeologists, was occupied by humans during the Mesolithic period that immediately followed the last withdrawal of the ice sheet. Fishing vessels working the North Sea have dragged up tools like barbed antler points and knapped flints as well as bones from animals like mammoths and lions.

The evidence suggests that Doggerland would have been a lush, food-rich environment for the hunters who lived there, with plentiful deer, aurochs and wild boar, not to mention an abundance of fish and birds to eat.

Dogger Bank, which usually gets a mention in the Met Office's Shipping Forecast, lies immediately north of the north Norfolk coast. These days it is a large submerged sandbank but once it would have been an upland area of Doggerland that remained an island for some time even after Britain had separated from Europe. Some 7,000 years ago it would have been possible to walk all the way to Dogger Bank from Cromer; a millennium or two earlier, it would have been possible to walk to mainland Europe – a point worth remembering for those a little over-obsessed with our 'Island Race' credentials.

The end of the Mesolithic period saw Doggerland and other lowland areas of the ancient world flooded, never to surface again. Perhaps it is the folk memory of this apocalypse that lies at the root of the many flood myths in cultures around the world? Perhaps Doggerland is the original Atlantis?

The point's western extremity is curved like a bird's claw – quite fitting really – and home to a visitor centre and colonies of nesting terns, also both common and grey seals. From Cley, it is a marvellous walk out to the end of the point: about four miles each way, but quite a tough four miles, as for most of the way it is a matter of trudging along pebbles – noisy work and tiring for the feet.

Halfway along the spit is a hut called, rather unimaginatively, 'Halfway House'. Many years ago, I camped near here for a night (which I am not recommending, by the way: this is a nature reserve and, quite rightly, it is not now allowed). What struck me most was the eerie sensation of hearing the sea slap against the pebbles on both sides of me, inducing an odd sense of claustrophobia.

9 GLANDFORD

Cley lies at the mouth of the **Glaven River** and the village of Glandford immediately to the south stands on the same river. There is a ford here by the watermill, too deep and tricky for most cars, and a footbridge. It's a charming spot full of birdsong and buzzing bees and the perfect objective for a gentle circular walk that might also take in Wiveton village and Wiveton Downs.

It may be just a tiny estate village, with Dutch-gabled cottages dating from the early 20th century, but Glandford does have its very own **Shell Museum** (✆ 01263 740081 ⬙ shellmuseum.org.uk ☉ Easter–Oct) next to the church – an eccentric place that has thousands of seashells in addition to quite a collection of fossils, birds' eggs and oddities such as a sugar bowl used by Queen Elizabeth I and a dried puffer fish. The museum also has a tapestry and painting by the much-lauded Norfolk fisherman turned artist John Craske. The **Natural Surroundings Wildlife Gardening & Wildflower Discovery Centre** (✆ 01263 711091 ⬙ naturalsurroundings.info ☉ May–Sep daily; Oct–Apr Tue–Sun) is located nearby, just south along the road to Letheringsett, within the walled confines of the Bayfield Estate, which also has a café. Follow the signs for 'Wildflower Centre' to find it.

10 WIVETON

A little inland from the coast on the Blakeney to Letheringsett road is the small village of Wiveton, with a church, an excellent pub and a neat row of cottages overlooking a village green – a sleepy place in the best sense of the word. You may notice a road sign here that says 'Slow You Down', which is Norfolk-speak for 'Slow'. Depending on your outlook, you might find this witty, slightly annoying or downright patronising. I tend to opt for both of the first two, while my wife, a Norfolk native, favours the third.

Wiveton Downs

Southwest of Wiveton stands the gorse-covered viewpoint of Wiveton Downs where there is an esker. An 'esker', as the information board will tell you, marks the past course of an underground river beneath a glacier. Some geologists scoff at this idea, however, arguing that if this were a true esker then it would be at right angles to the coast not parallel to it. Whatever, most locals come to walk their dogs rather than ponder

Quaternary geomorphology. The gorse is particularly impressive here in spring, with a custard-almond pungency that almost knocks you off your feet. Come on a bright winter's day and you may well see a ghostly barn owl quartering the gorse looking for prey. The views are lovely too: Cley Mill and Blakeney's St Nicholas's Church are clearly visible, as is Blakeney's Old Rectory snuggled away in the lee of the hill behind the church. Looking inland, you should see a well-appointed metropolis of pigs just to the south; that is, unless the bottom has dropped out of the bacon market by the time that you read this.

11 BLAKENEY

The village of Blakeney slopes down narrow streets towards the harbour from the coast road where its magnificent 13th-century church of St Nicholas is located. This is quintessential north Norfolk, with all the classic coastal village ingredients: a tiny harbour, flint-pebble cottages, fishing boats and quaint little shops.

This was an active port far more recently than neighbouring Cley, functioning as such until the early 1900s. Blakeney's eventual fate would be the same, however: the silting up of its estuary. It is this silting that characterises the coastal landscape here, with twisting muddy channels and creeks meandering out across the tidal flats of Blakeney Channel.

KAYAKING FROM BLAKENEY TO CLEY

Penny Edwards

I recently joined some friends on a Sunday morning in July when the tide was unusually high. We unchained the kayaks from the grassy area next to Blakeney Harbour and set off about 90 minutes before high tide, at about 09.00.

I had cycled out to Blakeney from Norwich and it felt good to be continuing to power myself, yet in a different medium. We made our way slowly past sailing boats and into New Cut – a channel joining Blakeney to Cley, created about three years ago to prevent flooding by the River Glaven.

It took us less than an hour to reach Cley windmill. We didn't disembark because we were aware that the tide would not remain high for long. On our return journey we stopped in New Cut to have a quick swim. We did this when the tide was near enough at its highest, and consequently the water was flowing so fast away from Blakeney that we found ourselves swimming on the spot making no forward progress whatsoever. After breakfast, I set off back to Norwich feeling as revived as if I had been away on a week's holiday instead of just out for the day.

Thankfully, the channels out to the sea are still navigable for smaller private craft at high tide and this is where Blakeney really comes into its own, as the village has become a favourite of north Norfolk's yachting set both for its moorings and for the unspoiled feel of the village itself. It is undoubtedly lovely but just a little unreal: a well-behaved ghost of the thriving port that it used to be. Even John Seymour writing about Blakeney back in the late 1960s in his *Companion Guide to East Anglia* reflected that: 'Certainly no fisherman could afford to buy a "fisherman's cottage" today,' adding, 'Blakeney is now what is called "select", meaning that many of its inhabitants have a lot of money. There is no "pin-table and Bingo culture" there'. Well, it is undoubtedly still select, and there is still no 'pin-table and Bingo culture' or 21st-century equivalent.

St Nicholas's Church, on the hill above the village, is well worth a look. You may notice something distinctly odd about this 13th-century church, sometimes referred to as 'the cathedral of the coast', when you first glimpse it. Above the chancel is a second tower that is much smaller than the main one to the west. This smaller tower was a 15th-century addition but its function is still a matter of debate. It used to burn a light as a beacon for Blakeney boats, but there is no reason why a second tower needed to be constructed especially for this purpose. Some think this incongruous addition may have been intended as a bell tower but, again, this makes little sense when the older, larger tower is far more suitable. The current church committee does not seem to have a firm opinion on this matter and invites visitors to write down their own suggestions on the pieces of paper provided. Simon Jenkins offers the thought that it may have been a private venture by a local patron wishing to rival the sponsor of the main tower. Undoubtedly, it does have something of the sense of a proud, if misguided, folly about it. Whatever the answer to this mystery, it is worth having a scout round and helping yourself to the generous free literature made available inside the church and, for a reminder of the long fishing tradition of this now somewhat sanitised village, take a look around the churchyard where you'll see plenty of fishermen's gravestones decorated with ropes and anchors.

¶¶ FOOD & DRINK

Blakeney Delicatessan 30 High St ✆ 01263 740939 ⊘ blakeneydeli.co.uk. Lots of locally sourced produce like cheeses and charcuterie as well as take-away salads, sandwiches and freshly baked pastries.

12 MORSTON: A SEAL-SPOTTING BOAT TRIP

⚓ Scaldbeck Cottage Campsite near Morston (page 308)

Beans Boat Trips (✆ 01263 740505 or 740038 ⏚ beansboattrips.co.uk) run from Morston Quay, with one-hour trips to view the seals and longer ones that land on Blakeney Point and spend up to an hour there. Times are dependent on tides. **Temples Seal Trips** (The Street, NR25 7AA; ✆ 01263 740791 ⏚ sealtrips.co.uk) which has a ticket office on Morston Quay, and **Bishop's Boats** (✆ 01263 740753 or 0800 0740753 ⏚ bishopsboats.com), operating from Blakeney Quay, both offer similar services.

There is not that much to Morston, another medieval port that has since silted up and now lies two miles from the open sea. Nevertheless, this is the place for boat trips out to Blakeney Point to see the seals.

Viewing these creatures is a slightly hit-and-miss business, despite their being 'guaranteed' by the boat companies. On an early May boat trip, Jason, one of the Beans Boats skippers, told me, 'We do get a few common seals but they come mostly later in the year. This time of year

MARSH SAMPHIRE

**Half-way down,
Hangs one that gathers samphire; dreadful trade!**

William Shakespeare, *King Lear*

The Shakespeare quotation above comes from a scene set near Dover and probably refers to the practice of gathering rock samphire, but it is marsh samphire (*Salicornia europaea*), sometimes known as glasswort or sea asparagus, that is the speciality of the Norfolk coast. The old name 'glasswort' comes from the medieval use of the plant's ashes to manufacture soap and glass.

Although it can be found at other locations around the British coastline, the finest samphire comes from the saltings of north Norfolk. Enjoyed as part of the local diet for centuries, samphire has started to appear on fancy upmarket menus in recent years, usually as an accompaniment to fish and seafood. It is harvested anytime between June and August before the plant flowers, but the sweetest is usually gathered early in the season. It is on sale at a limited number of outlets in north Norfolk in season but it is altogether more rewarding to forage for your own at low tide, providing you know what you are looking for and do not mind getting muddy.

Like most seasonal foods, samphire's short-lived availability is actually part of its appeal. It can be eaten raw in salads although the saltiness is quite pronounced; a light boiling or steaming helps to remove much of this. With its taste like asparagus dipped in seawater, eating samphire is a pleasure akin to stripping edible beads from a necklace with your teeth.

it's mostly grey seals – you can tell them from the common by their long, grey heads.' Out in Morston harbour, the seals were certainly a bit thin on the ground. 'You might want to call me a liar but, believe it or not, there are maybe around a thousand seals out around here altogether. They do well here – there's plenty of fish to eat and no predators for them.' Although the seals were not out in number, the birds certainly were. 'There's four sorts of tern out here. There's common tern, with their red beaks, and Arctic, who look pretty similar. Little terns are quite a bit smaller, of course, and then there's Sandwich terns, which are the biggest of all of them and have a sort of crest on their heads.' Terns were, indeed, everywhere, gracefully dive-bombing the water for sand eels, but I had also spotted some poetic skeins of sleek, dark geese flying about in the distance. 'They're Brent geese,' said Jason. 'They come all the way from Russia and they should have gone back home by now. I don't know what they are doing here this late. Maybe they know something we don't.'

Chugging back to Morston, past the bright blue warden's building on Blakeney Point, Jason told me about Morston's maritime history. 'That building was at the very end of Blakeney Point when it was first built but the spit has grown a lot longer over the last hundred years. Originally, it was a lifeboat station and the crew had to row 3½ miles out there from Morston just to reach it. They kept horses in stables out on the point and when the crew got there, they had to hitch the horses up to the lifeboat and drag it down to the shore. Then the crew had to row the lifeboat out to wherever the incident was. There was supposed to be a crew of 16 to man the boat but sometimes they had to make do with 12 or less. It took three or four hours just to get the lifeboat launched and when they had the job done they had to spend the same amount of time getting home again.' Clearly, the old days were not a time to be in any hurry to be saved. Still, the Morston lifeboat did manage to rescue over a hundred lives during its lifetime so it must have been doing something right. It finally went out of service in 1936 when Morston's rescue crew combined forces with the lifeboat at Wells.

13 STIFFKEY

Heading west from Morston towards Wells-next-the-Sea along a road bright green with shiny fresh alexanders in spring, you'll pass through Stiffkey, a village with both an odd name and an eccentric reputation. It has earned local renown for being the home of 'Stewkey Blues', blue cockles that are gathered on the salt marshes north of the village. It is said to be the mud that gives them their distinctive blue coloration.

The village is an attractive place of flint and pebble houses, and even the motor traffic on the busy A149 that passes right through can do little to assuage its obvious charm. The jury is still out on whether the village – and the river that passes through it – should be pronounced 'Stiff-key', as it is spelled, or 'Stew-key' in keeping with its famous shellfish. Opinions seem to differ, even between locals, so it's probably best to stick with the phonetic version lest you appear to be trying a bit too hard.

The east end of the village has the church of St John the Baptist alongside the ruins of an earlier church, St Mary's, in the same churchyard. South of this, **Stiffkey Old Hall**, the once spectacular property of the Bacon family, now lies in ruins and all that remains today is a gatehouse and part of one wing of the house. One of Stiffkey's former rectors, the Reverend **Harold Davidson**, who preached at the church and occupied the village's grand Georgian rectory during the interwar period, was a controversial figure who gained notoriety for attending the spiritual needs of fallen women from London. The Rector went on to become known as the 'Prostitutes' Padre' as a result – hardly the best moniker for a man of the cloth, especially in an isolated north Norfolk village. Such a crusade was an invitation to scandal whatever his true motives and, following accusations of licentious behaviour and falling out with the ecclesiastical powers that be, he was eventually defrocked at Norwich Cathedral and a more suitable replacement found. Bizarrely, Harold Davidson (no longer 'the Reverend' but still wearing full clerical regalia) met with a sticky end when he was mauled by a lion in a show at Skegness Amusement Park. His act had consisted of entering a lion's cage and talking about the injustices that had been meted out to him by the establishment. Unfortunately, one of the lions, Freddie, was unsympathetic to his plight and attacked him when he tripped over the tail of the other lion. These days, it is generally accepted that the charges against him were ill-founded and that he had inadvertently become one of the very first anti-celebrities created by the press.

Another controversial one-time resident of the village was Henry Williamson, the writer and naturalist alternately famous and notorious

---

1 Blakeney village. 2 Marsh samphire is at its finest along the north Norfolk Coast.
3 A boat trip from Morston to Blakeney Point to see the seal colonies is a highlight. ▶

HELEN HOTSON/S

LAURENCE MITCHELL

BEANS BOATS

respectively for his admiration of both otters and Nazism. Williamson bought a farm in the village in 1936 and lived here during World War II before eventually moving to Devon.

14 WARHAM

Halfway between Stiffkey and Wells-next-the-Sea, and a little further inland, is the flint and cobble village of Warham, which has the site of an Iron Age settlement nearby. There were two parishes here before the reformation, hence the village's two churches. Half a mile or so south of the church of All Saints, along a quiet lane, lie the round grass-covered earthworks of the Iron Age camp. Covering three acres, this was built by the Iceni in the 2nd century BC and is usually referred to as Warham Fort, although for many years it was known as 'Danish Camp' because it was thought to be the work of Viking invaders.

WELLS-NEXT-THE-SEA & HOLKHAM

15 WELLS-NEXT-THE-SEA

🏠 **Albert's Cottage** (page 308)

> There are few places in England where you can get so much wildness and desolation of sea and sandhills, wood, green marsh and grey saltings as at Wells in Norfolk.
>
> W H Hudson, *Adventures Among Birds*

The largest settlement between Cromer and Hunstanton, Wells-next-the-Sea is also the only real working harbour along this stretch of coast, even though it stands well over a mile inland. Really the suffix 'next-the-Sea' might be better described as 'quite-near-the-Sea'. Wells has seen service as a port for at least seven centuries although, as with the rest of this coastline, silting-up has been a major problem over the years. Lord Leicester of nearby Holkham Hall constructed a high embankment ('The Bank') in 1859 to reclaim 1,970 acres of salt marsh and as an attempt to protect the harbour. Unfortunately, this proved ineffective against the floods that devastated the coast in 1953 and 1978. These days, The Bank is a favourite walk out to the beach, woods, and caravan and camping site that lie north of the town, and you can continue along the pine forest and on to the vast beach that extends past Holkham Gap. The Bank also marks the stretch of the Norfolk Coast Path that leads into Wells. A miniature railway runs alongside The Bank. This might be a little too quaint for some tastes, but don't let this put you off – Wells has plenty more to offer.

Considerably less precious than Blakeney, Wells is an appealing little town with narrow streets of flint houses and an atmospheric waterfront that still has vestiges of its former life as a busy port. Most prominent is the granary with its overhanging gantry, which has been converted into holiday flats. The granary building itself on Staithe Street, the town's main shopping street, now serves as a small theatre. This is the main venue for the annual **Poetry-next-the-Sea Festival**, featuring poets and writers from East Anglia and beyond.

You may observe that there are notably more bungalows here than in Blakeney, as well as a few amusement arcades and gift shops along the harbour, but I think these humanise rather than devalue the place. One of the harbour fish and chip shops used to have a resident cormorant outside that would pester customers for a bit of cod as they sat on the quayside benches to eat. The bird has long gone but the chips remain as good as ever, as does the pleasure of tasting salt air along with your al fresco meal. In high summer there will inevitably be a queue snaking out of the fish and chip shops at the harbour, especially French's.

The harbour wall is also a great place for children who seem to love hoisting up small crabs on a line from the water below just as much as I did when I was a boy. On sunny days during the school holidays it can get so busy here that it is sometimes hard to find a space to dangle your line. These days, bacon seems to be the favoured bait.

Crabs and shellfish continue to be caught by local fishermen in Wells but **whelks** were the main industry here half a century ago when the port had its own fleet of special clinker-built boats. Once landed, the whelks were boiled in the town's boiling sheds close to the East Quay before being delivered around the country by train. Whelks are still brought in for processing today but the industry is a shadow of what it once was.

The strangely spelt *Albatros*, a 100-year-old Dutch clipper that formerly resided in Wells harbour on a more or less permanent basis, has an interesting history. The boat may have been used to assist Jewish refuges escaping from Nazi Germany and to supply the Dutch resistance with weapons. It was used to ship soya beans from Belgium to Norfolk from 1990 to 1996 and since then she has seen use by Greenpeace

as an environmental study centre for schoolchildren. The *Albatros* (⌗ willsofwells.com/albatros) made her last commercial trip in 2008. For many years she spent her days in Wells harbour moored at the quay near the fish and chip shops, selling beer and Dutch pancakes from its deck – something of a fall from grace for a sea-going vessel perhaps? In 2020 the boat was bought by a local café owner and later sailed to Maldon in Essex for an extensive refit. It is hoped that she will be returned spick and span to Wells Quay sometime in the near future. What I cannot understand is the choice of the boat's name. Have I, a confirmed landlubber, fallen into the trap of believing the old chestnut that the albatross is an unlucky bird for seafarers, or is it that Dutch sailors are exempt?

Apart from the quay itself much of the town's activity takes place along Staithe Street, which is lined with cafés, food shops, bookshops and gift shops. At the top, just beyond the Edinburgh pub, is a quiet Georgian square that has a leafy park at the centre of it – this is the Buttlands, where two of the town's best hotels and restaurants are located (see below). There is a stop for the Coasthopper bus service here, in addition to another down on the quay.

Wells & Walsingham Light Railway
⌁ 01328 711630 ⌗ wwlr.co.uk

As well as the mile-long miniature railway that runs along The Bank, Wells is also the home station of the Wells & Walsingham Light Railway. This claims to be the longest 10¼-inch gauge steam railway in the world, running all the way to Walsingham, a scenic journey of some nine miles, along the track bed of the old Great Eastern Railway. The service operates between March and October and takes 45 minutes with halts made at Warham St Mary and Wighton en route. The Signal Box Café next to the signal box at Wells is handy for a cake and a cuppa while you are waiting.

🍴 FOOD & DRINK

The Crown The Buttlands ⌁ 01328 710209 ⌗ crownhotelnorfolk.co.uk. Set in a 16th-century coaching inn overlooking the Buttlands, The Crown serves modern British cuisine and has a menu that includes a good selection of locally sourced fish and meat.

◀ **1** England's finest beach at Holkham. **2** The Marble Hall at Holkham Hall. **3** Wells-next-the-Sea harbour. **4** Flint and cobble buildings in Wells-next-the-Sea.

The Globe Inn The Buttlands ✆ 01328 710206 ⊗ theglobeatwells.co.uk. This 19th-century coaching inn, also on Buttlands Green and owned by the Coke family, has a restaurant that serves excellent seasonal food, much of which originates from the Holkham Estate. There is a courtyard for sunny weather and Adnams and Woodforde's ales on draught.

The Picnic Hut 73 Staithe St ✆ 01328 710436. This small café and sandwich shop on the main street down to the quay has something of a reputation for the quality of its crab sandwiches. It also serves cream teas.

Wills of Wells 1 Quayside ✆ 01328 710051 ⊗ willsofwells.com. This coffee shop, established in 2019, serves locally roasted coffee and artisan hot chocolate as well as a range of loose-leaf teas, cakes and pastries.

16 HOLKHAM

The estate village of Holkham serves as a mere appendage to the extensive grounds of Holkham Park and Holkham Hall. It also allows access to the grandest of Norfolk's beaches. The hall and park have walled gardens, a lake and a deer park, garden centre, gift shop and café, in addition to a Bygones Museum filled with artefacts of every description. The hall's grounds are used to stage regular summer musical events that range from Jools Holland to José Carreras, while the marble hall is occasionally used for chamber music concerts. Craft workshops, such as silversmithing and basketry, are also held at the hall through the year.

COKE OF NORFOLK: THE GREAT AGRICULTURAL IMPROVER

With Holkham Hall finally built – it took 28 years in all – and the Coke family's vast art collection installed, later generations, most notably **Thomas William Coke** (1754–1842), Thomas Coke's nephew, concentrated on improving the estate itself.

Thomas was far more interested in earth than architecture and would subsequently become known as 'Coke of Norfolk'. He went on to become the standard-bearer for the Agricultural Revolution with his application of four-crop rotation, an innovation for which modern farmers and even humble allotmenteers owe a debt for today. Although often credited with inventing this practice, it was more likely that 'Turnip' Townshend of Rainham Hall was the actual innovator here.

To the north of the hall, a tall column with sheep and cows carved around its plinth serves as a fitting memorial for this agricultural aristocrat and, if stately homes do not float your boat, then you might enjoy this more. This being Norfolk, even aristocratic pronunciations are not all that they might appear to be: Coke should actually be pronounced *cook*.

Holkham Hall

NR23 1AB ✎ 01328 713111 ⌂ holkham.co.uk ⊙ Apr–Oct noon–16.00 Sun, Mon & Thu;
pedestrian access at all entrances 07.00–19.00, vehicular access at north gate only between
09.00 & 17.00

Holkham Hall, the property of the Coke family, is a Palladian mansion that dates from the mid 18th century, its construction inspired by the Italian travels of Thomas Coke, the 1st Earl of Leicester, while undertaking a Grand Tour. It is undoubtedly striking but perhaps not to everyone's taste: purists might consider an Italian-Renaissance-style house to be somewhat incongruous up here in north Norfolk.

Building began in 1734 under the guidance of Lord Burlington and the architect William Kent, who were both keen admirers of Andrea Palladio's Renaissance style. What is most impressive is that the hall remains completely unchanged from its original form. Its Grand Hall contains classical statuary and art, with paintings by Van Dyck and Rubens.

You can walk or cycle through the estate's extensive grounds (no charge) but since this is a working farm dogs have to be kept on a lead.

Holkham Beach

No question, Holkham Beach is one of the finest in all England: a wide swathe of glistening sand backed by dunes and a thick stand of Corsican pines; the sea, a softly lapping presence or a thin line on the horizon, depending on the tide. This is the very beach that Gwyneth Paltrow walked along in *Shakespeare in Love* (1998).

"A wide swathe of glistening sand backed by dunes and a thick stand of Corsican pines."

Whatever the state of the tide, it's a wonderful beach for bathing and about as safe as it gets for children. Access is via Lady Ann's Drive opposite the Victoria Hotel and Holkham village. The provision for parking here is considerable but so are the crowds that come here on warm summer days. Once parked up, however, there is plenty of sand for everyone – the beach is a vast expanse that stretches as far west as the dunes at Gun Hill next to Burnham harbour creek, and east to The Run at Wells-next-the-Sea. Given the volume of traffic, arriving here on the Coastliner bus makes an awful lot of sense, as long as you don't mind the half-mile walk along Lady Ann's Drive from the main road. You'll save paying quite a steep car park fee too.

A Holkham Beach walk

✢ OS Explorer 24 or Landranger 132; start: Holkham Gap car park, 📍 TF891450; 4 miles; easy

It can be breezy here – it usually is – and lazing on the beach may not be to everyone's taste. Birdwatchers should find plenty of interest in the pinewoods behind the beach – rarities have turned up here over the years – but otherwise the best thing to do after a swim or a picnic is to go for a stroll. An enjoyable four-mile walk that takes an unhurried couple of hours is to bear right at Holkham Gap and head along the beach as far as the lifeboat station by the embankment at Wells-next-the-Sea. Then, reversing direction, follow the way-marked Norfolk Coast Path back west, keeping the pine plantation to your right all the way to the car park at Lady Ann's Drive. A shorter alternative is to turn left at Holkham Gap and follow the track that leads along the southern flank of the pinewoods until you pass a large pond and reach a bird hide with access to the beach along a boardwalk. The path continues past the hide and Meals House until reaching a crossroads in the woods. Turning right here will bring you to the beach at Burrow Gap, from where you can turn right and walk back to Holkham Gap and Lady Ann's Drive. An even shorter option, about a mile, is to turn right at the boardwalk by the hide and return to the start point by walking through the woods or by turning right along the beach.

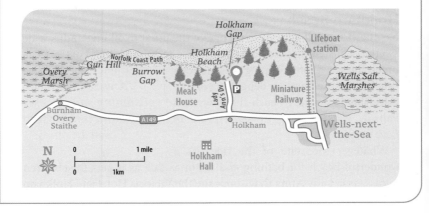

⅋ FOOD & DRINK

Victoria Park Rd ✆ 01328 711008 ⌂ holkham.co.uk. This fully renovated and spruced-up brick and flint pub at the entrance to the Holkham Estate enjoys considerable repute as both a restaurant and a convivial place to stay. Fresh local produce features strongly – Cromer crabs, Brancaster mussels and beef, game and eel from the estate. There is also a simpler lunchtime bar menu.

THE BURNHAMS

A whole family of Burnhams lie just west of Holkham in the valley of the unassuming River Burn: Burnham Overy Staithe and Burnham Norton on the coast road; Burnham Market, with its appendages of Burnham Westgate and Burnham Ulph, just to the south; and Burnham Overy Town and Nelson's birthplace, Burnham Thorpe, a little further inland. Burnham Deepdale lies a mile or two to the west of this group, and both Burnham Overy Staithe and Burnham Deepdale straddle the route of the Norfolk Coast Path. Such a tight cluster of villages means that six medieval churches lie within just three miles of each other. Ironically, Burnham Overy Town is the smallest of the group, hardly a village, although it was once the port in the medieval period. Similarly, Burnham Norton also has little to it other than a round tower church with a restored rood screen (at the very edge of the parish, almost in Burnham Market). In contrast, Burnham Overy Staithe, with its delightful boat-strewn creek, is perhaps the very epicentre of northwest Norfolk's yachting set, although Brancaster Staithe, which adjoins Burnham Deepdale to the west, might also claim this prize.

It is the largest Burnham, Burnham Market, that seems to charm the most, judging by the traffic weaving through it and the impressive array of smart cars parked in its narrow streets on any given summer's day. It is here where people gravitate to 'escape London' and discuss skiing holidays in the village's posh eateries. You might even spot a famous face 'getting away from it all'.

17 BURNHAM MARKET

🏠 **Bagthorpe Treehouse** at Bagthorpe Hall (page 308)

A picture-perfect village of attractive Georgian houses surrounding a green – is it any wonder that Burnham Market is so popular? How many villages of this size have such a selection of galleries and boutiques and even a posh hat shop? How many have such potential for fine dining? And how many get labelled 'Little Chelsea' because of their unashamed metropolitan atmosphere (or 'Burnham Mark-up' because of its near-metropolitan prices, or even 'Islington-sur-Mer')? Burnham Market is so upmarket that you almost expect to bump into minor royals or Hollywood A-listers whilst perusing the galleries here – in fact, there's a small chance that you might.

While it is certainly true that the village has attracted a disproportionate number of well-heeled second-home owners it is easy to see what all the fuss is about. If you are looking for a smart, yet unmodernised, rural idyll then look no further; if you seek the rural Norfolk of old then you might do better to try elsewhere. Either way, come and have a look around at least. The predominant dialect spoken around here may be that of South Kensington these days but that is not to say that genuine locals have disappeared from the scene altogether.

¶¶ FOOD & DRINK

Despite Burnham Market's haughty reputation you'll still find an excellent wet fish shop in the village, as well as an artisan bakery, a good independent bookshop – White House Books (✆ 01328 730270) – and even a couple of decent, unpretentious tea rooms. There is a **farmers' market** here on the first Saturday and third Friday of each month.

As well as the **The Hoste Arms** (✆ 01328 738777 ⬥ thehostearms.com), a long-standing favourite of the Sunday supplements at the heart of things in the village, Burnham Market has **The Burnhams Tea Room** otherwise known as Lucy's Tea Shop (✆ 01328 738908 🅵) on the market place for a light lunch or home-baked scones, **Gurneys Fish Shop** (✆ 01328 738967 ⬥ gurneysfishshop.co.uk) for locally caught wet fish, and **Groom's Bakery** (✆ 01328 736289) for cakes, pastries and 20 varieties of bread. **Humble Pie** (✆ 01328 738581 🅵) is a sumptuously stocked delicatessen and cook shop with lots of delicious Norfolk produce, perfect for foodies.

Located on the main road in the village of Stanhoe, three miles from Burnham Market, **The Duck Inn** (Burnham Rd, Stanhoe ✆ 01485 518330 ⬥ duckinn.co.uk) is an award-winning 'rustic-smart' gastro pub with creative and regularly changing lunch and dinner menus. The emphasis, along with inspired cooking, is on showcasing local produce like Norfolk crab and mussels and Holkham Estate beef. There's an extensive wine list and a choice of various East Anglian real ales.

18 BURNHAM THORPE

Horatio Nelson's birthplace no less and, although the original rectory in which he was born was torn down and replaced long ago, there is a plaque on the wall that commemorates the man whom many regard as one of the very greatest of Englishmen. The village pub, which unsurprisingly goes by the name of The Lord Nelson, does in fact date

---

1 Salt marshes near Thornham. **2** Burnham Deepdale's church of St Mary. **3** Pretty houses at Burnham Market. **4** Birdwatchers at Titchwell. ▶

from Nelson's time and serves as something of a shrine to his memory with all manner of memorabilia and paintings of marine battle scenes on its walls. The **church** next to the Manor House has more: a crucifix and lectern fashioned from wood taken from HMS *Victory*.

¶¶ FOOD & DRINK

Lord Nelson Walsingham Rd, Burnham Thorpe ✆ 01328 854988 ✐ nelsonslocal.com. This, the only pub in Burnham Thorpe, is both atmospheric and relatively unspoiled, and despite its claims to be 'Nelson's local' remains unpretentious. The Lord Nelson serves pub grub with an emphasis on fish dishes and local beef , along with real ales from Woodforde's and craft beers from its own FiftyTwo° North range. The pub's speciality is a herb- and spice-infused brandy it calls Nelson's Blood – an allusion to the story of Nelson's body being preserved in a barrel of brandy whilst shipping home for a state funeral.

19 BURNHAM OVERY TOWN

In a car at least, by the time you have said the name you have driven through it. Burnham Overy Town does have the church of **St Clement's**, with its odd-looking squat central tower. Historically, this village on the River Burn served as the harbour but this function switched to Overy Staithe at the end of the medieval period. One of the small cottages at the road junction has some curious recycled classical statues flanking its front door and there are the remains of an ancient cross, now reduced to little more than a hitching post, in the middle of the junction's central reservation.

20 BURNHAM OVERY STAITHE

Along with Brancaster Staithe further west, this small coastal village is a favourite of the sailing set. The fact that it has a chandlery but no shop or café says it all. The creekside harbour may be modest in the extreme but the village's seafaring credentials are impressive: Nelson learned to row and sail on the creek here and Richard Woodget, captain of the *Cutty Sark*, retired here to farm. As elsewhere, the harbour has long since silted up and these days Burnham Overy Staithe sees a very different type of craft sailing up its creek.

A sea wall stroll to the beach

For a wonderful short walk out to the beach from Burnham Overy Staithe, take a stroll along the sea wall that starts at the end of the road by the little harbour and zigzags its way above the saltings to reach the dunes; to the left you can carry on round past a point known as Gun Hill. Over the water is Aster Marsh, the eastern end of **Scolt Head Island**, mauve with sea asters in late summer. Keep going past Gun Hill (or take a short cut through the dunes) and you're on the same beach that extends round to Holkham Gap (page 62). This walk is even better if you extend it and begin at Burnham Deepdale, following the Norfolk Coast Path at the church opposite Deepdale Camping. The handy Coastliner bus service can be used to return along the coast road to the starting point.

FOOD & DRINK

The Hero Wells Rd ✐ 01328 738334 ⊘ theheroburnhamovery.co.uk. Burnham Overy Staithe's village pub is an unpretentious and cosy place for a drink or a tasty homemade meal after a walk.

21 BURNHAM NORTON & BURNHAM DEEPDALE

⋏ Deepdale Camping & Rooms (page 308)

Coming from the bright, fashionable lights of Burnham Market, **Burnham Norton** has the round tower church of St Margaret but no shop, café or pub. **Burnham Deepdale**, a little further on, has all of these facilities, along with the added appeal of easy walks out to the saltings and marshes. Other than that, the village centres on a strip of shops on the main road just before the eastern limits of Brancaster Staithe. Burnham Deepdale's **church of St Mary** is also well worth a look inside, having a Saxon round tower and a square Norman font that is carved to depict the Labours of the Months. Depending on the month when you visit, you can check what you ought to be doing in the agricultural calendar. In July, the 'labour' is mowing; in August, harvesting; winter is far more relaxed, with feasting in December and drinking in January.

Besides a handy garage and supermarket, there is a clothing store and a café here as well as the reception of the excellent **Deepdale Camping & Rooms** (page 308), which offers the opportunity to pitch a tent, park a campervan or motorhome or stay in a private or group room. The reception doubles as the **Deepdale Information Centre** (✐ 01485 210256 ⊘ deepdalebackpackers.co.uk), which has helpful suggestions for local walks and a good range of books and maps, including a stock of the wonderful hand-drawn Wilfrid George footpath maps. Deepdale Leisure Ltd, which runs all of these enterprises under the

CAMPING AT BURNHAM DEEPDALE

Donald (former Managing Director of Bradt Guides) and Darren (from the RSPB) spent a weekend polishing up their rusty camping skills in north Norfolk – and survived to tell the tale.

'Whether you're a seasoned camper or a first-timer just wanting to see what it's all about, the campsite (Deepdale Camping) at Burnham Deepdale is an ideal spot for a Slow experience. Days are filled with lots of low-impact outdoor activities, evenings are all about simple cooking on a stove or BBQ, or eating in one of the local pubs, and come bedtime you can retire weary but satisfied to the cosy interior of your canvas "bedroom".

'We hadn't camped for more than 15 years when we visited for the bank holiday weekend at the end of May, but soon got into the swing of things. Over the three days we were there we walked, cycled, went birdwatching and took umpteen photographs of the timeless coastal and inland landscapes, with their ever-changing skies, historic flint-built houses and churches, and captivating light that has inspired generations of artists. One evening, we cooked easy but nutritious meals on our stove; another day we spent a wonderfully memorable evening in the conservatory restaurant of the local pub watching a brilliant sunset over the marshlands, and sat in the outdoors wrapped up in fleeces with a bottle of wine as dusk turned to night. By the time we left we felt as if we had had a complete escape filled with three days of really healthy living, and what's more, we didn't use the car once.'

▲ See also listing on page 308.

same green umbrella, promotes green tourism in the locality and organises a music festival in September and a Christmas market. Deepdale Hygge was inaugurated in March 2017, a weekend that pays tribute to the latest Danish craze and which is described as being all about connection to the environment and life's simple pleasures. Courses, guided walks and other activities are on offer throughout the year, including the Deepdale Festival held in September, a weekend of live music. Deepdale Camping was awarded the East of England Sustainable Tourism award in 2009 and the EDP Tourism in Norfolk Award in 2010. More recently, the campsite was the popular-choice winner of the 2019 EDP Camping and Glamping Awards.

¶¶ FOOD & DRINK

Deepdale Café Main Rd, Burnham Deepdale ☎ 01485 210210 ☷ dalegatemarket.co.uk/deepdale-cafe. Serves everything from breakfasts to burgers and cakes. They open early (☉ 07.30), in good time to provide a full English breakfast for cyclists and walkers.

BRANCASTER TO HUNSTANTON

22 BRANCASTER & BRANCASTER STAITHE

🏠 **The White Horse** Brancaster Staithe (page 308) 🏠 **The Maltings** Brancaster Staithe (page 308)

Further west along the A149 coast road, Burnham Deepdale morphs almost seamlessly into **Brancaster Staithe**, which in turn leads into **Brancaster** proper. These villages have developed more than most as smart holiday centres and have more than their fair share of holiday lets and weekend sailors. If you doubt this, try **The Jolly Sailors** for a drink or a meal on a Saturday night and see if you can detect many Norfolk accents. Despite this, Brancaster Staithe has not given itself over to leisure craft entirely and there is still a viable whelk and mussel industry here. Leisure craft and fishing boats have separate staithes linked by a path. To reach the fishermen's sheds walk down the lane opposite The Jolly Sailors pub. The neighbouring leisure-craft staithe has a highly attractive row of 17th-century cottages at its entrance; the National Trust owns the 'Dial House', the one with a sundial above its porch.

"There are nesting colonies of Sandwich terns here in summer, the largest in the country."

Brancaster Staithe Harbour is the place to come to catch a boat over to **Scolt Head Island**, formed as a spit but later isolated by the sea and made into an island. There are nesting colonies of Sandwich terns here in summer, the largest in the country. Branta Cruises (✆ 01485 211132 🖉 brantacruises.co.uk) operate a year-round (weather-dependent) guided boat service across to the island on the *Laura May*. Trips vary between two and four hours according to season and customers' interests. Sailings are according to the tide so it is necessary to phone and make arrangements in advance. There are also unscheduled ferries in summer to the eastern end of the island from Burnham Overy Staithe.

The Romans built a fortress, **Branodunum**, in what is now Brancaster and used it as part of its Saxon Shore fortification scheme to protect the Wash from invaders (another fort, Gariannonum, was built at Burgh Castle near Great Yarmouth). Apart from the outline of its ground layout, nothing remains to be seen today. Other than sailing, the biggest draw in Brancaster these days is the Royal West Norfolk Golf Club, with a course that nestles between the beach and the saltings.

Up to Barrow Common

For a good overview of the coast at Brancaster, take a walk or cycle inland up Common Lane. In less than a mile, this narrow, alexander-lined road leads gently uphill to **Barrow Common**, where there is parking, gorse bushes aplenty and fantastic views over Brancaster harbour, Scolt Head, Brancaster golf course and even west across the Wash. On a clear day, you can easily see the wind turbines over on the Lincolnshire shore.

ACTIVITIES

Brancaster Millennium Activity Centre ✆ 01485 210719. Based in the 18th-century Dial House building at the entrance to the staithe, this centre organises a range of courses throughout the year that are mostly connected with art or wildlife. There are also activity days for children and family fun weeks that involve sailing, kayaking and mountain biking.

FOOD & DRINK

The Jolly Sailors Brancaster Staithe ✆ 01485 210314 ⬦ jollysailorsbrancaster.co.uk. This traditional 18th-century pub is known to everyone in these parts and has the advantage of a Coastliner bus stop right outside its door. The pub's own Brancaster Brewery provides a choice of five different ales to choose from and there is decent pub grub that includes curries and pub classics as well as stone-baked pizzas.

The White Horse Brancaster Staithe ✆ 01485 210262 ⬦ whitehorsebrancaster.co.uk. The interior is tastefully modern and the food good, featuring local seafood like oysters and mussels. The beers include Adnams, Woodforde's and Brancaster Brewery, and there is a lengthy list of wines from around the world. Also has accommodation (page 308).

23 TITCHWELL & 24 THORNHAM

⌂ **Titchwell Manor** Titchwell (page 308) ⌂ **The Music Room** Thornham (page 308), **Sea View Barn** Titchwell (page 308) ⚊ **Wild Luxury** Thornham (page 308)

The coast road passes through Titchwell on its way here from Brancaster, a village with marshes that are home to a 420-acre **RSPB bird reserve**. The reserve has a swish modern visitor centre and offers a good chance of seeing bearded tits and bitterns among its many breeding species, and geese, plovers and harriers in winter. If you still have not seen an avocet, the graceful bird used for the RSPB logo, a sighting here is virtually guaranteed as they are abundant on the scrapes.

Thornham was once a busy port but trade peaked here back in the 17th century when the River Hun was diverted in order to drain the marshes. Predictably, silting, and the inevitable arrival of the railway,

A Thornham coastal walk

✵ OS Explorer 23 or Landranger 132; start: Orange Tree, Thornham ⚲ TF733433; 1.5 or 5 miles; easy–moderate

A pleasant, varied but easy, circular walk can be made starting at the Orange Tree at Thornham. The Coasthopper service has a bus shelter here. From the bus shelter by the Orange Tree pub, take Church Street north past the church, bearing immediately right at the junction to continue as far as the wood, bearing left at the edge of the wood along the signed footpath. The Norfolk Coast Path soon turns left over a stile. Follow this path alongside a vast reed bed where you may well see marsh harriers quartering for prey in summer – blissfully unaware that they are supposed to stay within sight of birders at the nearby RSPB Titchwell reserve. The path emerges close to the staithe, with its chalk-built coal barn, where you can have a look at the boats.

If you want to extend the walk, you can carry on westwards along the coast path from here, past Gore Point to Holme-next-the-Sea, and return the same way back to the staithe. Then from the staithe head along Staithe Lane, turn left along Ship Lane past the Lifeboat Inn and the wooded grounds of Thornham Manor before turning right at the end past the terrace of white cottages and back to the main road.

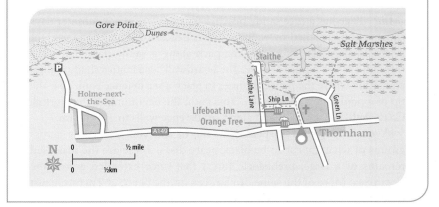

put an end to its harbour commerce. The massive floods of 1953, which washed away the railway line, sounded the final death knell.

A spread out, quietly affluent place, the village marks the western end of the transition zone of north Norfolk's vernacular architecture. East of here, to well beyond Cromer, the building material of choice is mostly flint (although the transition starts somewhere around Brancaster); here at Thornham, chalk is the main material, a clue to the local geology.

¶¶ FOOD & DRINK

Drove Orchards Thornham Rd ✆ 01485 525652 ⬧ droveorchardsfarmshop.com. Drove Orchards cover 40 acres of orchard growing over 160 varieties of apple, of which 120 are East Anglian heritage varieties. There are also pears, plums, gages and soft fruit. You can pick your own fruit in season and the farm shop here stocks a wide variety of fresh produce along with local meats, cheese, breads and beers.

Lifeboat Inn Ship Lane ✆ 01485 512236 ⬧ lifeboatinnthornham.com. This traditional 16th-century pub used to be the haunt of smugglers but these days it sees a more cosmopolitan clientele. The old bar has an open fire and gas lamps but there is also a new extension for swankier dining.

25 HOLME-NEXT-THE-SEA

Like Wells-next-the-Sea, Holme can hardly be described as 'next-the-sea'. The village is the point where the Norfolk coastline starts to twist south to face the Wash. It is also the 'elbow' of the combined Peddars Way & Norfolk Coast Path: the place where one ends and the other begins. It's a sudden change of coast and scenery, whichever direction you walk.

The village has a nice sandy beach, very popular on hot summer days, which can be reached by walking down Beach Road and turning right, or by turning just before the car park along a sandy path that leads through a NWT nature reserve. The boardwalk leads into a shady conifer plantation where the path continues to reach a sea defence bank near the tip of a pool called Broadwater. This path, the beginning of the Norfolk Coast Path, continues inland along sea defence walls to Thornham.

If you keep your eyes peeled on the beach, you may come across groups of what appear to be black peaty discs. These are the fossilised remains of a large, prehistoric forest that once extended across the North Sea. More of the same can be seen on the beach at Titchwell, just west of the sea wall and Brancaster golf clubhouse. The beach at Holme-next-the-Sea was put firmly on the map just over a decade ago with the discovery of a far more enigmatic arrangement of ancient wood, the so-called **'Seahenge'** (see opposite). A second timber circle has recently been discovered nearby, this time dating back to 2400BC, which pre-dates Seahenge by several hundred years. Holme may well have several more like this buried away in its vicinity.

THE SEAHENGE SAGA

Back in 1998, a particularly low tide at Holme beach revealed a circle of 55 oak timbers surrounding a massive upturned tree stump. The peat that had protected and hidden the circle for so long had been washed away by the tide and there were fears that further tides would sweep away the newly discovered site. As this was clearly some sort of ritualistic site, there was a strong argument for removing the timbers for preservation along with an equally vehement call to leave it well alone.

Debate raged as to what the original function was of what had become known as 'Seahenge' in the newspapers. Archaeologists suggested that the circle may have been a mortuary enclosure, while those of a less rigidly academic persuasion mooted more fanciful interpretations, such as a leyline centre. Spirits ran high and tempers frayed as those who would have the timbers removed clashed with those who wished to leave them be. Although this was mostly good-natured debate, the once-quiet beach at Holme became the setting for noisy argument between sensibly clothed archaeologists and dreadlocked, home-knitted jumper-wearing neo-druids, the latter performing improvised rituals accompanied by distinctly non-druidic instruments like didgeridoos and African drums.

The saga took an even more bizarre turn when, at a public meeting at the Le Strange Arms Hotel in Hunstanton, archaeologists, council officers and druids chanted together and used a 'talking stick' to symbolise the individual's right to speak uninterrupted. The meeting lasted five hours and reached some degree of accord but the circle's fate was already sealed.

The oak timbers were excavated and taken to Flag Fen near Peterborough. Analysis revealed that the circle was 4,500 years old and that the posts had not been positioned individually but placed in a circular trench. It was estimated that between 16 and 26 trees were used to build the monument, with at least 51 bronze axes employed, suggesting a community endeavour.

For many local objectors, the greatest fear was that the timbers might end up in the British Museum or somewhere similar, far away from Norfolk. These fears were unfounded, however: since 2008, the recreated Seahenge has taken pride of place in the Lynn Museum at King's Lynn (page 191).

With a leisure beach and wildlife reserve located next door to one another, there has always been the potential for a conflict of interests at Holme. The discovery of Seahenge added further tensions to the people-versus-wildlife debate. The words on everyone's lips these days, though, are global warming and what can – or should – be done to protect coastal wildlife against the effects of **rising sea levels**. John Hiskett, Senior Conservation Officer at the Norfolk Wildlife Trust, gave me his view. 'As sea levels rise, higher tides will squeeze coastal habitats against the shoreline and this will mean fewer habitats for wildlife.

The main losers will be those species that depend on these habitats and the bittern, for example, may be lost as a breeding species in north Norfolk if coastal reed beds disappear completely.'

So how can conservation bodies respond to this threat? 'We should help wildlife adapt to these changes by moving towards a more natural coastline. Freshwater habitats that are currently protected by sea walls will gradually be replaced by salt marsh – it is inevitable. At Holme, increased erosion means that we need to start considering some form of planned retreat now rather than live with the possibility of a catastrophic breach of the dunes sometime in the future.'

The award-winning Slow Travel series from Bradt Guides

Over 20 regional guides across Britain.
See the full list at bradtguides.com/slowtravel.

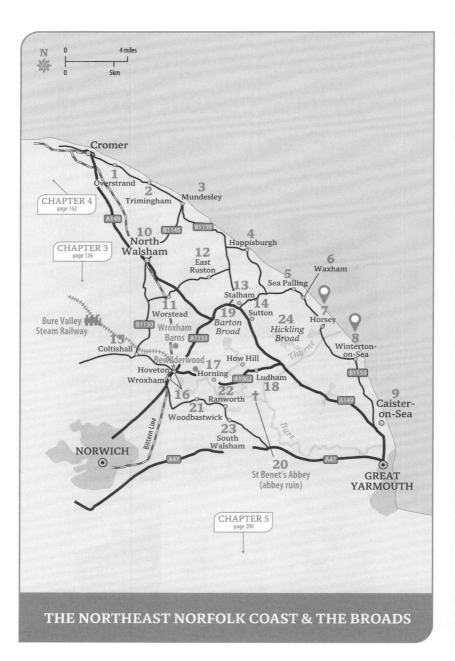

THE NORTHEAST NORFOLK COAST & THE BROADS

2
THE NORTHEAST NORFOLK COAST & THE BROADS

East of Cromer, the north Norfolk coast curves gently southeast towards **Great Yarmouth** and the border with Suffolk. The coast here is less spectacular than that further west but provides locals with pleasant spots for dog walking and fishing, as well as sunbathing and swimming in the summer months when the wind drops. It is an uncomplicated, calming landscape of sand, slate-grey sea, pebble banks and dunes, set against a backdrop of fields of grazing cattle and great swathes of sugar beet and barley.

Thousands of hedgerows were enthusiastically grubbed out in this part of the county back in the 1960s but, that said, even some of the larger expanses of grain seen inland from the coast are a far cry in scale from the geometric prairies in the Fens further west.

With quiet, old-fashioned villages like Overstrand and Mundesley, along with the slightly more bucket-and-spade atmosphere of places like Sea Palling, Norfolk's northeast coast is likeable but perhaps not as distinctive as the coast west of Cromer. Nevertheless, its safe sandy beaches and marram-grass-covered dunes make for great places for young families to potter about.

The villages that punctuate this stretch of the coast have little of the cosmopolitan gloss of places like Blakeney or Burnham Market in northwest Norfolk, but there are enjoyable corners: this is workaday Norfolk, and there are far fewer incomers and second home owners than elsewhere in the county.

The timber groynes that push out to sea along the length of this shoreline – sometimes mysteriously erased from view by the frequent sea mists – give a clue to the nature of the coastline in these parts. West of Cromer, it is a landscape in the making, with transported sand creating spits and extensive offshore sands. Here, it is one of occasionally brutal erosion. Dotted sporadically along this stretch of coast are houses *i* **TOURIST INFORMATION**

Broads website ⊘ broads-authority.gov.uk
Hoveton Station Rd ✆ 01603 782281
Ludham Toad Hole Cottage Museum, How Hill ✆ 01692 678763 or 01603 756096
Ranworth The Staithe ✆ 01603 756094

perched precariously on the edges of crumbling cliffs, with livelihoods hanging in the balance as the North Sea threatens to breach dunes and sea walls to flood valuable farmland. Measures to slow down the rate of coastal nibbling by the sea are hugely costly and ultimately don't often solve the problem. This can be hard to explain to those whose lives have always been based here.

Global warming is an altogether more sinister Sword of Damocles hanging over the region. With virtually all of northeast Norfolk sitting less than 20ft above sea level, things do not bode well for the future. Worst-case scenarios suggest that much of this coastline may disappear underwater by the middle of the century: a radical redrafting of the map of lowland Britain. For many, it is more palatable to limit concern to receding cliffs and menacing high tides.

Just inland from the coast is an area that really could not belong anywhere else in the country. **The Broads** dominate the landscape south of the small market town of Stalham: a sprawl of inland lakes linked by the River Bure and the shallow but navigable tributaries of the Thurne and Ant. Another collection of broads lies further south, east of Norwich along the River Yare, while a few more can be found across the border in Suffolk. They are all generally referred to as 'The Norfolk Broads'. For the purposes of this chapter, we will include just those northern broads clustered around the rivers Bure, Ant and Thurne – the very heart of Norfolk Broadland.

These sparkling bodies of water, previously assumed to be natural phenomena, were only proved to be artificial in the early 1960s, when research by Dr Joyce Lambert, a botanist, revealed that they had originally been medieval peat diggings that had become flooded over the centuries. With unique wildlife and landscape, and 28 Sites of Special Scientific Interest (SSSI) and nine National Nature Reserves

1 Ranworth Broad. 2 Hickling Broad. ▶

A COUPLE OF NORFOLK TERMS

Carr

A carr refers to a boggy wooded area that represents an intermediate stage between a fen or bog and dry woodland. Carrs are typically characterised by alder, willow and sallow trees, which have high tolerance of waterlogged conditions.

Staithe

This term, used in east and northeast England, comes from an Old Norse word for harbour or landing place and refers to a narrow manmade channel where boats were landed and unloaded of goods. Norfolk staithes are often used as moorings today.

within their boundary, the Broads have been awarded national park status, with the **Broads Authority** responsible for the area's management since its establishment in 1989.

The Broads are the one place that everyone associates with Norfolk (even though part of the area overlaps into Suffolk). Even David Bowie has made mention of them in one of his songs, although he was singing about 'Life on Mars' at the time. He also mentioned Ibiza in the same line, which hints at the frenzy that some parts of the Broads experience in high summer. At this time of year, the 'tourist honeypot' principle is amply demonstrated in the streets of Hoveton, where wannabe ship captains from the Midlands and elsewhere crowd the pavements, and Potter Heigham's medieval bridge has a lengthy tailback of floating gin palaces queuing to pass underneath. But this is just one face of the Broads; the other is a serene, watery wonderland of windmills, dykes and reed beds so rich with butterflies, dragonflies and exotic looking birds that it can feel almost tropical. It very much depends where you go… and when.

Not surprisingly, the busiest part of the Broads is around the boat hire centres – **Wroxham**, **Hoveton** and **Ranworth Broads**, and the River Thurne around **Potter Heigham**. Far quieter and more rewarding for landscape and wildlife are **Barton**, **Cockshoot** and **Hickling Broads**, the latter two having boarded walkways and water trails. **How Hill** near Ludham has special activities for children and a delightful walking trail through grazing marshes and woodland, and standing at a towering 40ft above sea level, the highest point for miles, also offers one of the best panoramas in the area. It is also one of the most reliable places to see swallowtail butterflies around midsummer. Another excellent place for an overview of the Broads is the tower of **Ranworth Church**.

Few of the settlements in and around the Broads are particularly attractive. Red-brick rules supreme and bungalow estates are the norm – perhaps the reality of living at sea level inhibits the urge to build a second storey. **North Walsham**, just outside the Broads network, is an unremarkable but nice-enough market town, while **Stalham** is mostly bungalow-land centred upon a workaday High Street. **Wroxham/ Hoveton** is very much a holiday centre between Easter and September when the Broads cruiser hire trade is at its peak. Outside this season, it is pretty humdrum. What comes as a surprise is the lack of really good **pubs** in the region. The fringes of the Broads are more fruitful territory, and recommendable places for a drink can be found in Winterton, Horsey and Woodbastwick.

GETTING AROUND

Travelling around the Broads can be problematic, given so much water. It's far from ideal car-touring terrain as it is so divided by rivers and great expanses of wetland that long, circuitous detours are necessary to travel from A to B. More frustratingly, you see virtually nothing from a car, other than the number plate of the vehicle in front. This is low-lying terrain and it is rarely possible to get views over the reed beds to the water beyond even when a road does pass nearby. The good news is that you don't really need to travel the length of the Broads to get the idea: you can very much slow down and get the Broads flavour just by exploring a very small area in detail.

PUBLIC TRANSPORT

Luckily, a surprisingly decent rail service passes through the western part of the Broads, which, with a bit of ingenious bus timetabling and a willingness to walk, makes much of the region reasonably accessible. The more-or-less hourly **Bittern Line** train service (⊘ bitternline.com) links the Broads with both Norwich and Sheringham on the north coast. Salhouse station lies some distance away from the quiet broad of the same name, but Hoveton & Wroxham station, at least, is convenient for Wroxham Broad, the epicentre of boating activity in summer, and also handy for occasional bus links deeper into the Broads.

Particularly useful stations for starting country walks from include Worstead and Gunton. The steam-powered **Poppy Line** from Sheringham

Weavers' Way
Public Footpath

to Holt, and the **Bure Valley Steam Railway** (☏ 01263 733858 🖥 bvrw. co.uk) between Aylsham and Wroxham, also link with the Bittern Line.

Bus services are rather sketchy but the **First in Suffolk & Norfolk** 12 service runs every half hour from Norwich Castle Meadow, Monday to Saturday in daytime, to Wroxham, while **Konectbus** 5B service runs five times a day between Norwich, Wroxham and Ludham via Stalham and Catfield. Sanders Coaches run between Norwich, Wroxham, North Walsham, Mundesley and Cromer, while their 34 service running between Stalham and North Walsham along the coast calls at Sea Palling, Happisburgh, Mundesley and places in between. Please note the only one of these services to run on Sundays and bank holidays is the Konectbus 5B.

RIVER CRAFT

Obviously, the very best way to see the Broads is on water. Self-drive **boat hire** options are numerous, and several companies like **Broad Tours** (☏ 01603 782207 🖥 broads.co.uk) at Wroxham, **Richardson's** (☏ 01692 668981) at Stalham (also Wroxham, day boats only), **Phoenix Fleet** (☏ 01692 670460 🖥 phoenixfleet.com) at Potter Heigham and **Ludham Bridge Boatyard** (☏ 01692 631011 🖥 ludhambridge.co.uk) offer quieter and less polluting electric boats for hire. An even more eco-friendly boat excursion is to follow a wildlife water trail around How Hill National Nature Reserve near Ludham using the *Electric Eel* (operated by the Broads Authority and booked from Toad Hole Cottage – page 110). There are also electric powered boat trips to be had at Hickling Broad organised by the **Norfolk Wildlife Trust** (☏ 01692 598276 🖥 norfolkwildlifetrust.org.uk/hickling), who also offer boat trips at Ranworth Broad (☏ 01603 270479).

CANOEING

Paddling your way around by canoe is probably the ideal way to get the authentic Broads experience and is one of the best means of sneaking up on wildlife too. Canadian canoes are very stable and easy to paddle even for beginners. They can hold up to three people and can be great fun

◀ **1** Paddleboarding is a great way to Explore the Northern Broads. **2** The 58-mile long Weavers' Way traverses the Broads from Great Yarmouth to Cromer. **3** Boat trips through the Broads are extremely popular.

especially for children. Hire centres can advise on routes and suitability according to experience but, generally speaking, headwaters are the most rewarding for novices while lower reaches tend to require more experience – more strength too, given the need to cope with tidal waters.

Starting from hire centres, you might for instance try heading upstream along the River Bure from Wroxham Bridge past Belaugh towards Coltishall, or exploring the Dilham canal as far as the disused lock from Wayford Bridge, or south along the River Ant to reach Barton Broad. Staff at canoe hire centres are generally happy to advise on times and distances for planned itineraries. **Bank Boats & Canoe Hire** at Staithe Cottage, Wayford Bridge near Smallburgh (✆ 01692 582457 ⌨ bankboats.co.uk), **Barnes Brinkcraft** at Riverside Road, Wroxham (✆ 01603 782625 or 782333 ⌨ barnesbrinkcraft.co.uk) and **Martham Boats** at Martham near Great Yarmouth (✆ 01493 740249 ⌨ marthamboats.com) all have canoes for hire, as does The Canoe Man at Wroxham (see opposite) and several other centres in the Broads.

CANOEING FOR NOVICES

For the uninitiated, canoeing is fairly intuitive really. I have a hopeless sense of balance but even I can manage it without too much trouble. The secret is to not stand up once you're in the canoe. It's best to make sure that anything that doesn't go well with water – cameras or electrical devices for example – is well-protected. In fact, it's easier just to leave these sorts of things behind.

Paddling is not especially hard work, although your shoulders and back may ache a bit if you are not used to it. Three hours is probably enough for novices – a six-hour canoeing session would leave most beginners pretty tired. Tidal currents should not present much of a problem unless you are a long way downstream but wind can slow you down and make it harder work just like on a bike.

As a humble canoeist, expect power boats to regard you in the same way that car drivers do cyclists – their attitude can range from courteous consideration to total and utter contempt. The further you can get away from them the better. Give anglers a wide berth, as canoes can scare away the fish.

The positives are considerable. You'll be getting good exercise and seeing river life close-up. You are likely to see plenty of kingfishers, herons and dragonflies and might even glimpse an otter.

One option is to take a **guided canoe trail** through the Broads, ideal for beginners. Mark Wilkinson, otherwise known as **The Canoe Man** (⟋ 07873 748408 ⟋ thecanoeman.com), offers a variety of guided canoe trails from spring to autumn between two and three hours' duration, more frequently during the school holidays. One- or two-night guided canoe and bushcraft trails take place about twice a month in the summer with camping or bivouacking on sites arranged with local farm owners ('wild camping' as such is not permitted in the Broads).

More comfortable are the canoe trails (from one to four nights) that make use of local B&Bs – these also offer an unguided option. Tipi camping trails that combine a Canadian canoe expedition with an overnight stay in a remote tipi lodge are another possibility.

PADDLEBOARDING

Stand up paddleboarding is now a popular alternative to canoeing and kayaking. Go Paddle (⟋ 01603 339105 ⟋ gopaddle.co.uk) in Horning rents paddleboards and can provide taster lessons and training sessions. Norfolk Outdoor Adventures (⟋ 01603 339133 ⟋ norfolkoutdooradventures.co.uk) at Hickling provide training for beginners and a range of SUP (stand up paddleboard) activities including nature and night adventures. They also do guided kayak tours. The Canoe Man at Wroxham (see above) also rents paddle-board equipment and offers regular evening tuition sessions in summer.

WALKING

The **Weavers' Way** takes a meandering 58-mile route through the Broads from Great Yarmouth to Cromer following footpaths, bridleways, riverside tracks and the occasional minor road. The whole route takes at least three days, although sections of it are ideal for half-day or day excursions. A particularly enjoyable section is between Potter Heigham and Hickling Green, taking in a stretch of the River Thurne and snaking around the south side of Hickling Broad. The seven-mile section from Stalham and North Walsham is also appealing as it has decent bus links between the two.

Another walking route through the northern part of the region is the **Paston Way**, which meanders between North Walsham and Cromer, taking in 15 historic churches as it goes. The spidery, wandering route, waymarked in the North Walsham to Cromer direction, is anything but a straight line, but it does offer some rewarding walking and several intriguing detours.

The **Norfolk Coast Path** now extends all the way from Cromer to Hopton-on-Sea on the Norfolk-Suffolk border. The total distance from Cromer is 38 miles. In contrast to the rather linear walking available along Norfolk's northwest coast, the area has many other walking possibilities, and circular routes are easy to organise if you don't mind the odd short section of minor road. With few contours on the map, it goes without saying there are no uphill struggles. The downside of this is that, away from water, the terrain can sometimes be a bit dull, but alongside river or broad, it can be a delight. Several of the rivers have footpaths that follow them for miles but seeing the Broads themselves on foot is not so easy as most lack waterside paths.

CYCLING

Exploring the back lanes by bike is a delight, but not the busy main roads like the A149 and A1151. As the terrain is almost perfectly flat, you won't be needing those low gears. Using bridleways and minor roads, it is possible to travel around the region far more efficiently than in a car, avoiding long detours. There's still a lot of water to get round, though, and it takes very careful routing to avoid the main roads. Unfortunately, the former ferry across the River Bure from Woodbastwick Fen to Horning is no longer in service for cyclists or walkers.

For those without their own bikes, **cycle hire** is available at Clippesby Hall (✆ 01493 369221 ⬧ clippesbyhall.com), which incidentally has an excellent touring and camping park with pitches set out in natural woodland; Broadland Cycle Hire at BeWILDerwood near Hoveton (✆ 07747 483154 ⬧ norfolkbroadscycling.co.uk), who provide free cycling maps and offer a delivery service to accommodation in the area; Bike Riders in North Walsham (✆ 01692 406632); and the tea rooms at Stokesby (✆ 01493 750470).

The **Bittern Line** (page 24) is a highly convenient means of taking your own bike in or out of the area. Those turning up on the day can transport their bike on a first-come first-served basis – each train is able to take up to four bikes. In summer it is probably best to book in advance (✆ 0845 600 7245).

The Broads Authority produce a useful **leaflet** called *The Broads by Bike* that can be picked up from any visitor centre or viewed online at

✎ thebroadsbybike.org.uk. This shows an orbital cycling route around the Broads and suggests a variety of day and half-day itineraries. These can be downloaded as pdf files from the website. One really good ride of around 15 miles that takes in Potter Heigham, How Hill and Ludham, begins and ends in Clippesby and gives a good overview of the region. A similar-length route starts at Hoveton's BeWILDerwood and follows quiet country lanes to Neatishead and Barton Turf where there is access to the boardwalk and viewing platform at Barton Broad. Another possibility is to follow the nine-mile Bure Valley Path that follows the Bure Valley Railway between Wroxham and Aylsham. Bicycles can also be carried on the Bure Valley Railway trains, space permitting, for £3.50.

THE COAST: OVERSTRAND TO CAISTER-ON-SEA

1 OVERSTRAND

🏠 **The Green House**, Thorpe Market (page 309)

Overstrand lies just two miles east of Cromer as the gull flies. Originally a place of crab fishing like its big-sister neighbour, it has slowly developed into a quiet resort with a safe, sandy beach. Much lauded in the writings of Clement 'Poppyland' Scott, the village was favoured by the Victorian upper classes and soon became known as 'the village of millionaires'. Some of its grandest buildings date from this period. Overstrand Hall was designed by a young Edward Lutyens for Lord Hillingdon, while Gertrude Jekyll is said to have been responsible for the gardens at The Pleasaunce. The rather grand Overstrand Hotel, built at the turn of the 20th century, became a very popular hangout for the aristocracy and upper classes, and one of the most prestigious hotels along the east

"Overstrand's original church had been swallowed up by the sea centuries before, in the late 1300s."

coast. Unfortunately, the architects built it rather too close to the cliff edge and its foundations started to crumble within a matter of years. It finally collapsed in 1947, ironically as the result of a fire.

Erosion is a serious concern all along this coast. In the neighbouring village of Sidestrand, the village church was moved back, stone by stone, from the cliff edge in the 19th century, although the tower was left standing where it was. Overstrand's original church had been swallowed up by the sea centuries before, in the late 1300s. A new church, of the same name – St Martin's – was built in 1399 but this too fell into disrepair by the middle of the 18th century and was a ruin by the mid-1800s. A replacement church was built and consecrated in 1867 but this proved to be too small for local congregations and so in 1911 it was decided to restore and re-consecrate St Martin's.

THE LEGEND OF BLACK SHUCK

And a dreadful thing from the cliff did spring,
and its wild bark thrilled around,
his eyes had the glow of the fires below,
'twas the form of the Spectre Hound.

Old Norfolk saying

Tales of Black Shuck, a dark ghostly hound with terrifying fiery eyes, are commonplace throughout East Anglia, especially along the coast. The legend may have arrived with Danish raiders, with 'Shukr' being the name of the faithful, yet ultimately abandoned, canine companion of the Norse god Thor. Alternative derivations may come from *scucca*, an Anglo-Saxon word that means demon, or even 'shucky', a local dialect word meaning 'hairy'.

One of Shuck's most notable appearances was at Blythburgh in Suffolk in 1577 when he appeared at the church and terrified the congregation, killing a man and boy, causing the tower to collapse and leaving scorch marks in his wake. Not content with this, Shuck was reported to appear at Bungay, also in Suffolk, the very same day and put on much the same sort of performance at the parish church.

The Overstrand version of the Shuck legend has it that two friends, a Dane and a Saxon, were drowned whilst out fishing together with their dog. The Dane washed up at Beeston and the Saxon at Overstrand, while the dog's ghostly presence roamed the coast in search of both his masters. Anyone unfortunate enough to encounter Shuck on his nightly patrol would generally find himself dead within the year. Along with any number of supposed sightings elsewhere, Shuck was reported to have made his home in the ruins of Overstrand's St Martin's Church until the restoration work of 1911 drove him away. He is rumoured to haunt the coast road between Overstrand and Sheringham.

Legend or not, Shuck has been quite an influential figure in literature. Sir Arthur Conan Doyle probably heard of the legend whilst on a golfing visit to Cromer in 1901 and a terrifying spectral dog character subsequently appeared in his *Hound of the Baskervilles*, published the following year. The setting was transposed from north Norfolk to Dartmoor but the descriptions of fictitious home of the Baskerville family are strongly reminiscent of Cromer Hall.

A cliff walk to Cromer

A favourite outing from Overstrand is the walk along the cliffs to Cromer: a short, often windy, hike of just a couple of miles that offers a marvellous view over the resort and its pier as you approach from the east. This route, which also coincides with the last couple of miles of the Paston Way, is very popular all the year round. In autumn and winter, bushes that bear the brilliant orange berries of sea buckthorn flank the clifftop path. The berries look good enough to eat and they were, apparently, part of the diet of prehistoric man. Appearances can be deceiving though, as they taste unbelievably bitter. Sweetened though, sea buckthorn does make a delicious, if somewhat runny, jam – something I have sampled many times a long way from any ocean on breakfast tables in Kyrgyzstan!

2 TRIMINGHAM

Further southeast along the coast road from Overstrand towards Mundesley, the village of Trimingham has the rather unusually named **St John the Baptist's Head**. The only other church in Britain with the same macabre dedication is in Kent. Needless to say, neither of these is the true repository of the apostle's cranium (which is supposedly at Amiens Cathedral in France): the name dates from a medieval scam in which hapless pilgrims were lured by the promise of holy relics. Certainly, as holy relics go, the head of St John would have been a very impressive attraction – if only it had been true. What would have once been on display here, and most probably destroyed during the Reformation, was a full-sized alabaster likeness – a superb 14th-century example, probably very similar to that on display at Trimingham, can be seen in London's Victoria and Albert Museum. The church itself is a little on the squat side but it makes up for this by standing, like Napoleon on a soap box, at one of the highest points along the northeast coast – around 200ft above sea level.

South of here, beyond tiny Gimingham, is Trunch, a place that sounds like a dull blow to the head but is, in fact, rather more pleasant. The gazebo-like, Gothic font canopy of Trunch's **St Botolph's Church**, carved with animals that include squirrels, monkeys, dogs and even a pig wearing a bishop's mitre, is by far the most striking feature of this 14th- to 15th-century building, although its hammerbeam roof is quite splendid too. Knapton, the village immediately east of Trunch, also has the interesting **church of St Peter and St Paul**, with its early 16th-century hammerbeam roof timbers lavishly decorated with angels with outspread wings, 138 in total (according to architectural historian Nikolaus Pevsner), although the church itself claims 160 – or count them yourself and arrive at your own figure. The cockerel weathervane on the tower here is reportedly the design of the eminent Norwich School artist, J S Cotman, who gave drawing classes at nearby Knapton Hall.

3 MUNDESLEY & AROUND

Mundesley is more of a large village than a town. The railway station that brought the Victorian elite here in the 19th century has long since closed and the nearest station these days is the Bittern Line station in North Walsham. John Seymour describes Mundesley as 'a good solid respectable seaside town, and that is all there is to say about that.' He has a point, but it also has a fine Blue Flag beach for bracing walks and safe swimming – a great place for children to splash about. The very lovely beach, understandably very popular with local families on warm summer weekends, has a café and a shop selling the usual seaside requisites – flip-flops, beach balls and shrimp nets. On the concrete promenade next to the shop stands a neat terrace of brightly painted beach huts that add a splash of colour to an otherwise grey scene on an overcast winter's day. It may not quite have the grandeur of Cromer but at least it makes an effort. The tiny **Maritime Museum** ($\mathscr{O}$ 01263 722068 $\odot$ Jun–Sep), on Beach Road and housed in an old coastguard lookout point, is worth 50p of anyone's money. Regrettably Stow Mill, a flour mill built in 1827 that lies just outside the village on the road south to Paston, can no longer be visited as it has, like so many historical agricultural buildings in these parts, been recently converted into a holiday let.

A little further along the B1159 coast road you reach the small village of **Paston**, where there is the magnificent flint and thatch **Paston Great Barn** built by Sir William Paston in 1581. At 160ft long and 60ft high this is one of Norfolk's largest barns. In recent years it has been fully restored by the North Norfolk Historic Buildings Trust. Paston Great Barn, now leased to Natural England, is also home to a maternal colony of very rare barbastelle bats and because of this the barn and outbuildings are closed to the public. Although the barn and courtyard cannot be visited, there is a small car park and interpretative panel on the eastern side of the barn and a footpath that takes you through the grounds to the south. The Paston family's dominant role in the village's history is brought to life through the legacy of the famous **Paston Letters**, a hugely historically important collection of 15th-century correspondence now kept in the British Museum and Oxford's Bodleian Library. The village's 14th-century St Margaret's Church has memorials to the family; the most striking is that of Katherine Paston, sculpted in fine alabaster in 1628.

PIONEER MAN IN NORFOLK

In July 2010, the surprise discovery of more than 70 ancient flint tools on a Happisburgh beach pushed back the date of the first known occupation of Britain by up to a quarter of a million years. The stone tools discovered by British Museum archaeologists are thought to be between 840,000 and 950,000 years old, making them the oldest artefacts ever found in the country, indeed, in all of northwest Europe.

These were most probably the tools of *Homo antecessor*, a humanoid species that lived as hunter-gatherers in the flood plain of the ancient River Thames, which in those times flowed through the territory that is now Norfolk. *Homo antecessor* or 'Pioneer Man', whose remains have been found in Spain, is the only human species currently known to have existed in Europe around one million years ago. It must have been this same species that walked across the land bridge that connected Britain with mainland Europe at the time to become the first settlers in what is now Norfolk.

The Happisburgh discovery suggests that early humans must have been able to adapt to the cold as the winters here were cooler than they are now, although summers were much the same. These early settlers would also have had to share their terrain with mammoth, rhino, hyenas and sabre-toothed cats. Clearly, there was a plentiful supply of free-range meat available at the time, if precious little edible vegetation, but certain difficult questions remain: did the early Happisburgh settlers have shelter and clothes, could they control fire?

Before this find was made the earliest evidence of human activity in Britain – a mere 700,000 years ago – was from Pakefield in Suffolk. So, not for the first time, Norfolk has trumped its southern neighbour.

In 2013, just a few years after the discovery of the flints, an even more astonishing discovery was made at Happisburgh, when a set of 800,000-year-old fossilised footprints were found on the beach on a newly uncovered layer of sediment. These were subsequently identified as the oldest known hominid footprints found outside Africa. Once again, it is believed that these belonged to our distant ancestor *Homo antecessor* although no hominid fossils have yet been found to confirm this. The footprints appear to indicate a group of adults and children moving through the mudflats of a river estuary. The river mouth in question would have been that of what we now know as the River Thames, which followed a far more northerly course 800,000 years ago.

Bacton, a little further east still, is another small seaside centre but the name is more frequently associated with the enormous North Sea Gas Terminal that lies north of the village. The terminal is actually closer to Paston than Bacton. You can't miss it, as you drive right past on the coast road, although perhaps you might like to at least try to do so. Both Paston and Bacton are quite attractive villages in their own right, although it is hard to see the attraction of the caravan site that is right next to the gas terminal itself: it offers an industrial outlook that only those homesick for Teeside could love.

Just south of Bacton, the ruined Bromholm Priory was an outpost of the Cluniac priory at Castle Acre in the Middle Ages, and an important pilgrimage centre as it claimed to have a piece of the True Cross. The impressive ruin that remains stands on private land; it can be viewed at a distance from a nearby public footpath.

¶¶ FOOD & DRINK

Ship Inn 21 Beach Rd, Mundesley ✆ 01263 722671 ⚲ mundesley-ship.co.uk. Above the beach, in an 18th-century flint and brick building, this friendly local pub, or 'restaurant with rooms' as it now calls itself, serves Woodforde's Wherry and other locally brewed guest beers and ciders. The bar and restaurant menu offers well-priced food that uses seasonal, locally sourced ingredients; the Sunday roasts here are especially noteworthy. Both dog- and child-friendly, it has a cosy open-log fire in winter. The breezy beer garden with trestle tables overlooking the beach is home to a converted boat used for serving chargrilled burgers, kebabs and ice creams.

4 HAPPISBURGH

⚑ Lanterns Shepherds Huts & Glamping (page 309)

Continuing southeast along the coast past Walcott, which, frankly, is a bit of a grim low-rise sprawl next to a popular but bleak-looking beach, you arrive at Happisburgh, an instantly recognisable place thanks to its distinctive red-and-white banded lighthouse (painted in camouflage colours during World War II), the oldest working lighthouse in East Anglia. Happisburgh, pronounced 'Hazeboro', was put on the map back in 1990 when the repainting of the **lighthouse** became the object of a *Challenge Anneka* television programme, in which the presenter

---

1 A traditional pretty village sign at Happisburgh. 2 Walking along the dunes at Winterton-on-Sea. 3 Caister Castle. 4 The tiny Mundesley Maritime Museum. ▶

landed her helicopter and ran about badgering locals into revamping their village icon. The 'challenge' was to smarten up the dowdy-looking structure with a repaint in 48 hours. The task took almost two weeks apparently – although they didn't mention this in the television programme as this went rather against the spirit of things. They used the wrong type of paint too, which soon started to peel, so the lighthouse required an expensive repaint later on. They still talk about this event in the village – the next best thing to *Antiques Roadshow* coming to town. 'Put on the map' is perhaps an unfortunate choice of words as the twin threats of coastal erosion and rising sea levels currently threaten to erase parts of the village from the map altogether. Take a look at the cliffs from the end of Beach Road and you'll get the picture.

The lighthouse (⌂ happisburgh.org/lighthouse ☉ late July–Sep Sun), was built in 1791 following a severe winter storm off the northeast Norfolk coast in 1789 in which 70 ships were wrecked and 600 men lost. Before that, apart from distant light from Cromer and Winterton, the only navigation aid had been the soaring tower of Happisburgh's **St Mary's Church**.

These days the village is perhaps better known for its connections with distant prehistory – the flint tools and early hominid footprints found on the beach (page 91) – but the existential crisis that faces us all is particularly noticeable in Happisburgh and along this stretch of coast. It is here, perhaps more than anywhere else along this coastline, where the effect of the raw power of the North Sea can best be seen, as every year, without fail, a little more land is chipped away by winter gales and high tides. The tenure of the caravan site next to the cliffs here looks increasingly precarious, and right next to this there is a tarmac road that, quite literally, ends at the cliff, crudely severed by gravity and deposited on the beach below. This is now a road going nowhere – concrete blocks have been put in place to block it just in case a mischievous sat nav encourages an innocent driver to follow it to the beach below. Coming here, you cannot but wonder how long the famous lighthouse will continue to stand, despite its location on a low bluff a little way inland. The village church, with its perpendicular flintwork and domineering tower, seems a better bet, although even here it is surely only a matter of time. Having said all of this, the clifftop path at Happisburgh is an excellent place to walk on a crisp winter's day, when the sea is at its wildest and the brutal reality of coastal erosion is almost visceral.

Hardy surfers in wet suits can sometimes be seen on such days – latter-day anti-Canutes who, rather than deny the incoming tide, embrace it.

5 SEA PALLING & 6 WAXHAM

Sea Palling, south of Happisburgh and four miles east of the market town of Stalham, is another fairly nondescript coastal village with a nice beach that has boasted a Blue Flag award for several years now. The drone of jet skiers speeding along the foreshore might spoil your peace, however. Right next door is **Waxham**, a smaller village that has a partially derelict church (St John's) next to a 15th-century gatehouse that once belonged to Waxham Hall. Originally there were two villages, Waxham Magna and Waxham Parva, but the latter has gone the way of much of this coastline and been washed away to sea. Nevertheless, there's a nice small beach here, backed by sand dunes.

Waxham Great Barn is one of the longest historic barns in the country. The building, which has featured in the BBC's *Restoration* series, was built in the early 1580s by the Woodhouses, a wealthy local family. Architectural salvage was common in those days if any material other than flint was to be used, and the barn's construction recycled parts of three monasteries closed by Henry VIII. The barn is actually a little larger than the slightly earlier one at nearby Paston and the roof may well have been built by the same carpenters.

Caroline Davison from Norfolk County Council's conservation department told me, 'The roof structure at Waxham barn is the same and was built only two or three years later. I like to think that the Woodhouses were making the point that they were the dominant family in the area, so they deliberately built their barn a bit bigger.' The Norfolk Historic Buildings Trust now manages the barn as a visitor centre on behalf of Norfolk County Council. It is open to the public in the summer months and on Sundays throughout the year and has a café adjacent to it.

¶¶ FOOD & DRINK

Dunes Café Coast Rd, Waxham NR12 0DY ✐ 01493 394931 ⬧ dunescafe.weebly.com ☺ Apr–Oct. Adjoining the enormous Waxham barn, this bright, family-run café uses locally sourced ingredients for its cakes, scones, breakfasts and lunches. Breakfast served until 11.30, hot food until 15.00. From the café's courtyard tables you can enjoy the aerial spectacle of swallows and house martins swooping around the barn while you eat.

A Horsey Mere circuit

✳ OS Explorer OL40 or Landranger 134; start: Horsey Mill car park, ♀ TG456223; 5 miles; moderate

One of my favourite walks in Broadland begins and ends at Horsey Mere, a broad just west of the village. The handy car park next to the staithe is alongside a four-storey windmill, restored by the National Trust. Horsey Mere, which also belongs to the National Trust, is a small, picture-perfect broad with thatched boathouses and sedge warblers calling from the reed beds. I have seen marsh harriers flying overhead here on several occasions – and, in the winter months you might spot hen harriers and day-flying barn owls. There is also a permanent colony of cranes in the fields around here, although they are not easy to see – I finally spotted two feeding in a field near the windmill on what must have been my tenth visit. The lovely thing about this walk, which is probably at its best on a clear, crisp winter's day, is that it gives you a taste of everything the area has to offer in the space of an easy five miles: reed beds, lake, river, farmland, marsh, beach, dunes and the North Sea itself.

A marked footpath leads through reed beds around the north side of the mere, along Waxham New Cut and over grazing marshes to a picturesque drainage pump before turning right to cross fields to the coast road. From here, a track leads over dunes at Horsey Gap to the beach, a favourite haunt of grey seals in winter. This is also highly popular with visitors in winter, especially during the week between Christmas and New Year. A mile or so southeast along the dunes, there's a muddy, pot-holed track that leads inland past an old World War II defensive pillbox to reach the road at Crinkle Hill. The 'hill' part of the name should be taken with a pinch of salt – round these parts 'hill' can mean almost anything above the horizontal; this one is about 6ft above sea level, perhaps a little less. The road leads back to the village past the Nelson Head pub, which has a telephone box by the door and a large beer garden – a tempting stopping point before the short leg back to the car park.

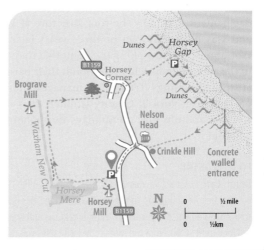

7 HORSEY

The coast road from Sea Palling turns inland slightly to pass through the village of Horsey, which has the best of both worlds in being close to the coast but also at the very edge of the Broads. Standing only a couple of feet or so above sea level, the village has always had a fractious relationship with the North Sea just over the dunes and was cut off completely for four months in 1938 when all of the villagers had to be evacuated. The village is tiny but manages to retain a pub, a nice old barn and thatched church, and easy access to a beach. Roman coins have been found in the area on several occasions and so despite its obvious vulnerability, Horsey has been settled for a very long time.

¶¶ FOOD & DRINK

Nelson Head The Street ✐ 01493 393378 ⬧ thenelsonhead.com. This country pub has a red telephone box immediately in front of the entrance, and a log fire and cheery, warm interior within. Outside is a huge beer garden. Fresh local food is served lunchtime and evening, all day in summer, and there's a selection of real ales including Woodforde's.
Poppylands Horsey Corner ✐ 01493 393393. Located on the coast road just before Horsey Gap, this popular tea shop serves coffee, cake, sandwiches and light meals. There's plenty of 1940s wartime memorabilia on display here, even down to the music played, because of the young owner's personal interest in the period. Thankfully, they draw the line at including wartime austerity dishes on the menu. Upstairs is a small gift shop.

8 WINTERTON-ON-SEA

Winterton's Holy Trinity and All Saints' Church is distinguished by its noticeably tall tower, the third highest in Norfolk, but steeples on steroids make good sense along this occasionally treacherous coastline: they stand out as beacons in this pancake-flat terrain. Local tradition sometimes claims that Winterton's church tower is 'a herring-and-a-half higher than Cromer'. Unfortunately, this is not true: it is, in fact, 35ft shorter.

Daniel Defoe, who visited the village in 1722, remarked that all its houses seemed to be constructed out of the timbers of wrecked ships – a reflection on the hazardous nature of the coastline here. Most of the ones he commented on would have come from the fleet that was wrecked in the fatal storm of 1692. The danger of shipwreck can seem real enough if you come here on a winter's day when thick sea mist blankets the shoreline and stretches for a mile or so inland obscuring everything from view.

The **Winterton Dunes Nature Reserve**, north of the village, is a large hummocky stretch of sand dunes stabilised by marram grass that are home to a large colony of rare natterjack toads. Plenty of birds nest here too – little terns, ringed plovers and stonechats – and dragonflies

Winterton walk: dunes, fields & woodland

※ OS Explorer OL40 or Landranger 134; start: Winterton beach car park, ♥ TG498197; 5 miles; easy–moderate.

Starting and ending at Winterton, this rewarding circular walk takes in pretty well all that the area has to offer: sand dunes, wildlife, wind turbines and woodland. It is about five miles – two hours – in total, but easy going and varied. You might prefer to do the whole walk in the other direction if you want to keep the coastal stretch for the finale.

From the beach car park, head north towards Winterton Dunes Nature Reserve until you reach a marked footpath beyond the nature reserve sign. Continue along the sand dunes keeping the perimeter fence to your left. After a mile or so, the reserve ends at Winterton Ness; turn left here along the public footpath to Winterton Holmes. Turn left again towards the wind farm along a concrete farm road, which turns sharply right after another few hundred yards. When the track finally divides, turn left along the estate wall, heading towards the wind turbines alongside woods. At the end of a small plantation to your right, turn left and follow the path past the entrance and left towards Manor Farm. To the right, almost hidden, is the ruin of St Mary's Church. From Manor Farm, head east down Low Road past the duck pond to return to Winterton.

While Winterton retains the slightly isolated feel of the northeast coast, Hemsby, the neighbouring village, just a mile away, seems to belong firmly to Great Yarmouth's gravitational field. In Hemsby, you are starting to venture into a hinterland of caravan parks, amusement arcades and crazy golf that stretches all along the coast from here through Yarmouth and Lowestoft as far as Kessingland in Suffolk.

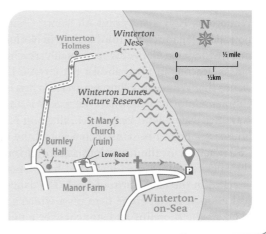

flit above the ponds. You can often see seals offshore here too: there is usually a colony of them on the beach to the north. In winter you might well see a flock of snow buntings on the beach. Other colonists found among the dunes to the north here are the odd naturist (and, perhaps, even odder naturalist) along with concrete pillboxes constructed during World War II as anti-invasion defences. In 2005, a landslide resulted in some of these toppling on to the beach near the car park.

Clearly visible from Winterton is the Blood Hill wind farm at nearby Somerton, one of the first erected in the UK, as well as the more extensive offshore wind farm at **Scroby Sands**, built in 2003 and 2004. Of course, wind farms are not popular with everyone, least of all those who fear living in their shadow. 'Nimby' might sound rather like a Danish place name but around here it means something completely different.

⑪ FOOD & DRINK

Sadly, the popular Winterton Dunes Beach Café that once stood in the beach car park at Winterton is no longer there. It was demolished in 2021 in anticipation of its concrete base falling into the sea.

The Fisherman's Return The Lane, NR29 4BN ⏱ 01493 393305 ⏣ fishermansreturn.com. This 300-year-old traditional brick and flint pub has a good range of local ales, including Woodforde's and Blackfriars. 'Keeping it local' is the motto on the bar menu: fresh fish is delivered daily from Lowestoft while meat is sourced from local butchers.

9 CAISTER-ON-SEA

Virtually a suburb of Great Yarmouth, Caister offers much the same as Hemsby, except for the nearby remains of **Caister Castle**, a 15th-century moated castle built between 1432 and 1446 by Sir John Falstaff, the inspiration for the Shakespeare character. The Pastons inherited the castle from Sir John but before long the Duke of Norfolk, an enthusiastic and serial castle-grabber, took control of it having laid siege for a year. When he died, it passed back into Paston hands until the 17th century when the new London owner decided to tear most of it down.

The castle (⏣ caistercastle.co.uk ⏱ mid-May–Sep) now serves as home to the largest private collection of motor vehicles in Britain, and includes a minor star of *Chitty Chitty Bang Bang* and an 1893 Panhard et Lavassor, the world's first proper motor car. The 90ft tower remains intact and can be climbed for a gull's eye view of the surrounding area.

A CAISTER PHOENIX

As with all of the northeast Norfolk coast, erosion is a fact of life. The Manor House Hotel, a largish building that once stood proudly in the town, was finally abandoned to the elements during World War II after much of its shoreline had been destroyed by environmental erosion. The hotel is said to have completely disappeared from view by 1948, never to be seen again. But not quite: in March 2013, following a wild night of northeasterly gales, a large chunk of the hotel's brickwork dramatically re-emerged from the sands like a proverbial phoenix from the ashes. Elsewhere, at nearby Hemsby and Hopton, World War II concrete pillboxes were revealed for the first time in years.

The huge amount of sand scoured from the beach to reveal these half-forgotten buildings is no doubt already halfway along the Norfolk coast, perhaps a future sand spit in the making.

Caister is also well known for its lifeboat and never-say-die fishermen, whose slogan, 'Caister men never turn back', says it all.

The word Caister comes from *castrum*, the Latin for camp: hidden rather unglamorously behind back gardens of semis and bungalows are the labelled knee-height walls of the late Roman fort (free access), built as a defence against Saxon raiders around AD200 and in use until the end of the following century, that gives the village its name. This is not to be confused with another Roman 'Caister' in the county – Caister St Edmund (Venta Icenorum) close to Norwich, a Romano-British settlement which has altogether more impressive town walls.

INTO THE BROADS PROPER: NORTH WALSHAM TO THE RIVER BURE

10 NORTH WALSHAM

This market town, just beyond the Broads, is the most important urban centre in northeast Norfolk. Having said that, it is still pretty low-key. The Bittern Line between Norwich and Sheringham passes through the town, as does the Weavers' Way long-distance footpath. There is no river but the now-disused North Walsham and Dilham Canal, which connects with the River Ant and Broads system, skirts the town to the northeast.

In keeping with Norfolk's radical tradition, the town became a focus for a rural uprising in support of Wat Tyler's Peasants' Revolt back in 1381, when a local dyer Geoffrey Litester headed a group of rebels calling for the abolition of serfdom. Workers' rights were not high on the agenda in the 14th century and, unsurprisingly, their pleas fell on deaf, and highly unsympathetic, ears. The rebels were attacked by none other than the Bishop of Norwich himself, Henry Despencer, who, if historic accounts are correct, rather enjoyed the bloodshed. The bishop, being a man of the cloth, was at least good enough to grant Litester absolution before having him drawn and quartered. Litester's quarters were subsequently dispatched to Norwich, King's Lynn, Great Yarmouth and his home village 'so that rebels, and those that rise above their place, may learn how they will end' – they did not do things by halves in those days. Bishop Henry erected three crosses to mark the crushing of the uprising, one of which can still be seen on the Norwich road just south of North Walsham.

Like Holt, most of Tudor North Walsham went up in flames, on this occasion in 1600, and most of the town's larger buildings date from the Georgian period. The town centre is a pleasant enough place to wander but the only real sights as such are the **Market Cross**, sometimes referred to locally as 'the gazebo', which has stood on the spot since 1550 but has been restored many times since, and **St Nicolas's Church** with its partially collapsed tower and rood screen covered in paintings depicting the apostles.

11 WORSTEAD

This solid, distinguished-looking village with its seemingly oversized church has a long historic association with the medieval Norfolk wool trade. The clue, of course, is in the name, as the village became well-known for producing a particular type of cloth. 'Walsham' cloth was light and for summer wear, while 'Worstead' was heavier. The first cloth description soon went out of common use, but the village still gives its name to worsted, even though it has not been produced in the village for centuries. Worsted cloth was introduced to East Anglia by Flemish immigrant weavers and the soft-textured but hardwearing material became highly sought-after from the 13th century onwards. Back in the medieval heyday of Norfolk's weaving industry, Worstead was a thriving place with two churches – more of a town than a village – but as the wool trade shifted to the mill towns of the north of England, its economy started to dwindle. There are still a few weavers' cottages there,

PUNTS & WILDFOWLING

NO

THE NORTH WALSHAM & DILHAM CANAL

Few expect to find canals here in Norfolk, far away from England's industrial heartland, and this modest stretch in northeast Norfolk is the county's sole example. It was created by the canalisation of the upper reaches of the River Ant and the locks installed were made a little wider than average in order to accommodate Norfolk wherries. The canal is a little less than nine miles long and begins at Swafield Bridge, just north of North Walsham, ending where it reaches the River Ant at Smallburgh near Stalham. Opened in 1826, it was mainly used to transport animal bones and phosphates to the bone mills at Antingham, although grain, coal and building materials were also carried by the wherries. The canal was sold off in 1885, but the money from the sale – some £600 – mysteriously went missing in the care of the company solicitor. He was never seen again.

Today, very little of the original canal, last used for a cargo journey in 1934, is navigable – just a couple of miles at the Smallburgh end – although there are plans to restore some parts of it for pleasure craft. It is best explored by following footpaths along its banks south of the villages of East Ruston and Honing. A canoe is an even better option: hire one at Wayford Bridge and paddle along Tyler's Cut to reach the staithe at the Honing Road bridge at the end of the channel, from where you can easily walk into Dilham village with its Cross Keys pub.

characterised by their high ceilings, lofty enough to accommodate a loom. Perhaps more remarkable is that Worstead still has an active, if rather symbolic, Guild of Weavers who sometimes put on demonstrations of their ancient craft.

St Mary's Church, built with wool money in 1379, stands tall in the centre of the village and has a number of noteworthy features other than its sheer size: an impressive hammerbeam roof, box pews and a finely painted dado.

The **Worstead Festival** (⊘ worsteadfestival.org), the largest village festival in Norfolk, held each year on the last weekend in July, gives villagers the chance to show off a bit and makes for a fine day out. This is the perfect excuse for displaying rare breeds and prize farm animals and demonstrating country crafts from ploughing with heavy horses to sheep shearing, beekeeping and falconry. Classic farm vehicles and vintage cars are dusted off to take part in a parade and there is usually live music in the village square.

◀ 1 The North Walsham & Dilham Canal. 2 East Ruston Old Vicarage Garden. 3 Exhibits at the Museum of the Broads, Stalham.

12 EAST RUSTON

Halfway between North Walsham and Stalham, close to the route of the Weavers' Way, this sprawling village is home to the **East Ruston Old Vicarage Garden** (℘ 01692 650432 ♂ eastrustonoldvicarage.co.uk ☉ Mar–Oct Wed–Sun & bank hols), a rather special 32-acre garden. It's less than two miles from the coast and vulnerable to onshore winds but the shelter of a belt of pines helps to maintain a relatively warm microclimate. Themed garden areas include the Californian Border and Desert Wash, a Tree Fern Garden, Sunken Garden and so on, as well as a wildlife flower meadow and cornfields sown with native species that have become rare in this age of herbicides. A pot of tea taken on the lawn here on a hot summer's afternoon with bees buzzing in the borders is an unbridled pleasure. The garden is not in the village itself but further east towards the coast along the Bacton Road, just beyond East Ruston church: guided tours led by gardener Alan Gray take place once or twice a month throughout the spring and summer months.

13 STALHAM & 14 SUTTON

These are two separate villages on the bend of the A149 at the northern limit of the Broads, both linked to the River Ant and Barton Broad by staithes. **Stalham High Street** is a hotchpotch of small shops and architectural styles but the town is probably best known locally for its supermarket that shall be nameless (but which rhymes with 'al fresco'), which, after years and years of planning permission being turned down, eventually took over the traditional saleground next to the bypass. It was inevitable, I suppose, that something as unfashionable as a weekly market and auction would finally give way to yet another 'out of town' shopping centre.

Stalham does, however, have an interesting **Museum of the Broads** (℘ 01692 581681 ♂ museumofthebroads.org.uk ☉ Mar–Oct daily) down at the staithe, where you can see a mock-up of a wherry's cuddy (page 119) and plenty more relating to the working life of the Broads. The museum puts on occasional events in the summer and runs river trips on *Falcon*, a Victorian steam launch on some days. The tiny **Firehouse Museum** (℘ 01692 582781 ♂ stalhamfirehousemuseum.info ☉ Easter–Sep) on the High Street is a fittingly eccentric place, the second-oldest fire station in the UK, built in 1833, with a 1902 fire engine and an array of fire-fighting paraphernalia on display.

Sutton has **Sutton Mill** just east of the village – at nine storeys high, the tallest remaining windmill in the UK (sold in 2018 to a private buyer and not open for visitors). The mill was built around 1789 on the site of a former tower mill.

15 COLTISHALL

🏠 **Norfolk Mead Hotel** (page 309)

Coltishall, better known as the site of an RAF base that existed to the north of here until recently, is actually quite a pretty village that sits in a bend of the River Bure. Formerly important for its malthouses and as a loading point for wherries travelling the Bure as far as Aylsham, the village's river trade fell into decline with the arrival of the railway line in 1879. Navigation beyond Coltishall became altogether impossible when the lock gates at Horstead were destroyed in a flood in 1912, and even today this remains the end of the line for boats venturing up from Wroxham.

Coming from Wroxham, the river bends sharply at Belaugh before it reaches Coltishall, and having passed the village meanders sluggishly through lovely woodland west of **Great Hautbois** – superb, safe canoeing territory that is often frequented by school groups. Great Hautbois – pronounced 'Hobbis' – gets its odd name not from 'high woods' or oboes but from the Alto Bosco or Haut Bois family,

---

A riverside walk from Coltishall

❄ OS Explorer OL40 or Landranger 134; start: Coltishall bridge, 📍 TG267198; 4.5 miles; easy–moderate.

An enjoyable **circular walk** from Coltishall is to follow the footpath along the north bank of the River Bure through woodland as far as Mayton Bridge at Little Hautbois, where you can cross the bridge to the south bank and cross fields via Hall Farm back to Horstead and Coltishall. I say 'enjoyable' but last time I walked it after a long period of rain the nettles along this path grew so tall that even my face got stung. Normally though, it is far more manageable and a lovely waterside excursion through dappled shade in the company of dragonflies. A lengthier alternative is to continue northwest from Little Hautbois towards Lamas and Buxton, then return along the river path on the south bank as far as Little Hautbois bridge before taking the route described above.

who acquired land in the area just after the Norman conquest. The village of Great Hautbois was the head of navigation of the River Bure in medieval times. As well as the Victorian church of Holy Trinity, the same parish also has the round tower church of St Theolbald out in the fields west of Great Hautbois Road, an atmospheric late Saxon/early Norman semi-ruin that lacks a roof over the nave and aisle. There's a Little Hautbois too, halfway to Buxton, a tiny place that consists of just eight houses, one of which used to be a pub. Formerly, it was important enough to warrant its own church. The church has all but disappeared today but traces of its foundations can apparently still be seen in the grounds of Little Hautbois Hall.

¶¶ FOOD & DRINK

A Piece of Cake The River Rooms, Church Cl ✆ 01603 736090 ⌂ coltishallcakes.co.uk. This traditional-style tea room, in premises that used to be the old Salvation Army hall, serves homemade cakes, light lunches and breakfasts. Depending on the weather, there are inside tables or an outside walled courtyard to choose from.

Recruiting Sergeant Norwich Rd, Horstead ✆ 01603 737077 ⌂ recruitingsergeant.co.uk. In the village of Horstead, just south of the bridge that leads into Coltishall. The pub menu here makes use of Swannington Farm meat and local seasonal vegetables. Real ales include Adnams, Greene King and Woodforde's.

16 WROXHAM & HOVETON

These two villages are practically joined at the hip – or rather, at the bridge. Many people, especially visitors, tend to refer to the whole settlement as Wroxham, much to the annoyance of Hovetonites. Effectively, for those who come here to hire a boat, lick an ice cream or shop at Roys, the business end of the village is immediately north of Wroxham Bridge – in Hoveton.

Wroxham (I have lapsed already – it should actually be Hoveton) is famous for two things: as the epicentre of the **broads cruiser hire** trade and self-appointed 'Capital of The Broads', and for Roys, the 'world's biggest village store', a local enterprise that is ubiquitous hereabouts. Ask any local, 'Where's Roys?' and they will know what you mean, although they might be incredulous that you need to ask. They'll point you towards Roys supermarket, anyway.

Roys was founded back in 1899 by two brothers, Arnold and Alfred Roy, to meet the needs of holiday makers visiting the Norfolk Broads.

Now it has branches throughout Norfolk and, to its credit, prides itself on selling locally sourced produce. Roys of Wroxham is well known throughout Norfolk but, technically, as all of the Roys commercial property lies north of the bridge, it really ought to be called 'Roys of Hoveton'.

Hoveton is anything but a typical sleepy Norfolk village. Once you cross the narrow bridge over the River Bure you'll find the

"Once you cross the narrow bridge over the River Bure you'll find the place heaving with people in the summer."

place heaving with people in the summer. However, even if you do not wish to step out on to a motor cruiser here, it's still a good place to rent a canoe and paddle upstream. Canoeing downstream, alongside a flotilla of inexpertly, and sometimes erratically, piloted hire-boats on their way to Wroxham Broad is not everybody's idea of fun but to strike out north along the River Bure towards Belaugh and Coltishall is well worth doing. **Canadian canoes** can be hired from Barnes Brinkcraft at Riverside Road (🖉 01603 782625 or 782333 🖱 barnesbrinkcraft.co.uk) or The Canoe Man (🖉 0845 4969177 🖱 thecanoeman.com) at Norfolk Broads Tourism and Activity Centre, right beside the road bridge.

Hoveton Hall Gardens
🖉 01603 784297 🖱 hovetonhallestate.co.uk
Popular for their azalea and rhododendron displays in late spring, these attractive and peaceful gardens are just north of the town of the same name. Various walks lead through woods and around a lake, and a walled garden has an ornamental wrought iron gate in the form of a spider. Tucked away in the woods is an 18th-century ice well, a brick-lined pit formerly used for storing ice for the house. The woodland has several adventure trails for children and there are suggestions as to what may be seen in terms of birds, butterflies and dragonflies along the way. Buzzards and hobbies are sometimes seen in summer, as are swallowtail butterflies occasionally.

BeWILDerwood
🖉 01692 633033 🖱 bewilderwood.co.uk ⏲ Apr–Sep daily; Oct–Mar w/ends & half terms
A little way along the A1062 Horning Road, BeWILDerwood describes itself as a 'curious treehouse adventure park'. Certainly, it's designed to exercise and stimulate the mind as much as the body.

It's a magical place for children – forest folk like Mildred, the vegetarian Crocklebog who lives in Scary Lake, and the Twiggles, litter-hating goblin-like figures, are BeWILDerwood residents, as is a giant spider called Thornyclod.

BeWILDerwood's environmental pedigree is certainly impressive too. The treehouses, ropewalks and boardwalks are all built from sustainable wood, while the 50 acres of marshland and woodland that make up the site are entirely pesticide-free, guaranteeing that no harmful chemicals leak into the broads. If that were not enough, some 14,000 broad-leaved trees have been planted since the park's creation and the food on site is mainly locally sourced and organic. BeWILDerwood won the British Guild of Travel Writers award for best new UK tourism project in 2008; as Jane Anderson, who nominated the park for the award, attests it 'harks back to a pre-PlayStation, pre-mobile, pre-iPod era' even if its creator Tom Blofield does admit to having been partly inspired by the 1990s computer game Myst. In 2009 BeWILDerwood won a worldwide award from the Themed Entertainment Association (TEA), and in 2021 was recognised as a Tripadvisor Travellers' Choice award winner for Amusement and Theme Parks. BeWILDerwood is open year-round and those under 92cm/3ft tall go free. Bikes are available to rent at the **Norfolk Broads Cycling Centre** in the car park (🖉 07747 483154 🖉 norfolkbroadscycling.co.uk) which also provides useful free cycling maps.

Wroxham Barns
🖉 01603 783762 🖉 wroxhambarns.co.uk

A couple of miles north of Hoveton along Tunstead Road, Wroxham Barns is a range of 18th-century barns and farm buildings that have been converted into craft workshops. Here, you'll find such things as woodturning, pottery and stained glass, all made on site with the finished goods being sold from the workshops. Several enterprises sell local produce, such as the Norfolk Cider Shop (🖉 07596 159747), which stocks both cider and apple juice produced by the Norfolk Cider Company and stages occasional demonstrations using antique apple pressing equipment. Animal-loving children are well catered for as well, with a **Junior Farm** that provides an opportunity for children to get up close to animals in a farmyard setting, offering activities like feeding rabbits and goats and grooming ponies.

BARTON BROAD, HICKLING BROAD & AROUND

17 HORNING

Heading east from Hoveton along the A1062 the first place that you come to is Horning, which, from a boating point of view, lies downstream along the River Bure beyond Wroxham Broad, **Hoveton Great Broad** and **Hoveton Little Broad**. Horning functions a little like a mini version of Wroxham. Firmly given over to the hire cruiser trade, it's all Edwardian thatch roofs and mock Tudor cottages but pleasant enough nevertheless and certainly a lot quieter than its riverside neighbour. Sadly, the seasonal passenger ferry that used to cross the river here from the Horning Ferry pub to Woodbastwick no longer operates. From Horning, the River Bure meanders east through the Bure Marshes, with channels connecting it with Cockshoot Broad and Ranworth Broad, both ripe for exploration by curious boaters.

18 LUDHAM, HOW HILL & AROUND

The next village reached by taking the road is Ludham, a pleasant, typical Broads village that does not sit on the river itself but just to the north of it. The village clusters around a crossroads with a pub and a church, and a road opposite the pub leads south past attractive houses with large gardens fronting on to **Womack Water**, a tributary of the River Thurne that serves as a staithe for boats. If you visit on Ludham Open Gardens Day, held every other year in June, you will get the chance to see some of these gardens. Horsefen Road, which leads south along the eastern bank of Womack Water, is similar, with some thatch-roofed barns, the parish staithe and a couple of boatyards. A staithe along here serves as headquarters for the **Norfolk Wherry Trust** (⊘ wherryalbion.com) where the 124-year-old wherry *Albion* is moored

"How Hill, while undoubtedly the highest point for miles around, still only manages to reach about 40ft above sea level."

when it is not out on charter. Given so many water's-edge back gardens, it is perfectly possible for many Ludham residents to visit each other by boat, as I am sure some of them do.

The River Ant joins the Bure just south of Ludham and, a little way along this, How Hill rises above the river with its gardens, woodland and manicured lawns. Lest this sound too dramatic, I should add that How Hill, while undoubtedly the highest point for miles around, still only manages to reach about 40ft above sea level. It is a hill, nevertheless – a welcome meniscus in this overwhelmingly two-dimensional landscape.

How Hill House is a residential Broads Study Centre that hosts courses and conferences and is not usually open to the public, although holiday courses and special events are organised by the **How Hill Trust** (✆ 01692 678555 ⌖ howhilltrust.org.uk). A narrow road with passing places leads up from a junction just before Ludham and there is a free car park on the left just before the main building. How Hill's Secret Gardens are open for all to enjoy and can be accessed via the wood at the rear of the house. These woodland gardens were established by Edward Thomas Boardman, the original owner of the house, in the early 1920s. With oaks, hornbeams, sweet chestnuts and many exotic species, these are probably most spectacular in late spring when the azaleas and rhododendrons are at their finest, or in autumn when the leaves are turning. The large meadow close to the public car park – Fisherman's Field – is a popular spot for locals to take picnics, play cricket and fly kites. A track leads across this down to **Toad Hole Cottage**, a small marshman's cottage containing a museum and information centre (✆ 01692 678763). A **wildlife walking trail** starts from here, but even better is the **water trail** that lasts for about an hour and makes use of the *Electric Eel* electric boat.

A Broadland water trail on the *Electric Eel*

Maximum 6 passengers; book in advance at Toad Hole Cottage ⊘ the *Electric Eel* leaves every hour on the hour 11.00–15.00 on weekends, bank holidays, Easter week & half terms in Apr, May & Oct, & Jun–Sep daily 10.00–16.00

Taking me out on the *Electric Eel* at How Hill in late May, Paul, the boatman, gave me the low-down on traditional Broadland ways and how, with encouragement from the Broads Authority, some aspects of the traditional economy are currently being revived. After gliding past a kingfisher's nest in the bank where, perfectly on cue, such a bird darted past us like a rocket-propelled jewel, Paul pointed out a couple of small windmills next to the water where the sails had been removed. 'Do you see what they've done there?' he asked, just a little exasperated. 'Would that be anything to do with Health and Safety?' I ventured. 'Yes, absolutely right. They said they were a hazard for walkers. Can you believe it? They're 9ft above the ground for heaven's sake.'

We soon turned off the River Ant down a narrow tributary to leave the diesel-engine throb of the motor boats far behind. This really was another world, a minimalist landscape of reed, water and a blue slice of sky. Reed has been harvested for centuries in the region for use as thatch but the industry went into decline back in the Victorian period when the railways made cheap pan-tiles and slate available to all. Nowadays, thatch is back in fashion, and there's considerable demand for reed harvested in the Norfolk Broads, as well as the sedge that is used to 'top' the thatch. Reed harvesting is clearly not an easy job. 'You need to be a special character to be a reed cutter,' said Paul. 'It's hard, laborious work and, in the winter when you have to do the cutting, it's freezing cold too. The sedge has to be cut in the summer months and that's just the opposite: there's mosquitoes to bother you and your hands get cut up from gathering the sedge.'

"This really was another world, a minimalist landscape of reed, water and a blue slice of sky."

Although reed-cutting is clearly no career for lonely, work-shy rheumatics, there is enough demand for the Norfolk product that the Broads Authority have been training up the young and willing over the past few years and employment has been created for at least a dozen local cutters. There is no question about quality according to Paul. 'Polish reed is a bit cheaper but it doesn't last anywhere near as long. Most thatchers reckon that Norfolk reed lasts for anything between 80 and 100 years.'

After an hour of squeezing through narrow, reed-fringed channels, we head back to How Hill Staithe. On the way, we stop off at Reedham Broad, a recently reclaimed body of water that has resident bitterns and summer-breeding marsh harriers – a pair of which were quartering the reeds on the other side of the water, painstakingly searching for voles and mice. 'This was a reclaimed meadow with cows on it just 30 years ago but the Broads Authority have encouraged it to revert back to nature. It's manmade, I suppose, but then so are all the broads.'

FOOD & DRINK

Alfresco Tea Room Norwich Rd, Ludham ✆ 01692 678384. Opposite Ludham's St Catherine's Church, this is a fine place for afternoon tea and cakes. There's an indoor tea room and even a small, al fresco element — two tables outside in the back yard.

19 BARTON BROAD

The **River Ant** twists north past How Hill to open into Barton Broad, one of the finest and most unspoiled of all these bodies of water. Barton Broad is the second largest body of water in the broads system and is managed as a nature reserve by the Norfolk Wildlife Trust. Hemmed in by reed beds and swampy stands of alder, the broad is barely approachable by road and the only meaningful way to visit – other than walking along the short boardwalk – is by canoe or boat.

An excellent boardwalk starts from the car park near Gay's Staithe. To reach it, you first need to undertake a short half-mile walk along a footpath and lane to arrive at the start. The trail soon splits into two: one direction leads to a viewing point that looks over the southern edge of the broad, while the other takes a short circular course through the alder carr. It's very green and humid here, with warblers warbling in the trees, dragonflies hawking the moist air and yellow irises pushing up through the sedge. Watch out for mosquitoes though; they can sometimes be a nuisance on warm, still days.

A decade or so ago, Barton Broad was heavily polluted with nutrients from agricultural and sewage run-off but the multi-million-pound **Clear Water Project** has improved the water quality dramatically, even to the point of attracting otters back to the area. Back in the 1960s, the water here was a toxic chemical soup of phosphates (from sewage) and nitrates (from farms). Now, with investment from bodies such as the Millennium Fund and, fittingly, some detergent manufacturers, there has been a dramatic transformation. This is mainly thanks to painstaking suction dredging that has removed the nutrient-rich mud at the bottom of the broad and its channels. Although otters are present, you are far more likely to see herons, grebes, terns and a variety of ducks. Swallowtail butterflies are relatively common at the right time of year – between May and July – too, thanks to the presence of milk parsley, a scarce plant that provides food for their caterpillars. The waters of Barton Broad host an open regatta each August Bank Holiday organised by the Norfolk Punt Club, and the broad is also used by the Nancy Oldfield Trust to provide sailing and canoeing access for the disabled.

1 How Hill House and gardens. 2 The 60ft wherry *Albion* is today maintained by the Norfolk Wherry Trust. 3 Edwardian thatch roofs and mock Tudor cottages line the river Bure at Horning. 4 The board walk at Barton Broad. ▶

Barton Broad has three villages that just about touch it – **Irstead**, **Barton Turf** and **Neatishead** – none of which could be described as a metropolis, although Neatishead does have a pub and a shop. Barton Turf has an interesting church with fine paintings on its rood screen but no other facilities whatsoever. Such a distinct lack of facilities may, in fact, represent a temptation for those in search of peace and quiet. A friend of mine who moved to Neatishead from London a dozen or so years ago told me: 'I've got used to living there; I've become a country boy now. Neatishead's got most things we need, like a pub and a restaurant. It's a lovely place to live. Every Saturday morning, we take the children for a walk along the boardwalk at Barton Broad and if we want a taste of big city lights then we just drive into Wroxham and go shopping at Roys. I hardly ever go into Norwich these days, let alone London.'

The stretch of the bank between Barton Turf and Neatishead is known locally as 'Millionaires' Row'. The posh, two-storey boathouses at the water's edge are just the icing on the cake, belonging as they do to large private houses in sumptuous surroundings set well back from the water. Barton Hall on the edge of Barton Turf village is where Lord Nelson's sister once lived and it is claimed that Nelson learned to sail on Barton Broad, presumably when he wasn't doing the same thing in Brancaster Staithe harbour.

Although it is hard to reach Barton Broad using public transport – Smallburgh or Stalham being about as close as you can get – the whole area west of Barton Broad makes for vintage cycling territory. With a bike, you might also wish to venture south of Neatishead to **Alderfen Broad**, another NWT reserve just outside **Irstead Street** – it's a decent circular walk too, starting in Neatishead. How Hill lies just across the marsh to the east but there is no direct way to reach it on either land or water.

Barton Broad by boat

I was lucky enough to tour Barton Broad by boat back in the days when the solar-powered *Ra* used to sail here (organised boat trips are sadly no longer available). As we progressed around the south end of the Broad, enjoying the sight of candy-striped grebe chicks riding on their parents' backs, Mike, the boat's skipper, pointed out a narrow channel leading off to the east. 'That's called Ice House Reach. There used to be an icehouse just down there. Ice was collected from the broad and stored there before it was transported all the way down to Yarmouth by wherry.'

Cruising up to the northern end of the Broads where the River Ant makes its entrance, we turned our attention to the water lilies dotting the water's surface. 'They're a really good sign of clean water', says Mike. Yellow water lily needs good water quality; white needs even better. What's remarkable is that they can lie dormant for years. Water lilies weren't here at all during the 1960s and 70s, when it was like a pea soup here. As soon as the water quality got better they started to appear again, growing from tubers that had lain dormant in the mud at the bottom for decades.'

The Broads, as everyone now knows, are an artificial environment, but it's easy to overlook the way that they have been altered to fit in with humankind's changing needs over the years. According to Mike, the River Ant did not originally pass through Barton Broad but passed just to the east of it. Irish workmen known as navigators were employed to cut a channel through to the broad so that wherries could be used to transport goods. 'Irish navvies did a lot of work in the Broads. They dug the channel here back in 1729 and there is even a Paddy's Lane in Barton Turf in memory of them.'

If you are up to it, an excellent way to explore the broad is to hire a canoe for the day from Wayford Bridge. To canoe south along the River Ant, cross Barton Broad, head up Lime Kiln Dyke to moor and visit Neatishead and perhaps have lunch before returning north, will probably take the best part of a day. It's a fairly energetic outing but, at the end of such a day, you will have better memories and a far more intimate impression of the Broads than will those who have chugged through them in a cruiser.

FOOD & DRINK

The White Horse Inn The Street, Neatishead NR12 8AD ✆ 01692 630828
⌂ thewhitehorseinnneatishead.com. This popular traditional inn tucked away in Neatishead village is probably the best bet for dining in the Barton Broad region. It sources food from plenty of local suppliers, including Swannington Farm, Pye Bakery and Direct Seafoods, who provide many ingredients for its varied menu. The pub also has its own brewery producing a range of real ales. What's more, it makes its own 'Hopton Gin', which is infused with hops to create a unique flavour.

CANOE HIRE

Bank Dayboat & Canoe Hire Wayford Bridge ✆ 01692 582457 ⌂ bankboats.co.uk

20 ST BENET'S ABBEY

Guided tours led by volunteers May–Sep 14.00 Wed, Sat & Sun; meet at the information board near the gatehouse

This atmospheric ruin was built on land granted by King Canute around 1020, probably on the site of a 9th-century pre-Viking hermitage. It's something of a rarity in having a pre-Norman origin and also for managing to survive the Dissolution. It did this by agreeing to a crafty swap of lands belonging to the Diocese of Norwich. Because of this, St Benet's is unique in being the only monastery in England that was not closed down by Henry VIII. The Bishop of Norwich continues to hold the role of abbot here and, once a year on the first Sunday in August, he arrives by wherry to preach an annual service at the site. The gatehouse contains a windmill, squeezed within its walls, that was put up by a local farmer at the turn of the 19th century. A more recent addition is the oak altar cross made from wood given by the Royal Sandringham estate. The Norwich School artist, John Sell Cotman, made a painting of the abbey in the middle of the 19th century, when it looked much as it does today, albeit with sails still present on the windmill. You can see this in Norwich Castle Museum in addition to another splendid painting of it by Henry Bright.

With a mysterious profile that combines these ecclesiastical and vernacular traditions, St Benet's Abbey is at its best viewed from the banks of the river at dusk, when long shadows help to enhance the numinous atmosphere.

For those lacking river transport, a visit to the site requires a detour south from the main road at Ludham – an easy cycle ride. The farm track that leads down to the abbey goes past a farmyard that has an enormous high midden of used car tyres of all shapes and sizes. So, if you were curious as to the fate of all the old tyres discarded in Norfolk, now you know. On foot, an even better way to reach St Benet's Abbey is to follow the permissive path that leads along the Ant and Bure rivers from Ludham Bridge, which takes around 25 minutes.

Following a conservation project under the auspices of the **Norfolk Archaeological Trust**, St Benet's Abbey now has better on-site information and improved access. A variety of special activities now frequently take place at the site – wildlife workshops, history days and storytelling. Information on these and pre-booking for regular guided tours can be made at ✑ norfarchtrust.org.uk/project/st-benets.

21 WOODBASTWICK

South of the River Bure, a minor road runs more or less parallel to the river and the A1062 beyond, connecting several villages on the southern fringe of the broads east of Wroxham. Salhouse village lies some distance from the broad of the same name – and its station lies even further away and is pretty useless for waterside exploration. **Woodbastwick**, the next village to the east, with a good pub and brewery, is an altogether better bet. Just east of the village, the road splits and a track leads down to the Bure where there is parking and a nature trail through the reed beds. **Woodforde's Brewery** (⌀ woodfordes.co.uk) next door to the Fur and Feather Inn runs occasional brewery tours that must be booked in advance (✆ 01603 720353). They have a shop and visitor centre too where, as well as bottles and beer-boxes, you can buy souvenirs that range from keyrings to T-shirts.

▌▌ FOOD & DRINK

Fur and Feather Inn Slad Lane NR13 6HQ ✆ 01603 720003 ⌀ thefurandfeather.co.uk. A very popular thatched pub with a fireplace and newspapers but no pool table or juke box. The food is mostly hearty English – steak and kidney pudding, venison pie, fancy burgers and the like – while the beer is excellent, and so it should be with the Woodforde's brewery right next door.

22 RANWORTH

Ranworth is a charming, dinky little village right next to Malthouse Broad, little brother of neighbouring Ranworth Broad. Ranworth's **St Helen's Church** is well worth a visit, not simply because it has some of the best screen paintings in the county and a beautifully illuminated antiphoner (service book) on display, but because it has a feature that offers something that geology does not in this neck of the woods – elevation. A steep, tightly curving staircase leads up 89 steps to the roof of the church tower. It's very narrow so try to avoid two-way traffic if at all possible. The view is undoubtedly worth the climb: the broad and river are laid out in front of you and Broadland comes alive and suddenly means a lot more than just blue and green shading on a map. From here, as well as from Ranworth and Malthouse Broads immediately below, you can see the Bure and Ant rivers, How Hill, the wind turbines near Happisburgh and even the coast at Yarmouth. On a really clear day, Norwich Cathedral spire is said to be visible.

Ranworth Broad is a NWT reserve of some importance, with a visitor centre, boardwalk and child-friendly nature trail along with the usual range of Broadland wildlife: plentiful wildfowl in the winter months and dragonflies and swallowtails in summer. There's also an enormous roost of cormorants, one of the largest inland roosts in the country. During World War II, a number of wherries met their fate in the water here, by design rather than by accident, sunk to obstruct enemy hydroplanes attempting to land here. More wherries were sunk in the post-war years to prevent erosion of the broad's banks. Indeed, this is where the wherry *Maud*, now happily afloat again, was dredged up from in the early 1980s.

The **boardwalk** to the NWT visitor centre (01603 756094) leads from the car park opposite The Maltsters pub, turning a corner past

BLACK SAILS IN THE SUNSET – THE NORFOLK WHERRY

Undoubtedly the most iconic craft on the Broads system, the Norfolk Wherry evolved as a cargo boat based upon the design of the earlier Norfolk Keel, a square-rigged, clinker-built vessel. Norfolk Keels started to vanish from service around 1800 and were succeeded by wherries that could be sailed using a smaller crew. The typical wherry was a shallow-bottomed, double-ended, single-sail boat fitted with a gaff rig; its sail was black as a result of weatherproofing with tar and fish oil. The tall mast was fitted with a counterweight so that it could be lowered to pass under bridges. Most wherries were capable of transporting around 25 tons of goods, which they would carry from boats anchored off the coast at Great Yarmouth or Lowestoft upriver through the broads system. Although once a common sight, they were in steep decline by the 1940s as cargo was increasingly transported by road and rail.

Eight wherries survive in Norfolk today, one of which spent 40 years in Paris as a houseboat before its return to the Broads in 2005. A few have been lovingly restored in recent years. The 60ft *Albion*, probably the best known, was originally used to haul coal between Bungay and Lowestoft. This vessel has had a colourful, if chequered, career: sinking near Great Yarmouth in 1929, to be raised three days later, and then losing her mast in 1931. Today, *Albion* is based at Womack Water near Ludham and has been maintained by the Norfolk Wherry Trust since 1949. The craft may be chartered with a skipper and mate for groups of up to 12 people, while members of the Trust have the opportunity to go on pleasure cruises several times a year at a reduced rate. In summer they hold open days when you can meet the crew and look around the boat for free.

As I was shown round the *Albion*, what impressed me most was learning that the 40-ton boat, and other wherries like it, were sailed using just a two-person crew. 'Man and boy, or man and wife, there was just two to private moorings and continuing a little along the road before it leads into woodland. A magnificent, and very ancient, oak tree stands near the entrance of the boardwalk, which continues through alder carr (page 80) until you reach the thatched visitor centre close to where Malthouse and Ranworth broads meet. The visitor centre has information and displays about the local area as well as maps, books and gifts for sale. The centre also runs regular wildlife sessions for children, with activities like environmental games and dyke dipping. There's an observation point here and fantastic views over the broad and back to Ranworth church. Hour-long boat trips aboard the Edwardian-style electric launch *Liana* can be booked at the visitor centre. These run three times daily June to September and at weekends and bank holidays in April, May and October.

sail it,' I was told. 'And if they didn't sail, they didn't get paid.' What goods did the wherry carry? 'It carried anything that needed to be carried – coal, bricks, flour, grain – and in the winter when there was ice on the broad it might carry ice down to Yarmouth too. This one worked mostly on the southern system – you know, on the Waveney – but it got about quite a bit.' From the deck you can't help but be impressed by the enormous tree-trunk of a mast that stands proud here. 'They lowered that while they were in motion as they approached the bridges. They were so good at doing it that they didn't even need to slow down.' Below decks, things are pretty cramped and you soon learn that the 'business end' of the boat – the storage area – is, in fact, most of the boat, and there is little space for frivolities like comfort. The sharp end has a tiny cabin called a 'cuddy' where there are two narrow and uncomfortable bunks separated by a cast-iron stove – cramped but somehow endearingly cosy.

Another wherry, the *Maud*, was moored in the next staithe, a slightly larger, 42-ton vessel. The skipper on board had sailed wherries in his youth, as had his father and grandfather before him. Massive rope-tying hands seemed to be part of the family inheritance. 'My dad used to carry a chain through the streets of Yarmouth on his way to the boat. He used to throw it in the water to slow it down.' The *Maud* worked right up until her demise in 1965 when she was sunk at Ranworth Broad as protection for the narrow spit of land separating it from Malthouse Broad. She was moved in 1976 to another part of the broad before being resunk. The boat was eventually rescued from the mud to be slowly and painstakingly restored five years later by Vincent and Linda Pargeter between 1981 and 1999. Now she is back on the water once more – a floating museum piece with far more history in her timbers than the photographic display in the hold could possibly hope to relate.

Welcome to Norfolk's award winning brewery
Brewery Shop & Pub Customer Parking

23 SOUTH WALSHAM & SOUTH WALSHAM BROAD

Clippesby Hall Touring & Camping Park near Acle (page 309)

A mile or two south of Ranworth, South Walsham sits astride the old Norwich to Acle road. The village is a quiet, rural place, with a pub, a post office, a village hall and some modern housing tucked away behind the old buildings.

The village is home to the lovely **Fairhaven Woodland and Water Garden** (01603 270449 fairhavengarden.co.uk), which comprises over 130 acres of mature oak woodland (one tree is said to be 950 years old), and shady bluebell and candelabra primula-carpeted glades divided by waterways with footbridges stretching across them. I once inadvertently dropped a telephoto lens into the water whilst crossing a bridge here. I managed to retrieve it, but it was never the same again: every image I've taken since has a little speck of South Walsham silt floating in the frame. Moral: do not try to change lenses when crossing water.

The gardens lead down to privately owned South Walsham Broad from where, between April and October, it is possible to take a short boat trip out on to the broad. These run regularly every day of the week in summer. The gardens are probably at their best in late spring when the naturalised candelabra primula and rhododendrons are at their prime, but every season has its charms, even winter. The Fairhaven Garden Trust has been run as a charity since 1975 and all gardening is done entirely organically using just leaf mould and compost as fertiliser. Both the trust office and the tea room, which is also open to those not visiting the gardens, are managed in a sustainable manner too.

Just north of the village, **South Walsham Broad** is linked to the River Bure by way of Fleet Dike. There's a footpath that leads past a boatyard all the way along the dike from a car park, and if you fancy making a circular walk from here it is quite a long six miles or so via the river and Upton Fen before you return to your starting point. There are no viable short cuts, but it is rewarding and varied.

From the car park, walk past the boatyard along Fleet Dike, where a number of hire boats are usually moored up. As you approach the confluence with the River Bure, you cannot help but see the unmistakable form of St Benet's Abbey ahead on the opposite bank; in fact, you will see

◀ **1** St Benet's Abbey. **2** Fairhaven Woodland and Water Garden. **3** Woodforde's Brewery. **4** Screen paintings at St Helen's Church, Ranworth.

it before you see the river itself. The path turns east and along the river, where there will be ditches full of reed and marshy grazing to your right and broads cruisers – and if you are lucky, possibly a wherry – plying the river to your left. Here and there, you'll pass clumps of gnarled old willows. In early summer, there'll be sedge and reed warblers singing in the reeds, dragonflies darting through the air and tortoiseshell, and perhaps even swallowtail, butterflies flapping around.

As the river curves southeast past a drainage pump, continue until it curves the other way and you can see a concrete farm track striking off south across the marshes. Follow this for some way as it zigzags across the marshes away from the river and you will eventually emerge at the far eastern end of the boggy woodland that surrounds Upton Broad. Although the zigzags might persuade you that you are heading the wrong way, don't be tempted to deviate across the marshes until you reach this point: I tried to once and ended up walking through Norfolk's largest nettle colony… in shorts – not to be recommended! A footpath leads from the farm track through a corner of the Upton Fen woods before reaching a road. Walk west through Cargate Green and take another footpath on the southern flank of the woods until you pass a large modern farm, Holly Farm, which has is a fishing pond.

The entrance to Upton Broad and Marshes NWT reserve is just down from here along Low Road, an important wetland site with rare dragonflies and butterflies like swallowtail and white admiral as well as many scarce water plants. It's a good place to see water voles too, with a waymarked trail and boardwalk for visitors. Back on the road, head across the T-junction to Pilson Green then turn right along the edge of a field where the houses start. Turn right when you reach the road and continue north along it a little way before taking another footpath that leads west after Town House Farm. This will take you back to the South Walsham Broad car park.

24 HICKLING BROAD

🏠 **Lawson Cottage** (page 309)

A water trail takes visitors by electric boat across the broad to visit boat-only bird hides & the Tree Tower, a 60ft-high observation deck. Boat trips last 1 or 2 hours (✆ 01692 598276 ☻ Easter–Oct; booking advisable during school holidays). You can also enjoy a combined water trail safari & supper on Tue & Thu evenings (Jun–Aug), two-hour evening water trails (May–end Aug 18.00 Wed) & a dawn chorus water trail on selected dates in late Apr & May.

Hickling Broad, the largest in all the system, is the classic Norfolk broad, with blue water, golden reed beds and white-sailed yachts bobbing on the water. It's off limits to power craft, and with a good footpath (the Weavers' Way) around its southern side, it is almost as enjoyable for walkers as it is for sailors.

The scope for **birdwatching** is excellent: you can often see marsh harriers hawking the reed beds here, and hear sedge, marsh and Cetti's warblers exploding with song within them. In summer, at certain times at least, swallowtail butterflies are just part of the scenery. Like Barton Broad, Hickling Broad is a nature reserve under the jurisdiction of the Norfolk Wildlife Trust, which has a visitor centre (⊘ Apr–Sep) and bird observation hides here. A water trail takes visitors by boat across the broad to visit the Tree Tower, a raised observation deck only accessible by the water trail, from where you can get a magnificent view over the broad to the North Sea coast beyond.

Early summer, when the swallowtails and dragonflies are out and about, is perhaps the perfect time to be here but even winter is good if you are wrapped up against the wind that blows straight from the North Sea. In winter, there is a daily **raptor roost** at Stubb Mill in the middle of the marshes just north of the broad, where you can witness birds of prey flying in to roost at dusk. This can be spectacular at times, with combinations of marsh and hen harriers, merlins, cranes and pink-footed geese. To visit, it is necessary to park at the NWT car park and walk half a mile or so to the viewing area.

Hickling village, just to the north of the broad, is a pleasant enough place to stop for refreshment. The village is split neatly into two parts – **Hickling Heath** and **Hickling Green** – with the former being of most interest to sailors because it is closer to the staithe. The pub here, the Pleasure Boat Inn, right by the staithe, used to serve the wherry trade. A young King Charles III spent a night here back in 1961 when his shooting party could not make it back to base. Seemingly, he was told off by the landlady for making too much noise whilst having a pillow fight. Hickling Green is mainly residential but has its own local, the Greyhound Inn. St Mary's Church, which lies a little way north of Hickling Green, has the curiosity of a horse-drawn hearse inside. Visiting Hickling Broad without a car is a challenge but far from impossible. Hickling village has bus services from Great Yarmouth and North Walsham, from where it is easy to connect to Norwich and Cromer.

South of Hickling Broad, straddling the busy A149, is **Potter Heigham**, a village resolutely geared to the boat hire trade. The village is best known in these parts for two things: its medieval bridge, under which many an inexperienced skipper has come a cropper, and Lathams, a super-cheap discount store. Less well known is its lovely round-towered St Nicholas Church tucked away at the edge of the village overlooking fields. The bridge dates back to 1385 and has a very low arch that can cause headaches (quite literally) to novice sailors. Fortunately, there is a bridge pilot to help boats safely through. There are dozens of waterside bungalows along the River Thurne here; one of them, downstream from the bridge, known as the 'Dutch Tutch' or 'Helter-skelter House', is fabricated from the bottom half of a helter-skelter that used to grace the end of Britannia Pier at Great Yarmouth and was the first residential building on this stretch of the river.

The popular 1940s entertainer George Formby regarded the Norfolk Broads as his second home and used to visit with his wife Beryl every summer from the late 1940s onwards. He even bought a riverside house at Wroxham but – when not performing on stage at Great Yarmouth – spent most of his time in Norfolk cruising the Broads waterways on his boat *Lady Beryl* that he kept moored at Potter Heigham. It is said that Formby took great pleasure in navigating his way beneath the village's treacherously low bridge.

Adventures in Britain

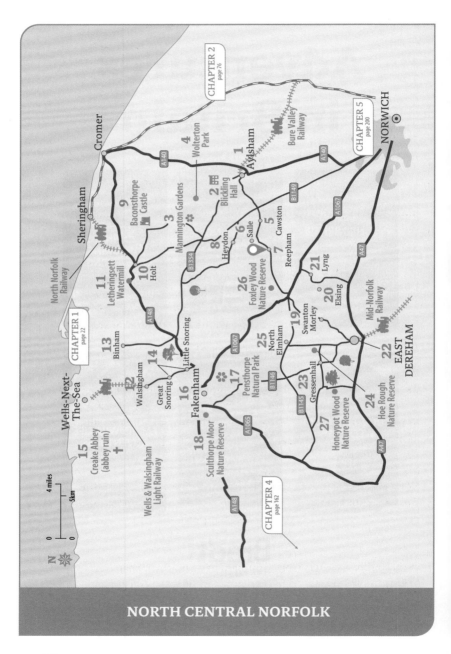

NORTH CENTRAL NORFOLK

3
NORTH CENTRAL NORFOLK

Norfolk's wool country that once was – this chapter covers the north coast hinterland and the gently undulating landscape of what is sometimes cheekily referred to as 'upland Norfolk'. It's a region of small, solid Georgian towns and massive wool-trade churches, grand estates and country houses: an enclosed landscape with lighter soils and fewer hedgerows than further south. The area is bounded, more or less, by the market towns of Aylsham, Holt, Fakenham and East Dereham, although there will inevitably be the odd diversion. The main rivers here are the Wensum and Bure, which slowly converge as you head eastwards across the county, before coming together at Breydon Water outside Great Yarmouth.

Visitors tend to rush through this part of the county en route to the Norfolk coast, which is a pity because there's plenty of interest here. And it's true to say that you'll probably find more of the traditional spirit of north Norfolk away from the coast than at it. Holt is close enough to the fashionable north coast to have its own claim as an alternative base for visiting that region, a reality reflected in its range of smart shops and places to eat. Aylsham is more overlooked, despite the fact that the presence of Blickling Hall just down the road brings in quite a few visitors. This is a shame as, for my money, it's just as attractive as Holt. Fakenham and East Dereham are a little more humdrum, but both pleasant enough market towns with their own merits.

There are some highly appealing villages. Reepham and Cawston have imposing churches, while Salle is just an imposing church without much in the way of a village. North Elmham has a Norman chapel and the site of East Anglia's former Saxon cathedral, while Little Walsingham, tucked away in lovely rolling countryside, has very much a living pilgrimage tradition. In between are sleepy villages like Heydon and even sleepier ones like, dare I say it, Great Snoring.

GETTING AROUND

This is straightforward enough: there are good roads to Aylsham and Fakenham from Norwich although it can take a long time to drive through the city's sprawling northern suburbs and satellite villages with their extensive new-builds. The main road to Holt branches off the Norwich to Cromer road at Norwich Airport and, once through a rather dreary commuter village, it's a nice drive through intermittent woodland and rolling farmland to reach the market town. East Dereham lies just off the A47 dual carriageway that links Norwich with King's Lynn. Away from these main roads, things are much, much quieter and you would get far more out of the experience by being on a bike.

PUBLIC TRANSPORT

The public transport network is reasonably good, with plenty of buses between Norwich and Aylsham, Fakenham and East Dereham, although Holt is better-connected with the coast than it is with the Norfolk capital. The fast, regular X1 service that links Great Yarmouth, Norwich, East Dereham and King's Lynn is ever-useful, as is the X29 that runs between Norwich and Fakenham. If you want to travel between towns within the area, like Aylsham and Holt for example, it's more problematic and will require a little more judicious juggling with connections; the website ⊘ traveline.info is useful. Two short heritage railway lines may also be of limited use: the Wells & Walsingham Light Railway (⊘ 01328 711630 ⊘ wwlr.co.uk ☉ mid-Mar–Oct 4 daily), and the Mid-Norfolk Railway (☉ late Mar–Oct 3 daily; page 245) between East Dereham and Wymondham.

WALKING

This isn't vintage walking territory, but you can find plenty of pleasant enough options for casual wandering, with numerous circular walks possible around the small market towns. The 1:25,000 OS Explorer maps 238 and 251 pretty well cover it.

The **Wensum Way** (page 154), a 12-mile route through fine central Norfolk countryside between Lenwade and Gressenhall, just north of East Dereham, is the central link in a cross-county route that combines with the existing Wherryman's Way, Marriott's Way and Nar Valley Way to provide a continuous footpath between Great Yarmouth and

ℹ TOURIST INFORMATION

Aylsham Aylsham Heritage Centre (🖉 aylshamheritage.com) in churchyard of St Michael and All Angels Church; Bure Valley Railway Station, Norwich Rd (🖉 01263 733903).
East Dereham Church House, Church St 🖉 01362 668214
Fakenham The Library, Oak St 🖉 07528 300103
Holt 3 Pound Lane, Market Pl 🖉 01263 712149
Walsingham Shire Hall Museum, 10 Common Pl 🖉 01328 820510

King's Lynn. Other than this, probably the most rewarding terrain lies in the area around Hockering and Foxley – both of which have gorgeous ancient tracts of woodland – or in open parkland of great estates, of which Blickling Park, Wolterton Park and Holt Country Park fit the bill nicely, with walks that take in lakes, pasture, woodland and sweeping views. You could also try sections of the Mariott's Way (see below), or the Weavers' Way and Bure Valley Walk that both terminate in Aylsham, or the Nar Valley Way from Beetley, near Gressenhall, north of East Dereham, to Castle Acre and beyond.

CYCLING

Exploring by bike is idyllic along the back roads of north central Norfolk, and areas like the quiet lanes around Heydon, Reepham and Salle are perfect for casual exploration, with plenty of alluring churches to investigate, strategic well-placed pubs for refreshment and great views.

The **Marriott's Way** is an excellent off-road path on a disused railway track running between Norwich and Aylsham along a curving route that takes in Reepham and Cawston. The Way, one of the country's longest paths along a stretch of disused railway track, follows the River Wensum west out of Norwich before curving northwards at Lenwade. It's not exclusively meant for cyclists: it's used by all sorts – leisure cyclists, Norwich commuters, dog walkers and so on – and you really don't need a mountain bike as the surface is mostly pretty smooth, compacted sand or gravel, although it does get rougher after Whitwell. Indeed, the surface of this track was the subject of some controversy in its early days when its compacted sand was found to cause staining. One irate dog walker complained of her pooch turning irreversibly orange as a result, and for a while the route become known to Norfolk County Hall insiders as 'the Tango trail'. The Marriott's Way is improbably curved:

the 180-degree Themelthorpe Curve that leads to Reepham was the sharpest bend in all of Britain's railway network. It was constructed in 1960 for moving freight, mainly concrete, from Lenwade but didn't stay in service for long as it was closed down in 1985.

AYLSHAM & NORTHWARDS

1 AYLSHAM

🏠 **Norfolk Courtyard** Foulsham (page 309) ⚑ **Deer's Glade Caravan & Camping Park** Hanworth (page 309)

In many ways, Aylsham is the archetypal Norfolk market town. Sitting squarely between Norwich and the coast at Cromer, it is distant enough from both to have an independent life of its own and is far more than simply a dormitory town or coastal jumping-off point. The town's market originated in 1519 thanks to a charter from Henry VIII. The small market square remains the heart and soul of the town today and the oldest building around it is the Black Boys Inn that has stood on the same site since the mid 17th century. There used to be a Black Boys pub in Norwich's Pottergate too but this was renamed some years ago in a nod to political correctness (casual racism and pub signs are not such strange bedfellows when you consider the number of Saracen's Heads and Turk's Heads found throughout the country that glorify the prejudices of the Crusades). The Black Boys would have always been the town's most prominent hostelry, serving as a coaching inn on the Cromer to Norwich run. Daniel Defoe is said to have stayed here – then again he did visit pretty well everywhere in the region.

There's a twice-weekly market in the square and a farmers' market on the morning of the first and third Saturday of the month. Equally well known, within the county at least, are the Monday sales auctions. Years ago, the Monday auctions used to bring all manner of old folk to town to buy and sell agricultural paraphernalia to each other. You could buy house-clearance rubbish for next to nothing. These days, it's quite a bit posher, with plenty of antique dealers perusing the items on offer. There's even a separate artworks sale that attracts national dealers.

Just north of the market square you'll find the church of St Michael and All Angels, where the landscape gardener Humphry Repton, who lived nearby at Sustead, lies buried in the graveyard. Repton's tomb has the following inscription, which celebrates the very essence of

PROUD TO BE SLOW

Aylsham has admirable green credentials. It proudly became plastic-bag-free in 2008 and even the new Tesco supermarket, opened in July of that year, claims to be the 'world's greenest supermarket', constructed as it was from sustainable materials such as recycled plastic. In recognition of Aylsham's enviable quality of life and very liveable nature, the town successfully became Norfolk's first **Cittaslow** (Slow Town) in 2004, the second town to do so in the country (Diss joined shortly after). Originating in Italy, the concept of a Cittaslow is that of a community that relishes good food, a relaxed living and working environment, and a high quality of life above more mundane concerns like the availability of supermarkets and car parks. In Norfolk, both Diss and Aylsham have managed to fulfil these criteria with consummate ease, although both certainly have supermarkets and parking too. Aylsham had to change very little to become a fully-fledged member as it already quite effortlessly ticked all the right boxes. This is easy to believe: Aylsham has always been 'slow', although perhaps 'laid-back' is a more fitting description for the town as it hurtles snail-like into the 21st century.

Aylsham's Slow Town standing is closely linked to its Slow Food credentials. **Slow Food Aylsham** (slowfoodaylsham.org. uk) was formed in 2004 in anticipation of its coming Cittaslow status. Slow Food Aylsham actively support local food producers and retailers and does their best to encourage people to shop locally. According to Slow Food 'convivium' leader Liz Jones, Aylsham sees itself as an 'unpretentious foodie town', and for a small town of just 6,000 to boast three butcher's shops, two greengrocers, two fishmongers, several cafés and a fortnightly farmers' market this seems a reasonable description. There's a food festival held in October that promotes local food businesses in addition to showcasing top local chefs in cooking demonstrations and highlighting the benefits of slow food to both the local environment and economy. In addition to a farmers' market and wine-tasting, the final event of the festival is The Big Slow Brunch held in the Town Hall on the Sunday morning. Tickets are available from the heritage centre in the churchyard (page 132).

impermanence and the cycle of life, and perhaps anticipates the Slow way of thinking with its eco-centric, altruistic outlook:

Not like Egyptian tyrants consecrate
Unmixed with others shall my dust remain
But mould'ring, blending, melting into earth
Mine shall give form and colour to the rose
And while its vivid blossoms cheer mankind
Its perfumed odours shall ascend to heaven.

The church itself is highly thought of too. Once, hovering at the church gate and dithering with a camera, I heard a voice in my ear exclaim: 'One of the best parish churches in Norfolk, that is. Well, according to Simon Knott anyway and he should know.' The voice came from a fellow visitor who, like me, was a devotee of Simon Knott's excellent Norfolk Churches website (∂ norfolkchurches.co.uk), an online labour of love by a modern-day digital Betjeman who, while not shy of expressing an opinion, is wholly generous about the churches he describes, even the humblest. We chatted for a while about the great churches of central Norfolk – Salle, Cawston, Reepham – me nodding sagely for much of the time as I flounder under a friendly-fire barrage of architectural terminology. It was flattering to be identified as a fellow church fancier even if I cannot always tell my apse from my aumbry. But that's what you do in 'Slow' old-fashioned places like Aylsham: chat to strangers about the parish church and arcane local history, and if given the benefit of the doubt, hold your ground.

"Years ago, the Monday auctions used to bring all manner of old folk to town to buy and sell agricultural paraphernalia to each other."

Within the churchyard itself you'll find the **Aylsham Heritage Centre** (∂ aylshamheritage.com), staffed by helpful volunteers, with old photographs, artefacts and displays about the town's history. The centre, which along with Bure Valley Railway station is one of two tourist information points in Aylsham, also organises a number of inexpensive guided walks through the town (book in advance).

The town is small enough to walk around in half an hour or so and my recommendation, after the market square and church, is to wander down towards the watermill at Burgh-next-Aylsham a little further downstream along the River Bure. Surprisingly perhaps, the section of the Bure that runs through the town was not navigable until the 18th century and, even then, wherries from the coast would struggle to reach the staithe. You can reach Burgh-next-Aylsham by following the Bure Valley Walk from the Bure Valley Railway Station. The railway (page 83) is a good way to arrive from Wroxham and the Broads. Heading southeast alongside the railway, turn left after about 1½ miles just before Brampton when you reach a small stream marked on maps as The Mermaid. Brampton itself is a pretty, if remote-feeling, little place, with a row of old cottages and a round-towered church.

SHOPPING

At **Erpingham**, just north of Aylsham, **Alby Crafts & Gardens** (albycrafts.co.uk) is a craft centre set in two courtyards of converted brick and flint farm buildings. Here, there's a range of shops and galleries as well as working studios where woodturning, stained-glass making and sculpture take place, plus a pleasant tea room, **The Artisan Café** (01263 761652 theartisancafe.co.uk), and gardens.

FOOD & DRINK

Biddy's Tea Room 16 Market Pl 01603 731278 biddystearoom.com. Located almost adjacent to the church, this child- and dog-friendly tea room and bakery is a sister of the original Norwich Lanes branch. This 'vintage inspired' tea room specialises in traditional afternoon teas served on tiered stands. Stocking 50 blends of loose tea (but only one type of coffee!), there are also breakfasts and light lunches to be had, as well as sandwiches and cream teas.

Black Boys Hotel Market Pl 01263 732122 blackboyshotel.co.uk. Right in the centre of things, this long-standing hotel and restaurant serves a fairly traditional English menu that includes local produce such as Cromer crabs and aged English beef from Swannington Farm.

The Conservatory 3 Penfold St 01263 734433. A bright café serving coffee and speciality teas, breakfasts, salads, jacket potatoes and afternoon teas, all using locally sourced ingredients wherever possible.

2 BLICKLING HALL

Blickling NR11 6NF 01263 738030 Apr–Oct, Wed–Mon; Nov–Mar Sat & Sun; National Trust

A couple of miles north of Aylsham, Blickling Hall has been in the care of the National Trust since 1940. Anne Boleyn may well have been born here, although there seems to be some uncertainty, but the building that you see standing today dates from after her time, the 1620s, and is a superb example of Jacobean architecture. The house attracts a large number of visitors, as do the formal gardens, but what cheapskates like myself often prefer is simply to walk (for free) the miles of footpaths that run through the estate. All manner of possible walks start either from near to the entrance or, further away, from the car park at Itteringham Common. Approaching the park from the Great Wood to the west allows for super views across oak-studded parkland to the lake and Blickling Hall beyond. You should also definitely check out The Pyramid, marked on most maps as a mausoleum. This is actually both of those things: a 45ft- high, pyramid-shaped mausoleum that holds the grave of John, the 2nd Earl of Buckinghamshire, who died in 1793. It's all rather esoteric and Egyptian in character, and quite a bizarre sight tucked away in this corridor of conifers and easily missed.

FOOD & DRINK

The Bucks Arms Blickling ✆ 01263 732133 ⬧ bucksarms.co.uk. A 17th-century former coaching inn close to the estate entrance that used to be known as the Buckinghamshire Arms but which has since been rebranded 'The Bucks Arms'. This has classic quality English food and real ales represented by the usual suspects – Woodforde's, Adnams, etc.

3 MANNINGTON GARDENS & WOLTERTON PARK

Contact details for both: ✆ 01263 584175 or 768444 ⬧ manningtongardens.co.uk

Not as well known as Blickling Hall but well worth a visit, nearby **Mannington Gardens** and **Wolterton Park**, which lie within a mile of one another, both belong to the Walpole family. Mannington Hall is not open to the public except by special appointment but its gardens are open in summer and make for pleasant walking. The Garden Tearooms, located within the gardens and run by Walpole's Kitchen, are open during garden visiting hours. If you just want to walk and not visit the gardens there is a car park charge (free for garden visitors). Wolterton Park, landscaped by Humphry Repton, is open year-round and has walks of varying length along a good network of public rights of way and permissive paths. Close to the car park there's a ruined flint chapel in the woods that was incorporated into a folly garden in the 19th century. The hall itself is also open for occasional 'Invitation to View' tours in summer.

Just south of Mannington Hall lies Itteringham, a charming small village straddling the River Bure. The poet George Barker (1913–91), much admired and financially supported by Graham Greene, lived here for many years. His grave lies in the churchyard marked by a granite book that bears the simple legend 'No Compromise'. George Barker's daughter, the novelist Rafaella Barker, continues the family literary tradition from her home in Cley-next-the-Sea.

1 Aysham's farmers' market. 2 Blickling Hall. 3 Black Boys Inn, the oldest building on Aysham's Market Square. 4 The double hammerbeam roof in Cawston's church of St Agnes. 5 Heydon village. ▶

🍴 FOOD & DRINK

Itteringham Village Shop ✆ 01263 587325 ⌖ ourvillagestore.co.uk ⊖ daily. A community shop that also claims to have the smallest café in the county, this was threatened with closure in 1994 after 350 years of business, but was bought out by the local community and has been run by volunteers ever since. As well as delicious snacks and good coffee, the shop defies its limited size by stocking an unreasonably wide range of greetings cards, art and design books (including one on the history of the shop), gifts, vegetables, bakery goods, bread, wine and beer, pretty well all of which is Norfolk produced. The shop also doubles as the village post office on two mornings each week, Mondays and Thursdays. Despite some uncertainties about the lease, at the time of writing both shop and café were still going strong.

Saracen's Head Wolterton ✆ 01263 768909 ⌖ saracenshead-norfolk.co.uk ⊖ Wed–Sun. Tucked away in isolation on a quiet lane close to the Wolterton Estate, this characterful country inn serves up local produce like Wolterton lamb and fish from the north Norfolk coast.

Walpole Arms The Common, Itteringham ✆ 01263 587258 ⌖ thewalpolearms.co.uk. This long-established country pub has recently reinvented itself as a Spanish tapas restaurant, offering over 30 options, so don't expect traditional English cuisine here. Locally sourced seasonal produce is used as much as possible. There's an impressive wine list, and Adnams and Woodforde's ales are on tap.

WEST OF AYLSHAM

West of Aylsham, the villages of Reepham and Cawston both have impressive, beautiful churches, while the massive wool church at Salle more or less stands on its own. Heydon is a handsome estate village. Reepham, Cawston and Salle all lie in close proximity to each other, which makes their oversized churches all the more remarkable.

5 CAWSTON

Cawston is a largish but compact village with a fascinating church. It lies in the heart of good cycling territory – the Marriott's Way goes right past the village and the local back roads are heaven-sent for those on two wheels.

The village's **St Agnes Church** is a marvel, certainly one of the most interesting in the county. Even before you enter, you encounter some fearful gargoyles on the parapets and a splendid Green Man and a dragon in the spandrels above the west door. Inside, there's a double hammerbeam roof strewn with huge angels, a rare 15th-century rood screen and wooden box pews. The local gentry had the comfy box pews while the hoi-polloi had to fend for themselves. The class system was as rife in church on Sundays as it was for the rest of the week outside. A friend from the village told me this that is where the expression 'go to the wall' comes from. 'If you didn't have a family pew in the church, you would have to "go to the wall". You'd have to stand up at the side for the service'. The stained glass is gorgeous but even better is the rood screen, created around 1460 and with about 20 paintings by Flemish artists – a series of saints, famous and less well known, including St John the Evangelist, St Jude and St Matthew (who wears glasses to read his book).

6 SALLE

There is not much to Salle village, pronounced 'Saul', a couple of miles west of Cawston, apart from a few cottages and a well-used cricket pitch. John Betjeman is reported to have said that, church-wise, you are either a Cawston or a Salle man. Personally speaking, as Sam and Dave (almost) once sang, I'm a Salle man. Really though, both have their charms and I would recommend visiting the two. Three would be even better: on a bicycle, you could make a three-cornered circuit through Reepham, Cawston and Heydon, taking in Salle along the way, using a combination of farm tracks, minor roads and a section of the Marriott's Way.

The spandrels above the door of St Peter and St Paul's Church here have no Green Man like at Cawston but, instead, a pair of scale-covered angels. Inside, there's a real sense of space, accentuated perhaps by the absence of stained glass in many of the windows. The church was in a terrible state at the end of the 19th century but restoration finally came with funds provided by Duleep Singh (the last Maharajah of Punjab) of the Elveden Estate in Suffolk. There is an enormously tall wooden font cover, supported by a sort of winch system, which dates from the 15th century, and distant angels and bosses high in the roof beams that retain some of their original medieval paint. If you want to see some bosses close up, go through the door at the northwest corner near the font where you'll find a narrow staircase leading up to a Lady Chapel, which has some wonderfully quirky bosses in the vaulted ceiling.

What I find most touching about the place are the carvings in the 15th-century misericord seats that have a variety of faces, some benevolent, some quite threatening. One looks like a tempestuous Greek god;

another, a gentle monk, his head polished from hands gripping on to him over the centuries. The best are two facing corner stalls that depict two monks deep in conversation, their faces pure medieval but also there's something quite contemporary about them too. There are animals too: a swan, a monkey, fish, a dragon swallowing its own tail and, perhaps most affecting, a representation of the *Pelican in her Piety* – a symbol of charity in which a mother bird draws blood from her own breast to feed her chicks, except the bird here resembles more a bird of prey. There are more fine bosses to be seen in the roof above the misericord benches. Helpfully, these have been photographed and displayed in a frame for easy viewing.

7 REEPHAM

⌂ The Dial House (page 309)

The largest of this trio, just south of Salle, Reepham is a small town with a fine marketplace that has the King's Arms, a 17th-century coaching inn, on one side, and what was once a brewery, the splendidly Georgian Dial House Hotel (formerly the old Brewery House), on the other. With a handful of old-fashioned shops meeting most of the needs of its residents, Reepham is a tidy, self-possessed sort of place – a bit like a smaller version of Aylsham just down the road. As well as a couple of cafés, a butchers, deli and farm shop, there are quite a few antique and crafts shops here too. Some might even consider the town as a smaller, alternative Holt although that is probably going too far – certainly, though, it is attractive.

"With a handful of old-fashioned shops meeting most of the needs of its residents, Reepham is a tidy, self-possessed sort of place."

Reepham is rare in having three churches (one of which is ruined) side by side and sharing the same churchyard – reputedly one of only two places in Europe like this. St Mary's Church is joined to Whitwell St Michael by a vestry corridor, while the third church belonging to Hackford parish burned down in the 16th century to leave just a fragment of wall. This unusual state of affairs features on the town sign that also shows the three sisters who were supposedly responsible for building all three churches – complete nonsense of course as they were built over a much longer period. The three-in-one churchyard actually came about by all three churches being built on the intersecting point of the respective parish boundaries of Reepham, Hackford and Whitwell.

A walk to Salle & back

❋ OS Landranger 133; start Reepham market place ♥ TG100229; 4 miles; easy.

This enjoyable short walk combines town streets and country vistas while taking in one of Norfolk's most beautiful and atmospheric churches along the way.

From Reepham's market place, walk down to St Mary's church before heading left along Norwich Road. Follow the path on the left that runs next to the road and then continues in the same direction as the Norwich Road curves away to the right. This path continues through trees to reach another road. Cross to Richmond Rise opposite, where a footpath leading from the first cul-de-sac to the right will soon bring you out on a narrow road. Turn left and walk uphill under the railway bridge. Reaching Cawston Road, continue along the footpath immediately across the road, which leads to Wood Dalling Road. At the road, take the footpath immediately to the right that leads along a field edge – the tower of Cawston's church can now be seen in the distance, to the right. The path turns a sharp right at the next field edge to follow another hedge towards a belt of woodland.

Follow the woodland edge north towards Salle's St Peter and St Paul's church, whose tower is now visible, as is the water tower at Salle Park. At the end of the trees, cross the sports ground next to the pavilion to arrive at the lych gate of the church.

Leaving the church, turn right past cottages then left at the next junction along Wood Dalling Road. This leads all the way back to Reepham, passing the old station and its café along the way.

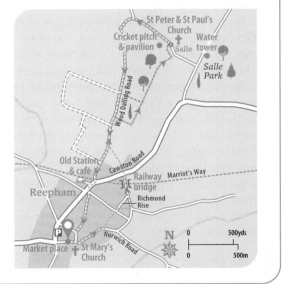

The town's successful **summer music festival** takes place in August; camping is available for the weekend at nearby Whitwell station. For a relatively small festival it is sometimes surprising who they manage to get to headline. In 2023 the main act was no less than 80s star Toyah.

🍴 FOOD & DRINK

Diane's Pantry 8 Market Pl ✆ 01603 920660. Right on the market square, next to the pub, this quirky little café doubles as a delicatessen. Good for light lunches, home-baked cakes, pastries and quiches.

Station Café Station Rd ✆ 01603 920707. In the old Reepham railway station building just north of the town centre, this is convenient for walks or cycle rides along the Marriott's Way – it's right beside it. Good value breakfasts and lunches plus daily specials.

8 HEYDON

North of Salle, Heydon Hall lies at the centre of a leafy estate of pasture and parkland. Over the years, the tiny estate village of Heydon, with its wide green and Earle Arms pub, has become well known, locally at least, as a popular focus for weekend outings. If anywhere in Norfolk deserves the accolade of 'hidden village', this does. Heydon became Norfolk's first conservation area back in 1971 and has won a couple of Best Kept Village awards.

Part of the explanation for the village's pristine status comes from the fact that there is no through road. You arrive at the village green by the pub, tea room and well and that's about as far as you can go on wheels. The estate's rented cottages that surround the green have attracted quite a bohemian community over the years and, in many ways, the whole village is something of a Victorian throwback. There's also a slightly feudal feel to the place, as everything in the village, including the pub, tea room, smithy and all the houses, is owned by the Bulwer Long family who have lived in the hall since 1640. This timeless quality has not gone completely unnoticed and Heydon's village green is beloved of movie location scouts – it has certainly featured in more than a film or two. If you remove the cars from the scene then nothing whatsoever gives the game away that Queen Victoria is no longer on the throne. The commemorative well in her name that dates from 1887 is, in fact, the village's most recent structure.

🍴 FOOD & DRINK

Earle Arms The Street ✆ 01263 587391 🖱 earlearms.vpweb.co.uk. With Adnams and Moongazer ales, a good selection of wines, and a changing menu that includes fresh seafood and game stews mostly sourced from local ingredients, this traditional and admirably unspoiled pub on the green is very popular at weekend lunchtimes.

Village Tea Room The Street ✆ 01263 587211 🖱 heydonvillageteashop.co.uk. Cosy tea room filled with china knick-knacks that serves light lunches, snacks and cream teas.

HOLT & AROUND

9 BACONSTHORPE CASTLE

The main reason for making a trip to the out-of-the-way village of Baconsthorpe is for a look at Baconsthorpe Castle, some way from the village along rutted farm tracks. The castle is more of a fortified manor than anything else. Henry Heydon started construction in 1486 and the Heydon family lived here for almost 200 years, expanding their property as their family wealth grew. It fell into ruin in the mid 17th century when the Heydon fortune went into decline and the family were obliged to take a sledgehammer to their property and sell it off for use as building materials.

"It must have been an odd and slightly creepy place to live, so far from anywhere else other than the farm next door."

The outer gatehouse, a later addition, has survived better than most, and this alone continued to be occupied until 1920 when one of its towers collapsed. It must have been an odd and slightly creepy place to live, so far from anywhere else other than the farm next door. With jackdaws noisily swirling around in the trees above the moat, it remains a lonely, atmospherically mysterious spot.

Half of the fun is getting here, along twisting country roads before striking out on farm tracks for the last mile or so. From the south you'll pass first through Plumstead, which just about typifies the rural landscape around these parts: a narrow sandy road and rolling fields; round bales of hay rising over a farmyard wall; an isolated phone box next to an overgrown churchyard; boxes of tomatoes and marrows for sale outside cottage doors. Cycle here and you will appreciate it even more, or you could drive here and then do a circular walk on arrival. There are even very occasional Sanders buses to the village from Holt, Cromer and Sheringham. The sign in the car park has some good walking suggestions including a circuit that takes in Hempstead and Baconsthorpe via Beckett's Farm and Ash Tree Farm. The nearest refreshment stops are Holt or Bodham.

10 HOLT

🏠 **Byfords Posh B&B** (page 309), **White Horse Barn** (page 309)

More cosmopolitan than Aylsham, Holt stands en route to Norfolk's prestigious north coast as an old market town that has recently found

DAVID BURTON/A

CHRISDORNEY/S

DIANA PAPPAS/A

renewed life; there's a confidence and sassiness here too that comes from its proximity to places like Blakeney and Cley-next-the-Sea. Almost all its buildings were reduced to ash on 1 May 1708, when fire raged through the town. The subsequent rebuild has resulted in a handsome Georgian centre, although one survivor is Gresham's School, Norfolk's most prestigious public school dating from 1555, which brings a certain amount of gravitas to the community.

The town centre has elegant colour-washed frontages and a handful of narrow lanes running off the high street. Immediately apparent is the staggering number of shops and services for such a small place; not just along the main streets but also set back from the High Street in a procession of courtyards – Feather's Yard, Old Stable Yard and the largest, Apple Yard, which has the excellent **Holt Bookshop** (✐ 01263 715858 ♲ holtbookshop.co.uk). Two more lie just off Albert Street – Lees Yard and Chapel Yard. In addition to the newsagents, chip shops and greengrocers that you might expect in a small Norfolk town, there are also a surprising number of clothes shops, galleries, bakeries, kitchen shops and antiquarian bookshops. Nowhere of similar size in East Anglia seems to have quite such a concentration of cafés and tea rooms. In late July the **Holt Festival** (♲ holtfestival.org) brings together a wide range of musical, comedic and theatrical performances, along with literary events and lectures.

🍴 FOOD & DRINK

The Black Apollo 24 High St ✐ 01263 712495. A small café with a reputation for excellent coffee, roasted locally by the Salle-based Norfolk Coffee Company. Also cakes, breakfasts and light meals.

Byfords 1–3 Shirehall Plain ✐ 01263 711400 ♲ byfords.org.uk. An all-day brasserie and deli that also functions as a 'posh B&B' (page 309), Byfords is a Holt institution and serves up superb homemade food and snacks, and especially fine cakes and puddings. They can also provide for picnics by means of an online click and collect service.

Owl Tea Rooms White Lion St ✐ 01263 713232 ♲ owltearooms.co.uk. On the corner of White Lion Street and Church Street, this busy place that has claims as Norfolk's oldest tea rooms – established 1929 – serves light lunches, snacks and afternoon tea in cosy rooms behind the bakery and also in the small courtyard garden.

◀ **1** Baconsthorpe Castle. **2** Holt town centre. **3** The Shrine of Our Lady of Walsingham. **4** Butcher's shop and whole foods at Letheringsett watermill.

11 LETHERINGSETT WATERMILL

Riverside Rd, Letheringsett NR25 7YD ✆ 01263 713153 ⌨ letheringsettwatermill.co.uk
🕒 09.00–16.00 (15.00 in winter) Mon–Sat

Take the Fakenham road from Holt and you soon reach Letheringsett on the River Glaven, with a pub on the west side of the river and a watermill on the east. Letheringsett watermill sits behind a large millpond, a constant source of power for this, the only working watermill in the county. It's a solid, four-storey building with a shop on the ground floor that sells a variety of flours from the mill, in addition to a range of whole foods. There is also an antique shop on-site and a tea room overlooking the water. The mill can usually be seen working several days a week, although this is dependent on its milling schedule. Guided tours are available by prior arrangement.

NORFOLK'S DESERTED VILLAGES

Norfolk is estimated to have over 150 deserted villages within its borders – a figure that is greater than most other counties in England. This is commonly thought to be simply the result of the Black Death that ravaged the country in 1349 but often the reason for abandonment is more complex. Places that may have thrived in medieval times but which have long since been abandoned usually leave little evidence of their former existence other than crop marks in fields. Occasionally there is a ruin or two to mark the site. A good example can be found at Godwick close to the village of Tittleshall, a few miles south of Fakenham. **Godwick**, which was mentioned in the Domesday Book, existed as a village until the 17th century when it was abandoned after two centuries of gradual decline. Poor harvests and colder, wetter weather were probably the main reasons for the village's demise. Following its abandonment the land belonging to the village was bought by the Coke family of the Holkham Estate, who in turn sold it in 1958 to pay for death duties. A solitary ruined church tower remains today surrounded by rough grazing land populated by indifferent sheep. Closer inspection of the site reveals earthworks that show where the houses, mill, village pond and street would once have stood.

Other villages in this part of north central Norfolk that were mentioned in the Domesday Book but deserted by the late medieval period include Little Bittering near Gressenhall and Pudding Norton close to Fakenham, where another ruined church tower stands near the roadside marking the site of the abandoned medieval village. Perhaps most evocative of all is **Egmere**, where the dramatic ruined tower of St Edmund's Church stands on a mound just south of the Little Walsingham to North/ South Creake road.

The present mill dates from 1802, although one stood on the same site at the time of the Domesday Book. The mill was converted to diesel power in the 1940s but was reconverted to waterpower in 1984. Mike Thurwell, who started restoring it in 1987, had absolutely no experience of milling at all when he took the place on but today it's a highly successful enterprise. 'I can't keep up with demand,' he told me when I visited some years ago. 'We produce about 3½ tons a week at the moment but we could easily get rid of eight tons. We've just got two new millstones from Holland made from German quartz – they cost £3,500 each – but I don't know how good they are yet as I'm still running them in.' Running in new stones means that the flour produced needs to be sent off for inspection until it is declared fit for human consumption. 'The test flour can be used for pigs as they don't mind a bit of grit in their diet.'

Different millstones are used to produce different grades of flour. 'The French burr stones we use to make white flour, and we use the Derbyshire for wholemeal. With the new stones up and running we should be able to increase production up to about seven tons of flour a week.' Did the mill ever run dry? Was there ever a danger of power failure? 'You're joking,' says Mike dismissively. 'There's a million gallons of water out there in the millpond. Every bit of water in the river goes past this mill.' Mike passed away in July 2013 but his daughter continues to run the business.

AROUND WALSINGHAM & FAKENHAM

12 WALSINGHAM

🏠 **The Old Bakehouse** (page 309)

'England's Nazareth', it likes to call itself, although 'Norfolk's Lourdes' might be equally appropriate. Walsingham is actually two adjoining villages, Little Walsingham and Great Walsingham, and in true Norfolk topsy-turvy style, Little Walsingham is the larger of the pair.

The village has long been famous as one of Britain's foremost pilgrimage centres, a tradition that began just before the Norman Conquest in 1061 when a Saxon noblewoman had a vision of the Virgin Mary here. A wooden replica of the house of the Holy Family in Nazareth was constructed and an Augustinian priory founded in the 12th century to enclose the chapel. This set the ball rolling for what would become an important European pilgrimage tradition which continued until the time of Henry VIII when the shrine and priory were destroyed as part of the Dissolution, despite the fact that the monarch had made his way here from Cambridge in his youth. The pilgrimage was re-established at the end of the 19th century and has gone from strength to strength ever since.

Both Catholic and Anglican **pilgrimages** take place here. The largest annual event, the Anglican National Pilgrimage, takes place here each Whitsun, when there is usually a good deal of heckling from hard-line Protestant pickets who view the proceedings as shameless popery. Numerous other pilgrimages happen throughout the year and the quaint narrow streets of Little Walsingham are sporadically busy almost year-round. Summer attracts quite a number of non-pilgrim visitors too. Whatever your take on religion, Walsingham is certainly an attractive place that has not allowed itself to become too fazed by centuries of Marian mayhem. In fact, it is probably its very status as a pilgrimage centre that has, by and large, kept the village so untainted by modern development.

It's an interesting place to wander and reflect on what has or hasn't changed over the centuries. Today's pilgrims mostly come by coach or car and are generally better-scrubbed and less disease-laden than those who would have gravitated here in medieval times. No doubt the charlatans, quacks and dodgy corrupt monks who would have preyed on hapless pilgrims are thinner on the ground too. In terms of buildings, all that is left of the original Augustinian priory is a large arched window that stands in the abbey gardens, a Norman gateway and two wishing wells. You must pay to enter the abbey gardens and pass through the tourist office by the 'pump' to do so; it's sometimes mistaken for the Anglican shrine, which is in a modern building just down the road, while the Roman Catholic shrine is at the Slipper Chapel outside the village. The pump, in fact a 16th-century octagonal pump-house with an iron brazier on top, has pride of place in Common Place, the square that is Walsingham's heart, with the tourist office, Shirehall and Bull pub all surrounding it.

The **Shirehall Museum** served as a hostel in the 16th century but was converted into the Shirehall at the end of the 18th century. The courtroom is now part of the museum, which gives a good overview of the village's history as a pilgrimage site. The **High Street**, a very pretty street composed almost entirely of timbered houses, leads off Common Place. Along here, you'll find a few gift shops, the evocatively eroded Norman gate of the priory, a crocodile or two of pilgrims in peak season, and splendidly old-fashioned tea rooms like The Swallows and Read & Digest. The gift shop on the corner has such a large choice of jam and candles that you could almost imagine this becoming a place of pilgrimage in its own right.

A couple of miles south along a narrow road at Houghton St Giles you'll come to the **Slipper Chapel**, a restored 14th-century building that houses the contemporary Catholic shrine. This has long been considered the last staging point along the pilgrimage route to Walsingham and the done thing, for the pious at least, was to remove footwear here and continue the last stretch into Walsingham barefoot. Numerous kings have performed this act of piety in the past, even Henry VIII, although few do it today. While the hardcore devout may be thinner on the ground these days, they are certainly still out there. A few years ago, I remember seeing a man hauling an enormous cross along the hard shoulder of the Fakenham road just outside Norwich. Quite obviously, he was Walsingham-bound. The only concession that this modern pilgrim had made to ease his tough journey was to affix a little wheel to the bottom of his cross to make hauling slightly easier.

A pilgrimage footway still exists between Houghton St Giles and Little Walsingham but these days, rather than the road, the route follows the course of the former railway track that runs parallel. Following this firm-surfaced path brings you into Walsingham at the site of its former railway station, which now serves as a small **Orthodox chapel**, silver onion dome and all. I once met an Irish nun in an isolated Serbian monastery who, on hearing that I lived in Norfolk, asked me about Walsingham as she had lived here as a nun for several years. No doubt this would have been her former church. It's a small world sometimes.

‖ FOOD & DRINK

Read & Digest Tearoom by the Old Pump 54 High St ✆ 01328 821332. One of several old-fashioned tea rooms in Little Walsingham village. This one, which as its name suggests is opposite the old pump, has a cosy ground floor room and a larger upstairs area that has a library of books with sofas and chairs, hence 'read & digest'. There is seating outside on the street too. Honest home-cooked food including excellent scones and quiches.

13 BINHAM

Guided tours of the church & monastery ☉ May–Sep 15.00 Sun & Tue

Turn right off the A148 just beyond Letheringsett and head due west and you pass through a landscape of big fields and small villages – Saxlingham, Field Dalling, Binham. It is well worth stopping at Binham to see the remains of **St Mary's Priory**, all the more remarkable because, although the rest of the priory lies in ruins, its church has been patched up and had its aisles removed to become the village parish church.

In a landscape of flint and brick, churches made of stone are rare, and this one is a monastic ghost that looks all the odder for the ornate windows of its façade being blocked up with workaday brick. An architectural historian might talk excitedly of the priory's west window being the earliest example of Decorated tracery in England but you do not really need to know this in order to appreciate just how atmospheric it all is.

Apart from the stone used for the church, the rest of Binham village is made almost entirely of flint cobble – the extensive farm buildings, the cattle yard walls, the village cottages. You would be hard-pushed to find a flintier place, making the finely dressed imported stone of the priory church seem all the more precious as a result. With Blakeney port just down the road in one direction and the pilgrimage centre of Walsingham in the other, Binham with its priory must have been a bustling place back in the medieval period. Today, the village is the very antithesis of 'bustling'. This is, of course, the village that gives its name to Mrs Temple's Binham Blue, the delicious blue cheese produced just down the road in Wighton.

14 GREAT SNORING & LITTLE SNORING

Great Snoring isn't dull but it is certainly sleepy. It's actually quite a charming little village tucked into a fold of a gently sloping land. **Little Snoring**, close to the A148, is a little more wide-awake and, somewhat contrarily, quite a bit larger than its neighbour. Here, the rather unusual church of St Andrew is set slightly back from the village on a sloping site. The church has a round tower that has a windmill-like cap and what look to be dormer windows, but the really odd thing about the tower is

1 Fakenham Market. 2 Pensthorpe Natural Park. 3 St Mary's Priory, Binham.
4 Great Snoring. ▶

that it is detached from the main body of the church, which is of a later build. The suggestion is that there may originally have been two Gothic churches side by side on this site although no-one seems to know. There used to be an airfield beyond Church Farm next to the church that was a base for Mosquito and Lancaster bombers during World War II, commemorated by plaques in the church and a Mosquito and propeller on the village sign.

The gloss put on the area by its religious connections makes it easy to overlook the loveliness of the valley of the River Stiffkey hereabouts. From the Slipper Chapel in Walsingham, you can cross a ford to reach tiny Houghton St Giles and then continue up what seems like a surprisingly steep hill to reach Great Snoring. Stop halfway along just before Canister Hall Farm and you'll be rewarded by what I think is one of the choicest views in north Norfolk, looking west over the valley and the folded hills beyond – a scene that presents perfect counter-evidence for use in any 'it's all flat' debate. Returning on foot to Walsingham from Great Snoring the most scenic route to follow is the leafy, ancient **Greenway**, which has served as a pilgrimage route for at least half a millennium. With all those pious feet tramping the way before you it may come as no surprise that this route can become extremely muddy at times but, in the spirit of pilgrimage, surely it's a matter of 'no pain, no gain'?

15 CREAKE ABBEY

🏚 **Fox Cottage** South Creake (page 309)

Northwest of Fakenham towards Burnham Market and the coast beyond are the villages of **South Creake** and **North Creake**, both quiet, pleasant villages with greens, duck ponds and neat flint cottages. Just beyond North Creake you'll find the ruins of Creake Abbey, originally an almshouse founded by the Augustinian order which attained abbey status in 1231. Fire and the Black Death in the 15th century, and Henry VIII in the 16th, all contributed to the abbey's downfall and what remains is an evocative ruin in the keep of English Heritage.

¶¶ FOOD & DRINK

Creake Abbey Café and Food Hall North Creake ✆ 01328 730399 ⌂ creakeabbey.co.uk. Next door to Creake Abbey is this craft and arts centre with galleries and a popular café and food hall in a set of converted farm buildings. The food hall stocks locally sourced meat and charcuterie as well as Norfolk cheeses, beers and wines. A farmers' market, said to be the largest in Norfolk, is held here on the morning of the first Saturday of each month except January, and there are occasional special day events like Plant Lovers' Day in May.

16 FAKENHAM

🏠 **Garden Cottage** Wellingham (page 309)

A medium-sized market town on the River Wensum, Fakenham is more of a place to shop and do business than go out of your way to see. I feel a bit sorry for poor Fakenham as the town seems never to have fully

A NORFOLK CYCLING ODYSSEY

Sheila Rattray is a rare woman – in the very best sense. Having retired from her hospital job, Sheila, a mother of five grown-up children, decided that she needed to keep herself fit now that she would no longer be cycling the seven miles a day between her Norwich home and place of work. She resolved to make up the missing miles by making forays into the Norfolk countryside on her bike. The long-term aim was to visit all the villages marked on her road map – effectively, all of them. Insistent that she should start and finish at her Norwich home, those villages in the Fens of the far west of the county would prove to be the most problematic as they required 140-mile round trips. Sensibly, she chose long midsummer days to attempt these, pedalling off at first light to get an early start.

Although she had previously cycled as far as her home town of Montrose in Scotland on one occasion, Sheila thoroughly enjoyed her freewheeling day trips in Norfolk. 'I really like those wee roads that don't have white lines down them,' she enthused. 'I like all the wee flowers at the wayside too. Last year, I saw the biggest bank of cowslips I'd ever seen in my life. I enjoy looking at the stock in the

fields; it reminds me of growing up on a cattle farm in Aberdeenshire. I love to see the rivers too – especially when they flood – and the wee thatched houses in the villages.'

Sheila's preparation for an excursion was minimal to say the least. 'I don't take food – I'll maybe get something from a farm shop and I like an ice cream sometimes too.' She didn't take a map either. 'I'll follow the signposts and ask for directions. Talking to people, that's the thing – they're usually really friendly when they find out what I'm up to. I do like getting a bit lost too.'

Sheila completed her Norfolk odyssey in August 2013. Her last village was West Beckham where she met family and friends for a celebratory meal and drink. A friend had made her a T-shirt bearing the legend 'Sheila Rattray – I've cycled to every Norfolk village from my home', which she donned for a photograph before cycling back to Norwich. I asked her what she was planning to do next. 'Och, I don't know. Maybe I'll stop for a wee ice cream on the way home'.

Ten years later, while continuing to cycle a minimum of 100 miles a week, Sheila remains a keen participant in the annual Norfolk 100 cycle event.

recovered from being described in the *Daily Telegraph* as 'one of the most boring places on earth' a decade or so ago – a wholly unfair slight. The quote was actually taken out of context as it related to a scurrilous comment made in a guidebook about Fakenham on Wednesday afternoons when it is early closing day in the town. As any local will tell you, Thursdays – market day – are quite a different matter. While it's not the most dynamic of towns, I could think of many more places where I would rather not be. Its centre has a modestly attractive Georgian square that hosts a very lively weekly market on Thursday mornings and a farmers' market on the fourth Saturday morning of each month. The Thursday market really does seem to attract crowds to the town, especially representatives of the county's more senior demographic who dust off their bus passes for a good day out. There's also a town racecourse, the only other one in the county besides Great Yarmouth. Above all though, you also really have to warm to a town that has taken the trouble of opening its very own Museum of Gas and Local History (✐ 07470 341402 ✐ fakenhamgasmuseum.com ☉ Easter–Oct Thu & Fri), which is housed in the former gas works – a designated Scheduled Ancient Monument – that produced the town's gas supply between 1846 and 1965.

Fakenham Market

Fakenham's Thursday market has an air of perpetuity about it, as well it might. The town was originally granted a charter to hold a market in 1250, and the square beneath St Peter and St Paul Church where the market was first held is still busy on Thursdays. The market has long outgrown its designated territory in the square next to the church and now spills over into a large car park towards Cattlemarket Street some distance beyond. Here you can find anything from pot plants to plastic potties, scented candles to smoked sausages. The main market square is crowded with stalls selling fresh fruit and veg, paperback thrillers, sunglasses, army surplus clothing and suspiciously cheap vacuum-packed meat. The Cattlemarket Street extension tends to be a bit more 'fringe' and, as well as having an excellent local cheese stall and a man selling artisan bread from a table by a van, there is also a lot of old green bottles, cigarette card albums and unloved crockery. If you are looking for brass horses, china plates with dogs' faces or a 1966 *Blue Peter Annual* then this is the place. Admittedly, it is mostly retired people that come these days but

Fakenham Thursday market remains an important weekly event on the north Norfolk social calendar: a chance to catch up with friends, have a mardle ('chat') and do a bit of shopping at the same time.

¶¶ FOOD & DRINK

Taylors 5 Oak St ✆ 01328 851454. A town-centre café with several small rooms leading off a central seating area. Good for cakes, scones, coffee and light meals.

17 PENSTHORPE NATURAL PARK

Pensthorpe Rd, Fakenham NR21 0LN ✆ 01328 851465 🖰 pensthorpe.com

Just outside Fakenham on the Norwich road, this is the biggest local draw, a nature reserve with a large collection of waterfowl in natural surroundings. With a wide range of habitats, plenty of wild birds turn up too – 171 species recorded in total. The BBC television natural history programme *Springwatch* used to broadcast from here, which is quite a feather in the cap for the place if you'll pardon the (bird) pun. The park has several themed garden areas with imaginative plantings to explore, like the Millennium Garden and Wave Garden, as well as duck-filled lakes, wildflower meadows and a sculpture trail for both adults and children to enjoy. There are plenty of activities specifically for children too, like WildRootz, a two-acre adventure activity centre close to the entrance. The idea is to re-connect children with the natural world by means of imaginative play equipment and a network of artificial hills, tunnels and burrows. As well as a giant slide tower called 'The Worm', there are trees to climb, zipwires to zip along and shallow streams to wade through – a kind of eco funfair. Beyond the confines of the WildRootz area and the indoor Hootz House play area, youngsters can participate in more traditional pursuits like pond dipping and bug walks, while the red squirrel sanctuary seems capable of charming visitors of all ages. In addition to red squirrels, the Pensthorpe Conservation Trust has ongoing projects with rare and endangered bird species like corncrakes, curlews and turtle doves. It also presents a great opportunity to get up close and personal to Eurasian cranes, which while native to Norfolk remain pretty elusive in the wild. The Pensthorpe Explorer, which operates at weekends between the end of March and end of September, is another draw for children and adults alike: a specially designed Land Rover and trailer that weaves through the remoter parts of the reserve.

FOLLOWING THE WENSUM WAY ALONG THE WENSUM VALLEY

The Wensum Way, which stretches from Gressenhall Farm and Workhouse (page 159) to Lenwade, on the A1067 south of Reepham, is well worth considering if you fancy a long day-walk through quiet pastoral countryside. The snag is that although there is adequate public transport at Lenwade, the route's eastern end, there is little transport available to Gressenhall at the other, although a few buses do run daily from Dereham. Buses also run to Swanton Morley from Dereham, so walking just part of the route is an option too. The 12-mile Wensum Way passes through some delightful pastoral countryside, alongside or close to the River Wensum for much of the way. En route to Lenwade, it passes through the villages of Swanton Morley, Elsing and Lyng, each one charmingly picturesque in its own right. Perhaps more importantly, if you are walking, Swanton Morley and Lyng both have decent pubs too, as does Lenwade at the end.

18 SCULTHORPE MOOR NATURE RESERVE

Turf Moor Rd, Fakenham NR21 9GN ✆ 01328 856788 ⌖ hawkandowl.org

A little way west of Fakenham, just off the King's Lynn road, this 45-acre nature reserve managed by the Hawk and Owl Trust is a fine example of unimproved fen habitat. With over a mile of walkways threading through woodland and marshes there are plenty of hides and viewing platforms from which to observe the reserve's rich birdlife. As well as birds, the fen flora here is a treat in spring and early summer with a plethora of yellow flag, ragged robin and the like. Having easy access and wooden boardwalks running all the way around it, this reserve must be one of the best wildlife reserves in the country for those with restricted mobility. For those using public transport, the X29 Fakenham to King's Lynn bus service has a stop close to the entrance at the end of Turf Moor Road.

⫯⫯ FOOD & DRINK

Sculthorpe Mill Lynn Rd ✆ 01362 633001 ⌖ sculthorpemill.uk. Tucked away down a narrow lane beside the River Wensum, close to Sculthorpe Moor Nature Reserve, this 18th-century pub with rooms, formerly a watermill, has turned the heads of none less than *The Sunday Times* for the quality of its food and accommodation. It is also one of only two pubs in England to receive a Bib Gourmand from Michelin. Nevertheless, it still has a reasonable-value bar menu and its garden remains a lovely place to eat. The best thing of all, though, is the tranquil riverside setting.

19 SWANTON MORLEY

🏠 **Carrick's at Castle Farm** (page 309)

Swanton Morley has the large imposing 14th-century All Saints' Church, a landmark for miles around. There are also two pubs, one of which, The Angel, was once home to Richard Lincoln, a distant ancestor of President Abraham Lincoln. The village also has one of the best butchers in this part of Norfolk.

🍴 FOOD & DRINK

The Angel 66 Greengate ✆ 01362 637407 ⌖ theangelpub.co.uk. This handsome brick building dating back to 1610 was built by Richard Lincoln, a distant ancestor of Abraham Lincoln. Woodforde's Wherry and other guest real ales. Traditional pub grub lunchtimes and evenings, Sunday roasts and themed food nights.

Darby's Elsing Rd ✆ 01362 637346 ⌖ darbyspub.co.uk. This freehouse in the centre of Swanton Morley offers a wide range of food using locally sourced seasonal ingredients and a good choice of local real ales.

20 ELSING

Elsing, the next village on the Wensum Way, is reached by following a footpath alongside the Wensum bank for much of the way. You'll probably be in the company of wide-horned White Park cattle that tend to sprawl themselves across the track in places but this ancient rare breed, descended from Britain's original wild white cattle (actually feral in forests after the Romans evacuated Britain) with a lineage of more than two millennia, are gentle beasts it would seem. King James I is said to have knighted a joint of White Park beef after a particularly good lunch in Lancashire in 1617. This is claimed by some to be the origin of the term 'sirloin' but sadly its etymology is more prosaic: it comes from the Middle French *surlogne*.

Walking along the riverbank here in high summer you can enjoy hungry swallows gleefully skimming the water and flood meadows in perfect symbiosis with the fly-luring cattle – an evocatively bucolic scene. Of course, you could always spurn the river and drive or cycle instead – the roads in this part of the county are generally pretty quiet.

St Mary's Church is notable for its pillar-free nave, the widest of any parish church in the region, and its splendid brass commemorating Sir Hugh Hastings, the church's founder. T E Lawrence ('of Arabia' fame) is said to have visited the church on a cycling tour back in 1905 – perhaps he was an enthusiastic brass-rubber? The village really has not changed much since then. No doubt Lawrence would have supped a pint in the Mermaid Inn immediately opposite the church, a once welcoming hostelry that has stood here since the 16th century. Sadly it stopped trading in 2020 and now appears to be permanently closed.

21 LYNG

This village has a charming millhouse next to a river and weir. Curiously, there are also large anti-tank blocks next to the bridge that date from World War II – but if invading Germans had managed to penetrate this far inland then surely the game would have been up anyway? After Lyng, the Wensum Way winds past Sparham Pools, a group of wildlife-rich flooded gravel pits leased to Norfolk Wildlife Trust, before reaching Lenwade on the main A1067. From here, the Marriott's Way leads to Norwich if you are game for more foot-slogging; otherwise, there is a regular bus service, the X29 from Fakenham.

EAST DEREHAM & AROUND

22 EAST DEREHAM

🏠 **Greenbanks Hotel** (page 309)

> **Pretty, quiet Dereham, thou pattern of an English town.**
> George Borrow, *Lavengro*

So where is *West* Dereham, you might ask? Out in the Fens in the middle of nowhere is the answer, so just plain 'Dereham' will do when referring to this medium-sized mid-Norfolk market town – no one round here calls it East Dereham. If you made a cardboard cut-out of Norfolk and looked for the central point from which to suspend it, you would probably find it passes close to Dereham (although nearby Hoe is also a contender) – it doesn't get much more mid-Norfolk than this.

◀ **1** Hoe Rough Nature Reserve. **2** Sculthorpe Moor at sunrise. **3** Bonner's Cottages, Dereham, are now a small museum. **4** Morris dancers at Gressenhall Farm.

Although it is not immediately obvious, East Dereham's quite an ancient place. The churchyard of St Nicholas has Withburga's Well named after a daughter of the 7th-century Saxon monarch King Anna (yes, king!) who founded a convent here. Withburga's shrine became famous for its miracles until AD984 when the Abbot and monks from the monastery at Ely came trophy hunting and made off with her remains into the mists of the Fens.

The well is said to be filled from a spring that erupted from beneath Withburga's empty grave. You can find it by looking behind the church on its south side. The sunken well has hart's tongue ferns growing on its walls and, less evocatively, is flanked by geraniums in plastic plant pots. The town has a few literary connections too: George Borrow was born at the outskirts of the town at Dumpling Green, just a few years after William Cowper died here; there's a shrine to the latter in the church.

There's nothing to see of Dereham's Saxon past, and little of the medieval other than the church. What greets the eye is mostly the rebuild that followed post-Tudor fires, although there is a row of 16th-century cottages near the church known as Bonner's Cottages that have elaborate Suffolk-style pargetting. The buildings, which now serve as a cottage museum (𝒜 01362 853453 𝒹 derehamhistory.com ☉ May–Sep Fri & Sat), take their name from Bishop Bonner who lived here as a curate before his stint as Bishop of London. Bonner was anything but a kind and gentle soul: as an enthusiastic foot soldier of 'Bloody' Queen Mary's excesses, he sent many a Protestant heretic to a fiery death. As an interesting aside, 'bishy barnabee', a Norfolk dialect word for ladybird, quite possibly derives from Bishop Bonner too.

The most enjoyable way to arrive is by train on the **Mid-Norfolk Railway** (page 245) from Wymondham. You could buy a return ticket from Wymondham or, alternatively, just a single to here, continuing your journey by bus – there are frequent services east and west to Norwich, Swaffham and King's Lynn. Dereham station is something of a throwback to the 1950s and has quite a nice café, so if you don't want to bother going into town and you could easily while away half an hour or so here whilst waiting for the return train.

23 GRESSENHALL

For a thorough exposition of the county's social and agricultural history, visit the village of Gressenhall a few miles north of Dereham, where **Gressenhall Farm and Workhouse** (📞 01362 860563 🖥 museums.norfolk.gov.uk) is a combined museum and farm set in 50 acres of countryside. The approach is hands-on: while the 18th-century workhouse seems to ooze despair from the very fabric of the building, much of the history is told through the recorded lives of inmates. The collections gallery has all manner of fascinating artefacts including a hurdy-gurdy and a portable Turkish bath. Despite the gloomy atmosphere of the workhouse itself, this is a surprisingly good place to visit with small children. The punishment cell may be rather sobering but there are fun activities too – for children, at least – like dressing up in Victorian clothes and cart rides around the farm with enormous shire horses. Separate from the main building is a Victorian schoolroom, a chapel and small walled garden, and a restaurant and tea room with its own small garden. There is also a very well-equipped adventure playground next to an outdoor picnic area. As well as family events during school holidays, the museum stages special events days such as a Norfolk History Fair and Apple Day in October, which, with live folk music, Morris dancers and a huge variety of apples for sale, is always very well-attended. For walkers, the Nar Valley Way begins (or ends) at the museum, as does the Wensum Way that links Gressenhall museum with Lenwade on the Marriott's Way (page 154).

24 HOE ROUGH NATURE RESERVE

A little way east of Gressenhall, next to the village of Beetley, you'll find Hoe Rough, a Norfolk Wildlife Trust nature reserve of ancient grazing meadows and 300-year-old oaks alongside the River Whitewater, a tributary of the Wensum. If you take a stroll here you might well see basking adders in spring and, if you are really lucky, otters in the river. The reserve has its own small car park, just off the main road east of the small bridge.

Immediately opposite the car park entrance, over the road in a small triangle of grass next to Chapel Mill, you'll find a large stone that does not look as if it comes from these parts. It doesn't: this is one of many large glacial erratics found in Norfolk – lumps of alien (as in 'non-indigenous', not from Mars!) rock dragged here by ice during the last glacial period. Whether or not this particular stone was deposited precisely on this very spot is open to debate, as a previous owner of Mill House in the late 19th century was an antiquarian dealer who may well have had it placed here in front of his house. Nevertheless, it is unlikely that the stone could have been transported very far by horse and cart so it's probably local enough – 10,000 years or so is just about long enough to be awarded 'local' status around these parts. The stone is also rumoured to mark the dead centre of Norfolk, although this same geographical distinction is also claimed by a supermarket car park in nearby Dereham.

25 NORTH ELMHAM

A little way north of Gressenhall, you come to North Elmham, a large, rather sprawling village that was once connected to Dereham and Fakenham by the mid-Norfolk Railway. Plans are afoot to extend the Wymondham to Dereham Mid-Norfolk line as far as North Elmham, or rather reinstate it; for the time being, the village has The Railway pub, a station road and even a station building, but no railway.

North Elmham was the site of the Bishopric of East Anglia until 1075, but of the Saxon cathedral that stood here, virtually no trace remains. Instead are the flinty remains of a Norman church built by Herbert de Losinga alongside the earthworks of a 14th-century castle built by Henry le Despenser, a later Bishop of Norwich. The ruins occupy a pretty spot at the edge of the village surrounded by old chestnut trees.

26 FOXLEY WOOD & 27 HONEYPOT WOOD

Norfolk has some wonderful tracts of ancient woodland and two of these lie quite close to Dereham. The Norfolk Wildlife Trust manages Foxley and Honeypot woods, which are fine reminders of what much of central Norfolk must once have been like before widespread agriculture took hold. It is tempting to think of woods like these as truly wild places left over from the last Ice Age but, really, they are not. They have been rigorously managed over the centuries, albeit in a sustainable way. These days, of course, there is little demand for woodland products like hazel wands but the ancient art of coppicing is still practised, creating the dappled conditions needed for what have become quite scarce plants like primroses, cowslips and early purple orchids.

These woodlands are all habitats for butterflies and birds and, in springtime especially, for idyllic walks along the grassy rides. Northeast of East Dereham, just beyond Foxley and Bawdeswell (which are on the A1067), **Foxley Wood** is Norfolk's largest remaining ancient woodland.

It was intensively coppiced in medieval times and, as well as hazel, it yielded other woodland products such as tree bark used in the tanning industry. The bluebells are so well known locally that the woodland rides can get almost busy at bluebell time (late April–early May). Several waymarked trails penetrate the heart of the wood. Their margins are sometimes boggy following prolonged wet weather but if you stick to the central part of the ride it's usually not too wet underfoot.

Four miles west of East Dereham and just north of Wendling, **Honeypot Wood** is smaller and takes its name from a nearby medieval sewage dump or 'honey pit' – a euphemism if ever there was one. Like Foxley Wood, it is at its very best in spring when enough light filters through the canopy to allow woodland plants like twayblades, wood anemones and, of course, bluebells to flourish.

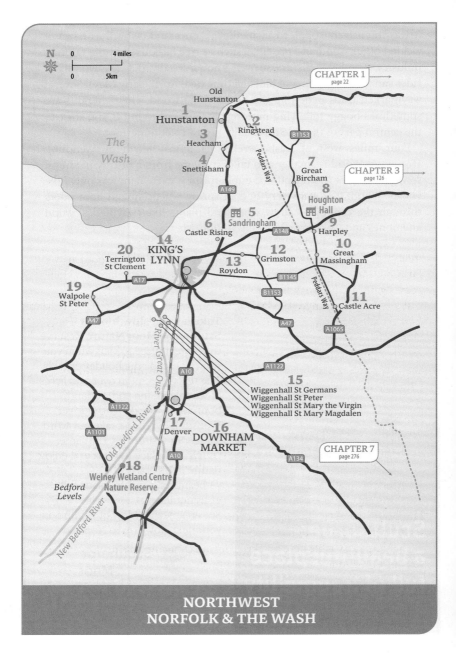

CHAPTER 7
page 276

N

0   4 miles

0   5km

The
Wash

1
Hunstanton

Old
Hunstanton

2
Ringstead

B1153

3
Heacham

Pedars Way

7
Great
Bircham

4
Snettisham

A149

8
Houghton
Hall

6
Castle Rising

5
Sandringham

A148

9
Harpley

20
Terrington
St Clement

14
KING'S
LYNN

12
Grimston

13
Roydon

10
Great
Massingham

B1145

19
Walpole
St Peter

A17

B1153

Pedars Way

11
Castle Acre

A47

A1065

River Great Ouse

A47

A10

A1122

15
Wiggenhall St Germans
Wiggenhall St Peter
Wiggenhall St Mary the Virgin
Wiggenhall St Mary Magdalen

A1122

Old Bedford River

17
Denver

16
DOWNHAM
MARKET

A1101

A10

A134

18
Welney Wetland Centre
Nature Reserve

Bedford
Levels

New Bedford River

NORTHWEST
NORFOLK & THE WASH

4
NORTHWEST NORFOLK & THE WASH

As you head west along the north Norfolk coast, it turns south just before the resort of **Hunstanton** and with a change of direction, comes a change of character. Instead of vast expanses of salt marshes, pebble cottages and silted medieval harbours we find ourselves in a zone of sandy beaches and low dunes, stone-banded cliffs and low chalk ridges inland. The coast runs down as far as King's Lynn, which once had a far more important place in the scheme of things than it has today but, there again, so did Norfolk as a whole.

It may seem strange to witness the sun setting out to sea – this is East Anglia after all. But the realisation that the Wash is just a rather wide inlet will come when, in fine weather, you see the wind turbines on the far Lincolnshire shore, or, on a very clear day, catch a glimpse of the 'Boston Stump', the improbably tall tower of Boston's St Botolph's Church. The Wash's beaches attract both holiday makers and wildfowl, with buckets, spades and suntan oil out in force at Snettisham in the summer months, and geese, ducks and waders feasting on the tidal mudflats and sandbanks offshore in winter.

Inland from the coast it is a different picture, with low chalk hills, quietly attractive carrstone and chalk-built villages like **Ringstead** and lush pasture with scattered patches of woodland. Further inland still and you edge into the light soils of what's sometimes termed as High Norfolk – the agricultural landscape of north Norfolk enclosure, with its hedgerows and woodland copses.

The slow pace of life here quickens only marginally in its urban centres, old-fashioned market towns like Swaffham and Downham Market that lie on the edge of this region and give way to the Brecks and the Fens respectively. On the whole though, smaller villages like Great Bircham and Great Massingham, both far from 'great', are generally more typical of this ultra-rural corner of the county. This is estate country too, with **Sandringham**, the Royal family's country retreat, being the prime example. The hall at **Houghton** is even more impressive and one of the finest country houses in East Anglia.

King's Lynn, once a thriving port, is central to the area and although it may seem unprepossessing on arrival, has a concentration of intriguing distractions centred around its historic core. South and west of here lie the spectacularly contour-free, drained arable region of the Fens, often associated with Norfolk but really far more typical of Cambridgeshire and south Lincolnshire than Norfolk as a whole. The Fens are not to everyone's taste, but have huge wide skies and distant horizons that are unsullied by anything as presumptuous as a hill or even a contour. Lines of straight poplars stretch into the distance like a French impressionist painting; pylons recede to vanishing point – you can almost sense the curvature of the earth.

The **Peddars Way** runs arrow-straight across this area, beginning uncertainly – or rather, ill-defined – in the heathland at Knettishall near Thetford but gaining confidence, and a more obvious surface, as it progresses through **Castle Acre** across the heathland and chalk ridges of west Norfolk to terminate at Holme-next-the-Sea. Such a linear, determined route suggests a Roman origin, and it was constructed as a military thoroughfare in their campaign to pacify Norfolk's warring Iceni tribes. When the Romans finally removed their sandals from these shores and high-tailed it back to Rome in time for the fall of their empire, the route came into its own as a thoroughfare for peddlers, thieves, drovers and pilgrims. There again, the route may well be even older – an extension of the undeniably ancient Icknield Way that was remodelled by road-mad Romans shortly after they arrived.

GETTING AROUND
PUBLIC TRANSPORT
Geographically west Norfolk is somewhat out on a limb and this isolation is reflected in its train connections. Rail services connect King's Lynn with Cambridge and London but there's no direct service to Norwich.

By **bus**, the situation is better but by no means marvellous. The Coastliner 36 service along Norfolk's north coast runs between Wells and Hunstanton before continuing south to King's Lynn, calling at villages along the A149 – Heacham, Snettisham, Dersingham and

ℹ️ TOURIST INFORMATION

Fens Tourism ⊘ visitthefens.com
Hunstanton Central Promenade ✆ 01533 774297 (King's Lynn TIC)
King's Lynn Saturday Market Place ✆ 01553 774297
Visit West Norfolk ⊘ visitwestnorfolk.com

Castle Rising. The X1, a direct, and reasonably quick, bus service, runs between Norwich and King's Lynn calling at East Dereham and Swaffham en route. Lynx (⊘ lynxbus.co.uk), the company that operates the Coastliner service, also has services running east to Fakenham via larger villages like Great Massingham and west to places in the Fens like Downham Market and Walpole St Peter. Unfortunately, some of the smaller villages, especially those in the Fens, are harder to reach.

WALKING

Some of the best walking in this part of the county is along stretches of the valley of the **River Nar**, a lovely chalk stream that has been designated an SSSI along its entire length. The river flows through Castle Acre, West Acre and Narborough, which all make good starting points for a circular walk.

The **Nar Valley Way** runs 33 miles from the Gressenhall Farm and Workhouse (page 159) all the way to King's Lynn. This links with both the Peddars Way at Castle Acre and the Wash Coast Path at King's Lynn. The Nar Valley Group of Parishes have produced a useful leaflet, *Footsteps through Time: Walks in the Nar Valley*, which outlines five circular walks starting in Narborough, Castle Acre or West Acre. You should be able to find the leaflet at tourist centres. Norfolk County Council also has useful information and suggestions for circular and short and long linear walks online at ⊘ norfolk.gov.uk/narvalleyway.

Close to King's Lynn, **Roydon Common** offers a bracing walk well away from habitation, and **Ringstead Downs** near Hunstanton is another good choice for short, leisurely strolls. To get close up to the Wash, explore the Peter Scott Walk, which runs a very tranquil ten miles along the sea bank from King's Lynn to the mouth of the Nene at Sutton Bridge in Lincolnshire (the great naturalist after which it's named lived in a lighthouse on the east bank of the Nene), with choice coastal and fenland views and some excellent bird-watching opportunities.

CYCLING

Cycling is enjoyable in much of this region, if you keep off major roads like the A149, and avoid the A47, A10 and A17 trunk roads at all costs. The terrain is varied and rewarding, and the hills are gentle. Best of all, is to take advantage of those sections of the **Peddars Way** which, doubling as a bridleway, can be used by mountain or hybrid bikes. The track is fine for mountain and touring bikes but sleek racers with tyres the width of a coin will not do well here.

THE NORTHWEST CORNER: HUNSTANTON TO CASTLE RISING

1 HUNSTANTON

🏠 **The Lodge** (page 310)

Rather like a smaller version of Cromer, Hunstanton – 'Hunston' if you live there, 'Sunny Hunny' if you take to the beach – is a seaside resort that came to prominence during the Victorian railway age. It has a somewhat different appearance and atmosphere to its north Norfolk competitors though, as among the mock Tudor of its seafront hotels are some built of **carrstone**, the tough gingery-red sandstone that gives character to this part of the county. Living in east Norfolk, I am so used to seeing only flint or brick used for domestic architecture that this corner of the county can almost seem like alien territory. But no, this is still Norfolk: the air, the accents, the pace of things – these are all constants. Norfolk is a wide county and Norwich and Great Yarmouth lie so far to the east that many people who live around here hardly ever travel there; instead, they look to King's Lynn or Cambridge for their ration of big city lights.

There are traces of Neolithic settlement in the area, as well as evidence of Bronze Age, Iron Age and Roman activity, but the town you see today is the result of planned development by artistocrat and amateur painter by Henry Styleman Le Strange of Hunstanton Hall in the mid 1840s, who encouraged investment in the railway line between the town and King's Lynn in an attempt to attract visitors to its fine sandy beaches. The venture was a success and well-to-do Victorians came in droves, even the Prince of Wales, later to be Edward VII, who stayed here while recovering from typhoid (perhaps his other favourite, Cromer, was considered a bit too fast-paced for this purpose).

LE STRANGE GOINGS-ON
AT HUNSTANTON BEACH

St Edmund's Point on the coast at Old Hunstanton makes reference to Edmund, the future King of East Anglia who is said to have been shipwrecked here, a mere 14-year-old boy, in AD855. Edmund would go on to become a religious cult hero and England's first patron saint after his matyrdom at the hands of Danes in 869 or 870. In the 13th century, the monks of Bury St Edmunds built a chapel on the cliffs above the spot where Edmund landed in gratitude for his safe deliverance. The ruins of the chapel lie close to an attractive white early 19th-century lighthouse, now a holiday let, whose light was extinguished at the outbreak of World War I never to be rekindled.

The beach at Hunstanton is one of the few places in Britain where the foreshore is privately owned. The Le Strange family, who have been lords of the manor here since shortly after the Norman Conquest, have in their possession a charter that states that as well as the beach itself they own 'everything in the sea as far as a man riding a horse can throw a javelin from the low-tide mark'. The hereditary title of Lord High Admiral of the Wash is also retained by the family. So the seaweed-covered rocks belong, technically at least, to the Le Strange Estate. If St Edmund had pitched up here a couple of centuries later perhaps he would have become the property of the Le Strange Estate too?

Hunstanton is pleasant enough, with a promenade, beach and sloping central green, but for my money, its greatest attraction lies north of the modern town centre in Old Hunstanton, where the gorgeous **banded cliffs** are made of layers of rusty ginger sandstone ('carrstone'), red limestone ('red chalk') with a white chalk layer on top. The cliffs – a perfect geology textbook illustration – are framed by a foreground of chalky sand and green, seaweed-covered rocks. With the setting sun lighting up the cliffs as it lowers across the Wash, and a painterly combination of red, white, green and blue, this is the sort of place that landscape photographers get excited about. The picturesque remains of a wrecked boat, the steam trawler Sheraton, on the tide-line beneath St Edmund's Point provide the final ingredient for a picture-perfect scene.

You can take a **boat trip** from the promenade. Searles Sea Tours (✆ 01485 534444 ⊘ seatours.co.uk) run a variety of trips to view seal colonies on sandbanks in the Wash, and they also do trips along the shoreline past the red and white cliffs and St Edmund's Point. Another option is to take a ride in a World War II amphibious DUKW to visit the wreck of the *Sheraton*.

Old Hunstanton, which is really just an estate village that has become a suburb of the larger town, has the remains – little more than an arch – of **St Edmund's Chapel**. This dates from 1272 and is reputed to have been built on the very spot where the saint landed when he arrived from Germany to become King of East Anglia. It's pleasant to stroll along the top of cliffs here, past the pitch and putt course, the ruined chapel and a converted white lighthouse towards the glitzier side of town. Better still though is to go one way along the beach, admiring the candy-striped cliffs, and return via the clifftop walk.

¶¶ FOOD & DRINK

Hunstanton seems to have a dearth of decent, traditional pubs. Your best bet is probably The Lodge Inn in Old Hunstanton or you could make your way out to the Gin Trap Inn in Ringstead (page 171). Many visitors tend to buy fish and chips from Fishers and eat them on the nearby green overlooking the sea.

Fishers of Hunstanton 2–4 Greevegate ⌀ 01485 532487 ⊘ fishershunstanton.co.uk. This traditional and conveniently placed fish and chip shop has been in business for over 60 years. Indeed, Fishers is so well known in the town that the queue can be very long here in summer.
The Lodge Inn Old Hunstanton Rd ⌀ 01485 532896 ⊘ thelodgehunstanton.co.uk. On the coast road next to the post office, the restaurant here serves imaginatively prepared food with an international flavour sourced mostly from Norfolk-grown ingredients. For a slightly less formal atmosphere you can also eat in the large airy bar. Accommodation available; page 310.
Norfolk Deli 16 Greevegate, Hunstanton ⌀ 01485 535540 ⊘ norfolk-deli.co.uk. This delicatessen specialises in local produce, especially cheese, of which there are 70 varieties, a dozen from Norfolk. It's also very good for breads, charcuterie, local beers and made-to-order sandwiches. Also sells themed gift hampers with a strong emphasis on local produce.

2 RINGSTEAD

A small, attractive village of whitewashed cottages just inland from the coast, and on the route of the Peddars Way, Ringstead is chocolate-box pretty, has a lovely pub and is a good starting point for leisurely walks along the valley of the Ringstead Downs immediately west of the village.

1 The knot spectacular at RSPB Snettisham. 2 The banded cliffs at Old Hunstanton.
3 St Edmund's Chapel and the lighthouse, Old Hunstanton. 4 Norfolk Lavender, Heacham.
5 A brown hare at Wild Ken Hill. ▶

The village's original church, St Peter's, is now long gone as a place of worship but its Norman round tower still remains a little to the south of the village.

Ringstead Downs

These are hardly the South Downs, but there are some similarities. Unimproved chalk grassland such as this is rare in Norfolk. Ringstead Downs is a short stretch of dry glacial valley, a far northern extension of the same chalk strata that make up the Chilterns and Cambridgeshire's Gog Magog Hills. The chalky soil ensures plenty of wildflowers that are rarely found elsewhere in the region, as well as a good show of butterfly species like Brown Argus and warblers in summer. On a sunny day, the gentle slopes here provide an ideal setting for a leisurely picnic, with butterflies fluttering by, the contented buzz of bees and the scent of thyme creating as much a sense of bucolic well-being as a 1970s shampoo advert.

Courtyard Farm

Ringstead PE36 5LQ ✆ 01485 525251 ⌖ courtyardfarm.co.uk

Courtyard Farm, just east of Ringstead village, is where the late Peter Melchett, former executive director of Greenpeace and tireless champion of ramblers' rights, farmed according to organic principles until his death in 2018. Happily, the organic tradition continues under the auspices of Melchett's partner, Cassandra Wedd, and Jay Wooton, who has been involved with the farm for a long time. The farm is welcoming to walkers and to walkers with dogs on leads too. There are two waymarked circular routes of around two miles and one of six miles on public footpaths around the farm, and more routes on permissive paths – a map can be downloaded from the farm website. Not surprisingly, given its organic credentials, Courtyard Farm is replete with wildlife, with plenty of typical farmland birds like skylarks and a thriving population of hares. Even driving past by car you can't help but notice the kaleidoscopic colour of the native annual wildflowers that grow in the field margins around here, an all-too-rare sight elsewhere in arable Norfolk.

"Not surprisingly, given its organic credentials, Courtyard Farm is replete with wildlife."

Courtyard Farm Trust also owns 90 acres of grazing marshes managed by Norfolk Wildlife Trust at nearby Holme-next-the–Sea (page 72), a haven for waders and wildfowl. Not wishing to turn its back on material culture in favour of wildlife, the farm has also commissioned works of art in two of its disused marl pits. Both use materials that reflect the local environment: *Carrstone Shale Wall and Boulder* by John Sands, which can be found in an old marl pit northwest of North Wood, and *Chalky Void (absence and presence)* by Martha Winter in North Wood itself.

¶ FOOD & DRINK

Gin Trap Inn High St ✆ 01485 525264 ⬧ thegintrapinn.co.uk. The oak-beamed bar has real ales such as Adnams and Woodforde's and a crackling fire, while the comforting food on offer is mostly locally sourced, with beef and pork from nearby Courtyard Farm and oysters from Thornham.

3 HEACHAM

🏠 The Summerhouse (page 310)

Heacham, just south of Hunstanton on the coast, has a beach but is probably best known for **lavender**. In summer, coachloads come from afar to view the bushes in their mauve, serried ranks. On a warm sunny day, the aromatic oils released from the plants permeate the air so much that the whole area is redolent of a National Trust gift shop. Lavender garden and distillery tours are available at Caley Mill Farm, headquarters of Norfolk Lavender Ltd (✆ 01485 570384 ⬧ norfolk-lavender.co.uk), where a tea room and gift shop sell all manner of lavender products. The company was founded in 1932 and lavender has been grown around Caley Mill since 1936. Henry Head, who has worked here for over 30 years, told me a little about the company. 'Here at Norfolk Lavender we've kept alive the great tradition of English lavender growing – for 60 years we were the only significant growers in the country. Caley Mill was a Victorian watermill built in 1837 but now it's our headquarters and we've got shops, a tea room and plant centre here, as well as our new Rare Breeds Animal Centre.' I asked him why this part of west Norfolk is so suitable for lavender growing. It is, after all, a plant that has its natural home on sun-baked Mediterranean hillsides. 'With one exception, all the varieties that we grow here were developed by us for their suitability for the local conditions. The locality is ideal: there's plenty of sunshine, free-draining soils and not too much rain.'

KING'S LYNN TO HUNSTANTON – A BETJEMAN TRAIN JOURNEY

There's a charming old film in the East Anglian Film Archive (⊘ eafa.org.uk/work/?id=1411) of John Betjeman travelling from King's Lynn to Hunstanton on the former Great Eastern Railway, stopping to admire the Edwardian splendour of Wolferton station along the way, a station so well-appointed for its royal passengers that it sports crowns atop its lamp posts. The film ends at the promenade at Hunstanton, Betjeman hamming it up delightfully as he inhales the bracing sea air in front of the pier.

Much has gone since the film was made in 1961 – the railway line, the poet himself and much else besides. The spectacularly long pier that appears in the documentary was washed away in a storm in 1978. The Sandringham Hotel seen in front of Hunstanton station is long gone too – demolished in 1967 – and the site of the former railway station now serves as a car park. Only half a century ago, this was a very different world – a black and white one in which poet laureates made unhurried documentaries about humble branch lines (now we have former Tory politicians in lurid jackets doing much the same), schoolboys wore caps and short trousers, and almost everyone who could afford it holidayed at a British coastal resort.

The village also has a curious association with Pocahontas and the village sign depicts the celebrated Powhatan Indian princess. Pocahontas married an English Virginian settler, John Rolfe, in 1614 and the two of them travelled to England together in 1616. At first, the couple spent some time in the capital, delighting the London set, but later moved on to live at Rolfe's country house at **Heacham Hall** for a while. The pair attempted to return to Virginia in 1617 but Pocahontas fell ill with smallpox before they had even left English waters. She was taken ashore before she died, to be buried at Gravesend. Many descendants of the Rolfe family lie buried at Heacham Church, a 12th-century building of Norman origin that is said to have the oldest church bell in East Anglia.

"In summer, coachloads come from afar to view the bushes in their mauve, serried ranks."

Now converted to holiday accommodation, Heacham's erstwhile **railway station** used to serve the now defunct King's Lynn to Hunstanton line, which operated for just over a hundred years between 1866 and 1969, when Norfolk was much better connected by rail than it is today.

4 SNETTISHAM

♠ **Rose and Crown** (page 310)

The beach here is enormous – wide and spacious – but the village is just as well known for its RSPB reserve. Both lie away from the village, around two miles to the west. There has been an important carrstone quarry here for centuries and much of the stone that you see in walls around this part of the county probably originates from here.

The Snettisham area has clearly been settled for millennia: a great hoard of treasure trove was discovered close to the village – 75 complete golden torcs (solid gold neck rings, which must have been almost too heavy to wear) and even more fragmentary ones that date from the 1st century AD, as well as a great deal of Romano-British jewellery, all now at the British Museum.

Snettisham's **St Mary's Church**, with its tall 14th-century spire, has been raved about by architectural writers Nikolaus Pevsner and Simon Jenkins for its west window, with its complex, lace-like tracery. The east and south windows were replaced after having been bombed by a Zeppelin in 1915 – the very first air attack on an English church, a unique honour of sorts. Compared to churches in Lincolnshire, St Mary's seems perfectly normal, as spires are not at all unusual in that part of the world. Coming from Norfolk though, it does look a bit odd, as if some sort of boundary has been crossed – an architectural aperitif for the world beyond the Wash.

At the shoreline, the tide can go out for miles here, leaving a vast area of mud and sand, ideal for feeding birds and games of cricket. Naturally, birds have the advantage of being able to fly away if cut off by rapidly incoming tides; strolling humans do not have this facility. The **RSPB reserve** (✆ 01485 210779) here really comes into its own during the autumn and winter months when high tides push tens of thousands of waders up on to the shoreline. The higher the tide, the easier it is to see the birds. Low tide require telescopes and an aptitude for identifying indeterminate blobs in the distant mud.

One of the greatest events here is the 'knot spectacular' that occurs when tens of thousands of small waders, mostly knot, take to the sky in shifting, swirling patterns of silver, black and white. These occur at spring tides in spring, late summer and early autumn, and a useful timetable of suggested visiting times can be downloaded from the RSPB website (⊗ rspb.org.uk). In winter, the highlight is watching vast

numbers of pink-footed geese leave the mudflats of the Wash at dawn for their feeding grounds inland: a thrilling sight on clear mornings when the rising sun reflects on their wings. Such a spectacle comes at a price, though, as it requires a very early start. Nevertheless, it is certainly something worth witnessing if you are staying in the area. Be aware that it is a fairly long walk from the RSPB car park to the reserve, but there's plenty to look for in the reeds along the way. The nearest bus stop for both beach and reserve is on the A149 at the Beach Road junction.

Snettisham Park Farm (✆ 01485 542425 ⌘ snettishampark.co.uk), with its entrance close to the church on the Bircham road, is a working farm that offers hands-on activities likely to appeal to children. Animals include what you would normally expect on a farm, plus deer and, even more exotically, llamas. Deer safaris feature a 45-minute commentated tractor and trailer ride, and there are a number of farm trails.

Also close to Snettisham is the farmland and reserve at **Wild Ken Hill** (⌘ wildkenhill.co.uk), which stretches across 4,000 acres of coastal scrub, freshwater marshes, woodland, pasture and arable fields between the village and the coast at Heacham. As well as a working farm engaged in sustainable and regenerative practices, Wild Ken Hill is a site of conservation and rewilding with lots of exciting ongoing projects. Its most celebrated rewilding project is that with beavers, the only one of its kind in Norfolk. Wild Ken Hill has been featured on the BBC's *Springwatch*, *Autumnwatch* and *Winterwatch* in recent years. Although this is private land that cannot be accessed without prior permission, there is a good range of daylight guided tours on offer, either on foot and in a farm trailer, such as Rewilding in Practice and Wader Watch, as well as Nature by Night, Bats, and Dawn Chorus tours that take place at night or in low light. In 2022 Wild Ken Hill organised the first one-day Gathering festival, which included workshops and many guest speakers involved in conservation and wildlife.

¶¶ FOOD & DRINK

Rose and Crown Old Church Rd, Snettisham ✆ 01485 541382 ⌘ roseandcrownsnettisham. co.uk. This whitewashed 14th-century inn has an imaginative menu that uses local produce where possible: all meat is outdoor-reared in Norfolk; mussels come from Brancaster, and vegetables are sourced from a local allotment. Also has accommodation; page 310.

◀ **1** The castle at Castle Rising. **2** The Dining Room of Sandringham House.

5 SANDRINGHAM HOUSE & ESTATE

Sandringham PE35 6EN ✆ 01485 544112 ⌂ sandringhamestate.co.uk ◌ house, museum & gardens: Easter–early Nov except for last week in Jul; country park: daily; discounted admission to the estate for those who arrive by public transport; free entry & parking for the country park

Adjacent to the village of Dersingham is the Sandringham Estate, with Sandringham House set in 60 acres of landscaped, wooded gardens, and best known as the place where the Royal Family traditionally spend Christmas. Queen Victoria's son, Edward the Prince of Wales, first came across the country house and estate here in 1861 and snapped them up forthwith (he rejected Houghton Hall, which was also offered for purchase). The Prince rebuilt the main residence to his own tastes in 1870 and landscaped the grounds, adding a ballroom later on, which sees use today as the venue for estate workers' Christmas parties. The author John Seymour describes the house as 'very ugly – like a huge and grandiose Victorian seaside hotel', but he does have a point as, scaled down in size, it wouldn't look too out of place sitting above the promenade in Cromer. Anyway, you can make up your own mind if you choose to visit.

The wooded grounds are, indisputably, quite lovely. For devotees of local vernacular style, the 16th-century church of **St Mary Magdalene** is widely considered to be one of the very finest carrstone buildings in existence. This is, of course, where the Royal Family traditionally comes to worship at Christmas and so you have probably glimpsed it already on television. The estate's **museum** has a large and rather bizarre collection of royal vehicles and some of the gifts given to the Royal Family over the years. The gift shop sells all manner of royal memorabilia but the estate farm shop is perhaps more appealing, with wares including local cheese, estate-produced rare-breed organic meat and a large selection of jams and chutneys.

Sandringham Country Park, which extends north from the visitor centre and car park to cover an area of nearly 600 acres, has open access and is free to visit. The park dates from 1968 when 350 acres of Queen Elizabeth II's estate was designated as a Country Park. It has been enlarged since then to create a large wooded area with free access to the public. The park has two waymarked nature trails and a sculpture trail as well as numerous woodland paths through stands of mixed evergreen and deciduous trees.

The Coastliner bus service between Hunstanton and King's Lynn provides a regular service to the visitor centre. The Sustrans National Cycle Route 1 passes nearby.

6 CASTLE RISING

Between Dersingham and King's Lynn, Castle Rising village is attractive in its own right. The village is old enough to get a mention in the Domesday Book. There's **St Lawrence's Church** with its Norman and Early-English features and the Hospital of the Holy and Undivided Trinity opposite, but what most come to see is the village's mighty Norman castle (✆ 01553 631330; ◌ castlerising.co.uk ◷ closed Mon and Tue in winter; English Heritage). This impressive and seemingly impregnable ruin, owned by English Heritage, has a typical Norman square keep similar to Norwich Castle's; it peeps over the top of the huge oval defensive earthworks that surround it and are believed to be Roman or earlier. Ruins of a Saxon and Norman chapel lie partly buried in the earthworks' north side.

Edward III made use of the castle to banish his mother Isabella, the 'She-wolf of France', after she had colluded with her lover in the death of her husband, Edward II, reputedly by a grisly method that required the unorthodox use of fire-stoking equipment. The means of this brutal murder is most likely pure myth, however, and some accounts even suggest that Edward II escaped to live in exile. For Isabella, it was a relatively liberal banishment, more a kind of voluntary house arrest, as she continued to move around the country relatively freely and did not go mad in her confinement as is sometimes alleged. Later occupants of the castle included the Black Prince and Richard II, and later still, Henry VIII, who sold it to the Howard family.

Opposite the church, the red-brick Hospital of the Holy and Undivided Trinity, also known as the Howard Bede House, is effectively an almshouse founded by Henry Howard, the Earl of Northampton, in 1614. It continues to house a dozen elderly ladies to this day who, following the statute set down by Henry Howard, must be 'able to read, single, 56 at least, no common beggar, harlot, scold, drunkard, haunter of taverns, inns or alehouses' – tough conditions indeed, especially the alehouse requirement. Once a year, in thanksgiving to their founder, the Howard Bede women march to church as a group wearing Jacobean costume and conical headgear. Who said tradition was dead?

EAST FROM SANDRINGHAM & CASTLE RISING

7 GREAT BIRCHAM

East of Dersingham, just beyond the route of the Peddars Way, and south of the village of Docking, lies Great Bircham, which is home to one of the best-preserved windmills in Norfolk. Like the village of Docking, this sits on a hill. Great Bircham is one of three villages that lie within the parish of Bircham: just north is Bircham Newton and to the east is Bircham Tofts.

Great Bircham Windmill

Great Bircham PE31 6SJ ✐ 01485 578393 ⟡ birchamwindmill.co.uk ☉ Mar–Sep daily

Just west of Great Bircham village, this mill has changed hands quite a number of times since it was built in 1846. Originally located on land belonging to the Houghton Estate, it was purchased in a derelict state by the Royal Sandringham Estate in 1939 before being sold on to a private owner in 1976. A thorough restoration project began in 1977, and by 1981 its four sails were back in place. The fully restored mill stands an impressive five storeys tall and has a cottage and long-established bakery attached, where bread is still baked today.

Special events are put on from time to time, with regular courses that teach arcane crafts like walking-stick carving and wool-spinning. There is also the opportunity to bake your own bread at the bakery. The tea rooms on the site of the old granary specialise in cream teas, so after indulging in one of these you might need the mill's cycle hire facility. Accommodation features a choice of a campsite, a holiday cottage and a shepherd's hut.

8 HOUGHTON HALL

PE31 6UE ✐ 01485 528569 ⟡ houghtonhall.com ☉ end Apr–Sept Wed, Thu & Sun & bank holiday Mon

Minor roads south and southwest of Great Bircham lead to the south entrance of Houghton Hall at New Houghton where you enter the estate's vast array of woodland and the deer park with an unusual herd of white fallow deer. This part of west Norfolk has been the seat of the Walpole family since the 14th century and the present incumbents, Lord and Lady Cholmondeley, are direct descendants of this long line.

Built in early 18th-century Palladian style, Houghton Hall is Norfolk's largest country house, and both house and estate reflect the flamboyant tastes of Norfolk 'new money' some three centuries ago. Planning regulations were less proscriptive in those days, and **Sir Robert Walpole**, England's first Prime Minister, who built the house in the 1720s, saw fit to pull down the nearby village of Houghton on purely aesthetic grounds as he claimed it spoiled his view. Houghton's Early English 13th-century village church of St Martin, however, was left well alone. So the unsightly villagers were moved to a new village, New Houghton, immediately south of the estate.

No expense was spared with the new hall: rather than use Norfolk brick, Walpole opted to build in Yorkshire stone, and the interior was sumptuously furnished and decorated with Old Masters. These are no longer at Houghton Hall as its paintings were sold to Catherine the Great, the Czarina of Russia, by Sir Robert's dissolute grandson, George, the third Earl of Orford, in order to pay off debts. His collection ended up in the Hermitage in St Petersburg, where it remains to this day. In light of this, the present incumbents were delighted when a large number of the masterpieces were returned to their home of 200 years ago, albeit temporarily, for a major exhibition in 2013 *Houghton Revisited* proved so popular that there is always a chance that something similar may happen again one day.

Aside from the house, the lush parkland surrounding the hall is well worth a visit if only for the spectacle of seeing a herd of around 600 white fallow deer. There is a permanent display of sculpture and landscape art in the grounds and walled garden too, featuring the work of renowned artists like Rachel Whiteread, Zhan Wang and Stephen Cox. Most impressive of these is probably *Skyspace* by James Turrell, a natural light installation with its own building tucked away in the woods. There's also a Richard Long piece, *Moon Circle*, located close to the ha-ha. The permanent work is supplemented by a summer exhibition most years, often in tandem with the start of the Norwich & Norfolk Festival – in 2019 this featured sculpture by Henry Moore, in 2020 works by Anish Kapoor, and in 2021 with sculptures by Tony Wragg. In 2022 the sculptor and woodturner Ernst Gamperl created a series of beautifully fluid wooden vessels for the house, made from a recently felled 300-year-old oak, a tree that had been planted when the estate was first established in 1722 by Sir Robert Walpole.

9 HARPLEY

South of the Houghton Estate, the pleasant but unremarkable village of Harpley has a decent pub and a highly atmospheric church. **St Lawrence's Church** is a curious musty place of decorated Gothic. The ridge of the roof is studded with angels with folded wings and the benches inside have carvings of all manner of wild animals – monkeys, bears and even mythical creatures – in addition to a pleasing carving of St James the pilgrim with his staff, satchel and shell. The village is also one of the highest in Norfolk but not the highest – that honour goes to Docking a few miles to the north.

Close to Harpley, to the northwest clustered alongside the route of the Peddars Way at Harpley Common, is a group of **Bronze Age barrows**. Although the tumuli look impressive marked on the OS map there is not much to see on the ground other than low grassy mounds. Nevertheless, they serve as a worthy reminder that this region has been populated for millennia – the proximity of the Peddars Way suggesting that parts of this ancient route might well date back to before Roman times.

¶¶ FOOD & DRINK

Rose and Crown Nethergate St ✆ 01485 521807 ⌂ roseandcrownharpley.co.uk. An intimate village pub with well-kept ales like Moon Gazer and Woodforde's, and good, unpretentious food made with locally sourced ingredients.

10 GREAT MASSINGHAM

Not far from Houghton Hall and the village of Harpley, and just south of its sister community of Little Massingham, Great Massingham is a very pretty village of 18th- and 19th-century cottages set against an impressively large and carefully mown green studded with daisies. The village has several ponds that originally were probably fish ponds for the village's former 11th-century Augustinian priory that today lies in ruins. It is possible that the village is actually much older than this and dates from as far back as the 5th century when the area was settled by a group of Angles and Saxons in the wake of the Roman withdrawal. The leader of this group may have been Maesron and the settlers known as Maersings, hence the village becoming Maersingham and later, Massingham.

1 Great Massingham. 2 Great Bircham Windmill. 3 Castle Acre Priory. 4 The village of Castle Acre. ▶

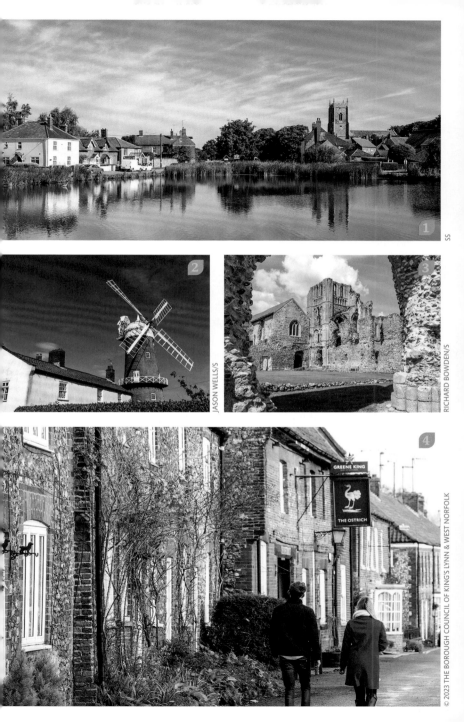

Mad Dog Lane, which leads from the village past council houses to the Peddars Way, does not appear to have any dogs – mad or otherwise – prowling along it but it would be interesting to know how this name came about. Perhaps the deranged animal escaped from nearby Kennel Farm? Given its sizeable ponds, ducks rather than dogs tend to sum up the character of the village – a detail that has not gone unnoticed by the local hostelry.

A small, private airfield just east of the village saw service as an RAF bomber base during World War II. Robert Walpole, the first English Prime Minister, was educated in the village and he appears on the village sign alongside a monk, an RAF bomber, a sheep and a tractor. Curiously, no ducks are represented.

¶¶ FOOD & DRINK

Dabbling Duck 11 Abbey Rd ✆ 01485 520827 ⌂ thedabblingduck.co.uk. Sitting comfortably alongside the village green as if it has always been there, the Dabbling Duck has long been regarded throughout west Norfolk for the quality of its food, which showcases the best of local produce. There's seasonal game from local estates and fish and shellfish from the coast and, as well as local beers and a lengthy wine list, the pub also boasts its own brand Mucky Duck gin.

11 CASTLE ACRE

Conveniently straddling the route of both the Peddars Way and the Nar Valley Way, Castle Acre makes a welcome stopover for hikers, but is well worth a visit even for those not inexorably striding towards Holme-next-the-Sea (where the Peddars Way ends). The village does contain, of course, a castle – an early Norman one in this case – but not that much survives other than its sprawling earthworks and a gateway. Far more impressive are the Norman ruins of Castle Acre Priory, founded just after the conquest in 1090, a highly atmospheric place to wander, especially late in the day with the sun low in the western sky. It may seem just like any other picture-perfect Norfolk village today – albeit a bit hillier than most – but, left to your own devices, it is still possible to get an inkling as to just how important Castle Acre was back in the Norman period.

The village sits on a low chalk hill above the River Nar, a compact place of flint and brick houses that take up the space of what would have been the outer bailey of the castle on the hill. The village's flint

SAXON CHURCHES IN WEST NORFOLK

The area immediately east of Castle Acre in west Norfolk is home to several small churches of Saxon origin. All Saints' Church at **Newton by Castle Acre** is one of the oldest in the county and has several surviving Saxon features such as a short central tower and a rounded chancel arch. The Church of St Nicholas at nearby **West Lexham** has a late Saxon tower, while St Andrew's Church at neighbouring **East Lexham** has a round tower with bell windows that is almost entirely Saxon. Immediately south at **Great Dunham**, St Andrew's is almost entirely Saxon in structure with a short square central tower with bell windows and nave that are clearly pre-Conquest.

This compact rectangle of sleepy west Norfolk contains more surviving pre-Conquest churches than any other part of the county. Given such a concentration of ancient buildings, it seems a little strange that they all exist so close to Castle Acre, a place that with its huge motte and bailey castle and Cluniac monastery seems so resolutely Norman.

16th-century gatehouse would have been the bailey gate. The priory is a little lower down to the east, in fields beside the River Nar's north bank. Down here there is a ford that you need to cross if arriving in the village by means of the Peddars Way. A raised footpath to the left of the road offers a route over the water as well as a fine view of the priory ruins to the left. But even this gets flooded sometimes – coming this way in the wet autumn of 2012 I found that the footpath was barely visible beneath a torrent of fast-moving floodwater. My own fault really, as the 'No Access – Flood' sign at the top of the road should have given me some idea of what to expect.

Castle Acre Priory

Castle Acre PE32 2XD ✆ 01760 755394 ☺ Apr–Oct daily; Nov–Mar Sat & Sun;
English Heritage

Founded by William de Warenne, son-in-law of William the Conqueror, the abbey was set up as a daughter priory of St Pancras at Lewes in Sussex, which in turn reported to the Cluniac Priory in Burgundy. The original priory was built within the walls of the castle but this proved too small and the monastery was soon moved to its current location. As is often the way with medieval religious orders, the priory went on to have a colourful and sometimes notorious life, with considerable friction between the Cluniac motherhouse and various English kings, notably the early Edwards, resulting in the priory being considered 'alien' and therefore heavily taxed. Not all medieval monks led blameless lives: in 1351, some of those at the priory were accused of 'living as vagabonds in secular habit' and the king felt it necessary to send his Serjeant-at-Arms to make arrests. Castle Acre Priory eventually became naturalised in 1373 and subsequently lost its connection with its French motherhouse.

Lying close to the route of pilgrimage to Walsingham, the priory set itself up in competition by selling indulgences to penitents on the first two days of August each year. The priory already had its very own relic, the arm of St Philip, but surprisingly this did not turn out to be a particularly big crowd-puller; in fact, it only earned ten shillings from its exhibition during the whole of 1533. With the advent of the Dissolution, the priory changed ownership swiftly several times over, passing through the hands of Thomas Howard the Duke of Norfolk, Elizabeth I, Thomas Gresham and eventually, the Coke family. It is now owned by English Heritage.

¶¶ FOOD & DRINK

In Castle Acre village itself, **The Ostrich Inn** (✆ 01553 611004 ⌂ theostrich.pub), a 16th-century former coaching inn, is a decent enough place for a drink or a meal. It has reasonable food, Greene King and Moon Gazer ales on draught, and a sunny outdoor beer garden. **Church Gate Tearooms** (✆ 01760 755551) and **Wittles Castle Acre** (✆ 01760 755577), both on Stocks Green, are convenient places for coffee and snacks. Wittles can also provide produce for a picnic.

KING'S LYNN & AROUND

12 GRIMSTON HEATH & 13 ROYDON COMMON

⌂ **Congham Hall Hotel** (page 310)

The road (Lynn Lane) that leads from Great Massingham to King's Lynn via Grimston and Roydon is vastly more pleasurable than the frenetic, speed-crazed A47 trunk road further to the south. It is wider than it appears on the map and surprisingly quiet, striking west across the lonely country of Grimston Heath. The road ranges relatively high for Norfolk but seems higher, almost as if it were upland country somewhere else in Britain. Grimston is a carrstone village without any great incentive for travellers to stop, as is Roydon, but shortly after the village is an off-road parking place to the left from where you can make an exploration of Roydon Common.

Roydon Common is a large area of heathland, looked after by the Norfolk Wildlife Trust, where heather thrives and sheep safely graze. The sheep, along with some ponies, are a fairly recent introduction as part of a management scheme to keep the habitat intact. A rough path leads towards an odd-looking isolated tower on a low hill. The tower is marked on the OS map as being among the conifers of Grimston Warren but the trees shown on the map have since been felled. 'Warren' is certainly right, as there is plenty of evidence of rabbits here. Occasional lapwings and curlews fly up from the heather, and hen harriers are not uncommon in winter. What is odd about this large area of heathland, just a stone's throw from the Wash, is how alien it seems to most of the rest of Norfolk. The view is impressive, with gentle valleys and plantations stretching into the distance and barely a village or church tower in sight. It might even be Exmoor or one of the flatter parts of the Pennines but just over the brow of the hill to the west is industrial King's Lynn, Norfolk's third largest town.

"The house was originally a 14th-century fortified manor house, founded by the Scales family on a large, moated platform."

Much of the terrain around here, like Snettisham to the north, is one of old and new carrstone quarries, the disused quarries returning to heathland if left to their own devices long enough. A little south of here, just across the B1145, you'll find evidence of another type of mineral extraction – sand – although not just any old sand but the finest and purest variety used for glassmaking. If you head into King's Lynn from here, along the B1145, you'll pass a swanky country park with sailing club and golf course at the smart dormitory village of **Leziate**. South of Leziate, just across the disused railway line, a large neo-Gothic castellated mansion hides behind high walls. This is **Middleton Towers**, a moated medieval house that is pure Gormenghast and looks unlikely to welcome strangers. The house was originally a 14th-century fortified manor house, founded by the Scales family on a large, moated platform. Not much remains of the original today but a bridleway leads off the road into woods just south of the complex to give you a closer look. In the early post-war years, Middleton Towers hosted speedway races and celebrities like George Formby were invited to open the proceedings. These days, it is clear that whatever goes on there is very much a private affair.

14 KING'S LYNN

Everyone driving into Norfolk from the Midlands or the North catches a glimpse of King's Lynn's outer reaches as they negotiate the huge roundabout on the A47. To be honest, it is not a wholly prepossessing sight: an industrial landscape of grain mills and pylons. Just west of the roundabout is a vast paper-recycling plant built of low, square blocks that themselves could even be made up of lofty blocks of old newspapers. With food processing still the biggest employer here, King's Lynn can, at first glance, appear to be a frozen-fish-finger wasteland – the natural domain of Captain Birdseye.

Having said that, it is best that you put all your prejudices to one side until you reach the town centre, as King's Lynn really does have quite a lot to offer, especially for those with an interest in maritime history. Still Norfolk's third largest town, King's Lynn has an important place in both Norfolk and English history. Its rich architectural heritage hints at its hugely eminent status as a port in former times and it still has the scent of distant shores in its nostrils and the dirt of sea trade under its fingernails.

Historic Lynn

King's Lynn was England's third biggest port in the 14th century, the medieval period's equivalent of what Liverpool was in Victorian times, and as a member of the Hanseatic League between the 14th and 17th centuries, it looked east to trading partners in northern Europe and the Baltic as far as modern-day Estonia. Plain old 'Lynn' became King's Lynn (or Lynn Regis) when the town became royal property following Henry VIII's dissolution of the monasteries and it was a royalist stronghold during the civil war a century later. In the aftermath of Norfolk's wool production years, grain exports became increasingly important from the 17th century onwards.

The railway came to the town in 1847, providing an easy London connection and with Sandringham coming to prominence in the later years of the 19th century the town regained some of the prosperity lost during the previous one. The modern town underwent considerable decline in the 1980s and in 1987 became, somewhat notoriously,

---

◀ **1** Roydon Common. **2** Walking on Grimston Heath. **3** The 15th-century guildhall, King's Lynn. **4** The view towards the customs house, King's Lynn.

the first place in the UK to introduce CCTV as a means of monitoring the activity of town centre ne'er-do-wells. Despite its position in the far west of the county, the language on the street remains firmly Norfolk, with none of the East Midlands cadences found a little further west in the Lincolnshire Fens. Portuguese, Polish and Lithuanian are also spoken, although perhaps not as conspicuously as a few years back.

The beauty of King's Lynn as a place to visit is that its historic core is small and easy to walk around. In a half-day you could see most of the major sights and get a feel for the place; a full day is a better option though. The town's most photographed building is its elegant square Custom House, built in 1683 by the local architect Henry Bell, which now serves as the town's tourist office. The helpful staff here can suggest a walking route that takes in all the main places of interest.

The customs house is on **Purfleet Dock**, the original harbour inlet along South Quay. Standing at the Custom House, you should notice immediately the figure of a sailor in a tricorn hat clutching a sea chart and looking out across the River Ouse. This being Norfolk, it is reasonable to assume that it's a likeness of Nelson but no, this honours the town's own son, George Vancouver, a sea captain credited with the discovery of the long-searched-for North West Passage and who went on to give his name to Canada's Pacific coast city. A decorative brass compass set into the concrete at the end of the dock associates various maritime aspirations with compass points – northwest is whaling, northeast is trade (and so on) – and has a roll-call of Norfolk mariners around it including Captain Vancouver, Captain John Smith and, of course, Admiral Nelson.

"The beauty of King's Lynn as a place to visit is that its historic core is small and easy to walk around."

Old King's Lynn certainly has plenty to see: the arcaded terrace of Hanseatic buildings with their distinctive narrow windows and jettied upper storey – the only ones in the country – and plenty of cobbled lanes and handsome Georgian merchants' houses. Town centre life revolves chiefly around two squares, **Saturday Market Place** and **Tuesday Market Place**, which both do exactly what they say on the tin. Tuesday Market Place is the more northerly of the two, just a block in from the Great Ouse River, and serves as a large car park much of the time. Dominating the market place is the impressive powder blue façade of the Duke's Head Hotel. The **Corn Exchange** here also has an impressive front to it. King Street running south has the Arts Centre, a restored 15th-century **guildhall**, and just beyond it a narrow alleyway, Ferry Lane, which leads to the dock for the pedestrian ferry across the river to West Lynn.

South of the Customs House is a warren of narrow streets filled with an impressive array of Tudor, Jacobean and Flemish houses, courtyards, warehouses and cottages. Most notable are **St Margaret's House**, a row of restored Hanseatic warehouses that date from 1475 and now house a café and a number of craft shops, but beside this there's plenty of interest at every corner.

Saturday Market Place has the enormous **St Margaret's Church**, which dates from 1101 and dominates the small square. It has twin towers, one of them much rebuilt after it crashed dramatically on to the nave during a storm in 1741. The south tower sports an odd-looking clock. Odd-looking that is until you realise that it gives you the time of the high tide and the phase of the moon. I am no expert on high tides but currently it does not seem to be very accurate.

Directly opposite, the chequerboard stone and flint Town Hall, or Guildhall of the Holy Trinity, which stands next to the Old Gaol House, looks at first to be of a single build but the original building, dating back to Tudor times, was enlarged considerably by the town's fathers in the Georgian period. I was lucky enough to be given a tour by a friendly curator, who, very keen to show someone around, explained the development of the building to me in detail. He walked me through to the paintings in the Georgian annex where there was a portrait of Nelson looking boyish and approachable, despite the sea battle raging in the background. 'This was painted six months after his death,' the curator informed me. 'He looks well, doesn't he, all things considered?' It was apparently a copy of a popular portrait around at the time. We moved on to a portrait of George Vancouver, King's Lynn's own son. 'You know, you used to be able to see his old house in the town centre. There was a plaque and everything. Well, that was until the 1960s when the planners knocked the old buildings down to put up a shopping precinct. They've knocked that down too now.'

Just east of the town hall is a small park that has an isolated tower with an arch beneath – **Greyfriars Tower** – all that remains of a friary established in the 13th century by Fransciscan monks. The southeast

WHALE BONES ON THE RIVER NAR

King's Lynn was once an important port for the whaling industry. Heavy investments in the trade were made in the late 18th and early 19th centuries and an act of 1771 encouraged the industry by withdrawing the obligation to pay duty on catches for whale ships and also by protecting the whaling crews from Royal Navy press gangs during the whaling season. Whale products found many uses: whalebone was used to make chair backs and brush handles and for use as stiffening in dressmaking (hence a 'whalebone corset'); whale grease was used to lubricate machinery and oil was used to make soap and also for street lighting – St Margaret's Church in King's Lynn was illuminated with whale-oil lamps until the mid 19th century. Whale bone was also ground down to make fertiliser. King's Lynn still has a few reminders of this trade today – the Greenland Fishery Inn and Blubberhouse Creek to the south of the town being most conspicuous, although the blubber houses that once stood here are long gone.

The whale trade made its mark inland too. Follow the Nar Valley Way along the bank of the River Nar a mile or so west of Narborough and you'll come across a very large cast iron waterwheel on the opposite bank. I was surprised to find this the first time I walked this route but thankfully two helpful women, Annie and Chris from the local ramblers group, just happened to be on the spot to explain its significance to me. 'That belonged to a bone mill that used to be here. They used to transport whale carcasses here all the way up the river from Lynn. This was about as far as the barges could go, and once they'd removed the blubber at Blubberhouse Creek they would bring the bones here for grinding. They would have to boil them down first though – to remove the fat.' I reflected on how such a process would probably not smell that good as Annie continued, 'I heard that they sometimes brought human bones here for grinding but I don't know if that's true or not'.

A little research showed that Annie was quite right – human bones had indeed been ground down for fertiliser here at Narborough. The whale trade had declined dramatically by 1820 and as a consequence bone mills such as this one had to depend far more on local farms and slaughterhouses for raw materials. Supplies also came to King's Lynn by ship from north Germany; these would sometimes include exhumations from Hamburg burial grounds. No-one seemed to mind that much as it was said that 'One ton of German bone-dust saves the importation of ten tons of German corn'. It was all 'grist to the mill', in a manner of speaking. The old waterwheel from Narborough Bone Mill also makes an appearance on the Narborough village sign although there is no indication of its former use.

In 2015 a restored railway carriage was set up on the site to serve as a visitor centre (⊘ bonemill.org.uk), although currently this only has limited opening days like on National Mills Weekend in May or on Heritage Open Days weekend in September. Volunteers continue to assist with research and further explore the site.

corner of the park has the **town library**, an Edwardian Gothic fantasy in brick and carrstone. Further east again is a much larger park with a Georgian Walk and the Red Mount Chapel, which, along with **South Gate** on London Road, dates from the time of the 15th-century fortifications of the town. Thanks to a bit of inspired, prescient design, the arch of South Gate is sufficiently large to allow modern-day double-decker buses to pass through it.

Lynn's museums

I find the most rewarding activity in King's Lynn is to take a leisurely amble along South Quay and try to rekindle the atmosphere at the height of its maritime trade, but there are some decent museums to investigate too. The recently expanded **True's Yard Fisherfolk Museum** (North St ✆ 01553 770479 ⊚ truesyard.co.uk) explores the town's maritime past. Pride of place must go, however, to **Lynn Museum** (Market St ✆ 01553 775001), in a converted Union Baptist chapel next to the bus station, and which has the reconstructed display of Seahenge (page 73). You'll also find displays on the town's past and oddities, like a Victorian cabinet of curiosities and slightly sinister souvenirs from the colonial era such as a demon mask from Persia and a skull from a West African fetish house. There is also a fair amount of hands-on stuff for children.

The Peter Scott Walk

If you're hankering after a long coastal hike along the Wash, consider the Peter Scott Walk that leads west into Lincolnshire from King's Lynn. The walk begins at West Lynn, easily reached by regular passenger ferry from South Quay. The path leads north along the west bank of the River Great Ouse as far as the Wash before skirting the south shore as far as the River Nene, where the lighthouse that Peter Scott lived in between 1933 and 1939 lies on the east bank. The village of Sutton Bridge, in Lincolnshire, lies about three miles inland from here. The walk is a little over ten miles in total but if you are depending on public transport you still have to get to and from the end/start point at the mouth of the Nene. One solution might be to take a bus to Sutton and then a taxi to the lighthouse and picnic place at East Bank, which is the furthest point the road goes northwards towards the Wash from Sutton Bank. You could then walk east along the south shore to West Lynn, taking the ferry to King's Lynn at the end of your walk.

🍴 FOOD & DRINK

Cobbles Tea Room 5 Hanse House, South Quay 🕽 01553 277 456 🖮 cobblestearooms. co.uk. A stylish old-fashioned tea room on South Quay, this is the place for afternoon tea and cake, served on antique plates with silver cutlery and proper tea pots.

Marriott's Warehouse South Quay 🕽 01553 818500 🖮 marriottswarehouse.co.uk. Formerly Green Quay, this converted 16th-century warehouse next to the river at South Quay has a daytime café menu offering sharing platters and sandwiches and an evening restaurant menu. Both offer a reasonable amount of local seasonal produce.

WEST INTO FENLAND

Heading west from King's Lynn, you experience a sudden and quite dramatic change of scenery. Instead of leafy hedgerows, scattered woodland and softly undulating valleys, there are wide expanses of black soil, scattered rambling farmsteads with ugly modern barns and occasional villages that have a more insular feel than further east.

Newcomers to East Anglia may assume that all Norfolk looks like this. It doesn't, of course – it is a misleading preface to what comes later with the slightly more undulating charms of High Norfolk – but at least a quarter of the county does consist of the Fens, even if a quarter of Norfolk's population most certainly does not live here. This is definitely the most overlooked part of the county (for good reason, you might say). But despite its relentless flatness and uncompromising scenery, Norfolk's Fenland has more to offer than just celery, fertile soil and easy cycling: there are a couple of quite extraordinary churches, spectacular winter assemblies of swans and wildfowl at places like Welney, and the comfortable market town of Downham Market.

15 THE WIGGENHALLS

South of King's Lynn, strung along the course of the Great Ouse River, are four villages prefixed Wiggenhall, each differentiated from the others by the name of its church: Wiggenhall St Mary Magdalen, Wiggenhall St Mary the Virgin, Wiggenhall St Peter and Wiggenhall St Germans. Strictly speaking, these are not of the Fens but in the Norfolk Marshlands – slightly higher land that has been inhabited for millennia. All four villages are pre-Norman, Saxon settlements with a timeless charm about them that is hard to find in the Fens proper. They also have some quite remarkable churches.

Two river walks around the Wiggenhalls

Three-mile walk ✽ OS Landranger 131; start: west side of Magdalen Bridge, Wiggenhall
St Mary Magdalen ♀ TF599113; easy **Eight-mile walk** ✽ OS Landranger 132; start:
Watlington train station ♀ TF612110; moderate

A recommended and easy **three-mile walk from Wiggenhall St Mary Magdalen**
crosses **Magdalen Bridge** (note this is the Magdalen Bridge by the village, not to be
confused with another of the same name near Lordsbridge a mile or so northwest) and heads
north along the east bank of the Great Ouse River, past tiny **Wiggenhall St Peter** and its
handsome roofless church to **Wiggenhall St Germans**, probably the most picturesque of
all the four villages. The river has always been the life-blood of the village and, for centuries,
this has been a favoured mooring place for Fen boatmen on their way to King's Lynn – a factor
that explains why such a small place used to
have three thriving pubs. Today it just has the
Crown & Anchor. Return along the west bank.

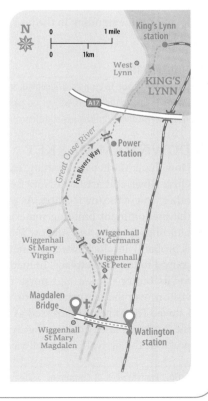

You can take an enjoyable **eight-mile
walk** by approaching the Wiggenhalls by
train from King's Lynn. The starting point
in this case would be **Watlington station**,
which lies at the halfway point on the train
line between King's Lynn and Downham
Market. From the station, head west to the
metal bridge over the Relief Channel and then
cross Magdalen Bridge just beyond it.

After crossing the Great Ouse to have a
look at St Mary Magdalen Church, re-cross
the river and follow the signposted Fen Rivers
Way north all the way to King's Lynn, passing
Wiggenhall St Peter, Wiggenhall St Germans
and the power station at Eau Brink Cut along
the way. The Fen Rivers Way terminates at
South Quay where you'll find a choice of
welcoming cafés , as well as some of King's
Lynn's most interesting sights, including the
Hanseatic warehouses and Custom House at
Purfleet Dock.

Of the four Wiggenhalls, **Wiggenhall St Mary Magdalen** has for me the most distinguished church. This lofty 15th-century building is a fine exemplar of medieval balance and proportion, with a plethora of medieval stained glass and fine carved benches. Earnest hagiographers may be interested to note that the church has a gallery featuring some obscure saints who have spectacularly failed to become household names: St Leger, St Callistus, St Britus… the list goes on.

St Germaine's Church at Wiggenhall St Germans has an altogether different appeal. Here it is the woodwork that attracts attention, with resplendent poppies carved in the bench-ends along with a variety of animated human figures that include musicians, drunks, various sinners and courting couples. All of the Seven Deadly Sins are represented: Avarice clutches bags of money; Anger wields a sword; Lust, my favourite (carving that is, not necessarily the sin), is represented by a loving couple standing in the jaws of a giant fish, presumably the mouth of Hell.

﹗ FOOD & DRINK

Crown & Anchor 16 Lynn Rd, Wiggenhall St Germans ✆ 01553 617340. A former Greene King pub close to the church, with wood-panelled lounge and outside tables by the river. Serves well-cooked British pub food along with Adnams & guest ales.

16 DOWNHAM MARKET

Downham Market stands at the eastern edge of the Fens, with the Great Ouse River and artificial New Bedford Drain running alongside each other west of the town centre. As with many other places in west Norfolk, the predominant building material here is carrstone, which gives the buildings a warm and mellow look. The town's most memorable sight is probably its clock tower, a fancy Victorian cast-iron structure that is central to the marketplace. In medieval times, the town was well known for its butter market and horse fair. It has had a handful of famous visitors over the centuries: Nelson came here to go to school and Charles I stayed (or rather, hid dressed as a clergyman) for a night after fleeing the Battle of Naseby during the civil war. The town was once a busy river port but the arrival of the railway soon took away much of this trade

---

1 Downham Market. **2** Cormorants at Denver Sluice. **3** A whooper swan at Ouse Washes, Welney Wetland Centre. ▶

LITERARY NORFOLK

In 2013 an article appeared in *the Guardian* newspaper that posed the question: Is Norfolk England's most secretive and strange literary county? It turned out that the author, Ian Sansom, was plugging his own book to some extent but he cited the large number of authors who have used Norfolk as inspiration for their storytelling. Crime novelists in particular seem to favour the county as a setting, and the names Elly Griffiths, P D James and Hilary Mantel were all mentioned as having chosen Norfolk as a literary backdrop. It appears that there is even now a genre called 'Norfolk Gothic'. Other writers have used specific Norfolk landscapes as a backdrop to their fiction: *Salt* by Jeremy Page makes atmospheric use the north Norfolk salt marshes around Cley and Salthouse, while the Norfolk Fens with their relentless flatness create a sense of menace in Graham Swift's *Waterland*.

Norfolk in literature is nothing new. Charles Dickens famously used Great Yarmouth beach as the setting for the Barkis family's upturned boat-house in *David Copperfield*, L P Hartley's *The Go-Between* paints a picture of rural Norfolk at the turn of the 20th century, while Arthur Ransome celebrates the watery landscape of the Broads in *Swallows and Amazons* and *Coot Club*. It is also likely that Arthur Conan Doyle used Cromer Hall as the inspiration for the hall in his *The Hound of the Baskervilles*; no doubt he would have made use the local Black Shuck legend (page 88) for inspiration too. The county is also the subject for much affectionate poetry by former Poet Laureate Sir John Betjeman.

However much the Norfolk landscape has served as a muse to writers from beyond its borders, the county has produced more than its fair share of its own writers too. The first of these was Julian of Norwich, whose *Revelations of Divine Love* was the first book written by a woman to be published in English. Later Norfolk-based authors include Anna Sewell of *Black Beauty* fame, who was born in Great Yarmouth and spent her later life just outside Norwich; George Borrow (*The Bible in Spain, Wild Wales, Lavengro*), born in East Dereham; H Rider Haggard (*She, King Solomon's Mines*), who lived at Ditchingham in the Waveney Valley; Henry Williamson, who farmed near Stiffkey for several years and wrote *The Story of a Norfolk Farm* while there. In more recent years, we have the author D J Taylor, and also Malcolm Bradbury, who set up the famous postgraduate Creative Course at UEA that attracted the likes of Ian McEwan and Kazuo Ishiguro. This list is by no means exhaustive.

Then there are the 'new nature writers' – Richard Mabey resides in Norfolk, as did Mark Cocker for many years before returning to his native Derbyshire, while the late, great Roger Deakin lived just over the Suffolk border close to Diss. Patrick Barker, author of *The Butterfly Isles* and *Badgerlands*, is another Norfolk-based nature writer. One of Norfolk's most famous writers in recent years is W G Sebald, who died in 2001 – a German native who taught at UEA. His book, *The Rings of Saturn*, which has attracted something approaching a cult following, is primarily focused on Suffolk but begins and ends in Norfolk.

following the construction of the Riley Channel, which succeeded in carrying the waters of the Cut-Off Channel to the main channel of the Great Ouse at King's Lynn.

17 DENVER

Just a couple of miles south of Downham Market, Denver is a relatively new village that dates from the time of the construction of the first Denver Sluice in 1651. The brains behind this project was Cornelius Vermuyden, a Dutch engineer commissioned to drain some of vast acreage of wetlands owned by the Duke of Bedford. The original drainage cut is no longer there but the so-called Old Sluice, which serves the same function as the original, dates from 1834, while the newer Great Denver Sluice was created in 1964. The wetland area between these two channels, generally referred to as the Ouse Washes, is allowed to flood in winter in order to keep the surrounding fields drained and as a result creates a vitally important winter habitat for wildfowl.

¶¶ FOOD & DRINK

Jenyns Arms 1 Sluice Bank ✆ 01366 383366 ⌂ jenynsarms.com. With a large dining conservatory, outdoor tables by the water, reasonable pub fare and Sunday roasts, this is handily placed for a visit to the area.

18 WELNEY WETLAND CENTRE

Welney, a small village sitting on the Norfolk bank of Hundred Foot Bank, one of the Fens' prime artificial water courses, is home to the splendid Welney Wetland Centre (✆ 01353 860711 ⌂ wwt.org.uk/welney) run by the Wildfowl and Wetlands Trust. This nature reserve has plenty of interest throughout the seasons but really comes into its own in the winter months when vast numbers of wild swans – both whooper and Bewick's – gather on the **Ouse Marshes** here to feed and avoid the far harsher conditions in Siberia and Iceland. One of the joys of watching wild swans here is the centre's heated observatory, which gives visitors a birder's eye view of proceedings while they languish in relative comfort – a far cry from shivering with a telescope outside at the mercy of the elements. The **swan feeds**, in particular, are quite spectacular, with the birds gracefully thrashing about for grain right beneath your comfortably warm nose. Children and adults tend to love this, even those not normally bowled over by natural history close up in the flesh. Feeds take place between the end of October and the middle of March around midday and just before sunset. Another feed takes place at around 18.30 by floodlight and this is usually the best attended, in bird terms, as many swans fly in to the lagoon to roost after dusk. For all the feeding times, it is best to arrive half an hour before.

The **eco visitor centre** has all the right-on credentials: loos that flush with rainwater, solar power electricity, geothermal heating and reed bed wastewater cleansing – plus a decent café, a gift shop and a pond room with giant models of creatures found on the reserve. In the warmer months, there are walks around the reserve and children can try pond-dipping.

19 WALPOLE ST PETER

The Walpoles – there are three of them – are unexciting dormitory villages filled with modern bungalow estates: here in deepest Fenland, it seems that even houses do not dare raise their heads above the parapet of what most of us regard as sea-level. How odd then that one of Norfolk's very finest churches can be found here, way out west in the agribusiness shabbiness of the Fens, far from the action and as close to Leicester as it is to Norwich. **St Peter's Church** in Walpole St Peter (obviously) is a worthy rival to that of Terrington St Clement; it's a magnificent and very large parish church that is sometimes referred to as the 'Queen of the Marshland'. It is unique in being the only church in Norfolk to receive a five-star rating from Simon Jenkins in his *England's Thousand Best Churches*.

20 TERRINGTON ST CLEMENT

The A17 west of King's Lynn is not a road one drives along for pleasure, and **Terrington St Clement** itself, a large and not particularly attractive village, has little to warrant a detour were it not for its magnificent parish church often dubbed 'the Cathedral of the Marshland'. **St Clement's Church** is a massive 14th-century masterpiece with impressive buttresses and a detached tower.

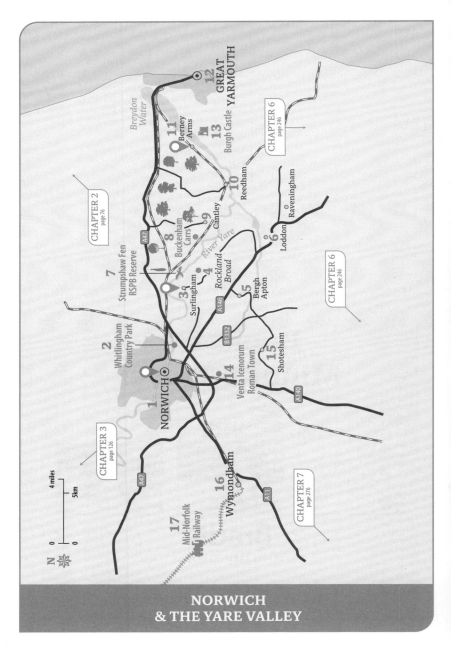

NORWICH
& THE YARE VALLEY

5
NORWICH
& THE YARE VALLEY

This area comes as something of a catch-all, a means of including parts of east and south Norfolk that don't conveniently fit in elsewhere. The River Yare that flows from central Norfolk to Great Yarmouth is perhaps an obvious point of focus: a natural conduit for river trade between Norwich and the coast. This same river also connects with the Broads at Breydon Water, and even has a couple of important minor broads of its own at Surlingham and Rockland. If the Yare Valley is a convenient means of incorporating uncooperative slices of east Norfolk, then the valley of the River Tas can be brought in to do the same for south Norfolk. The modest River Tas, which joins the Yare just south of Norwich (having quietly meandered up from south Norfolk), has nothing of the importance of the Yare, but it does link a number of villages that are worth a visit south of Norwich.

Norwich is a place of such importance that in a book like this it is almost tempting to ignore it in case it takes over the text completely. I will aim for the middle way of brevity. It is probably true to say that Slow philosophy has its heart in the villages and market towns rather than the cities, but Norwich is hardly your average city. At the other end of the River Yare stands Great Yarmouth, a large, slightly threadbare sort of place that some might prefer to avoid. It, too, has its own story to tell. The River Tas has no such urban centres, just a few likeable villages strung along minor roads in pretty rolling south Norfolk countryside. There's some interesting history and unsung places half-hidden away here in what is effectively Norwich's commuter belt.

"The River Yare was a vital waterway for trade until quite recently and remains an important area for wildlife."

As Norfolk's broadest river the River Yare was a vital waterway for trade until quite recently and remains an important area for wildlife, with the whole of its floodplain, as far as Norwich itself, lying under the aegis of the Broads Authority. It's a formidable barrier too that, strikingly, has only one crossing place between Norwich and Yarmouth. The nature writer Mark Cocker, for years a resident of the Yare Valley, points out in his fascinating book *Crow Country* that communities that can quite clearly see each other on either side of the river usually have absolutely no contact with each other, as such contact would require a massive detour. How different from the situation along the River Waveney (page 247) where villages on both the Norfolk and Suffolk banks visit each other's marketplaces (and supermarkets) without a second thought. It would make more sense in a way if Norfolk north of the Yare were deemed a different county to that south of the river. Those living in Langley Green south of the Yare tend to be more interested in getting into Norwich at weekends than they are curious about what happens in Cantley, north of the river, whose lights they can see at night.

GETTING AROUND

Travelling along the Yare Valley is easy enough, as long as you don't want to cross the river. If you do, then your only option is to take the car and passenger ferry at Reedham (page 234). The A47 runs between Norwich and Great Yarmouth, north of the River Yare, a dual carriageway as far as Acle. This continues as the southern bypass at Norwich and links to the A11 south before continuing west to East Dereham and King's Lynn. The section between Acle and Great Yarmouth – the so-called 'Acle Straight' – is a straight-as-a-die single carriageway across a wind-blown, windmill-studded marshland, and a road notorious for speed merchants and accidents. Heading south, the A140, an old Roman road, runs more or less parallel to the spidery course of the River Tas, to eventually cross the River Waveney near Diss.

PUBLIC TRANSPORT

This is better than average. A fast, regular **bus service** connects Norwich with Great Yarmouth, while the services that link Norwich with Thetford, Diss and Beccles also pass through south Norfolk towns and villages like Loddon, Long Stratton, Wymondham and Attleborough. The fastest east–west service is the ever-useful X1 that plies between Lowestoft and King's Lynn via Great Yarmouth, Norwich and Swaffham

𝒊 TOURIST INFORMATION

Great Yarmouth Maritime House 25 Marine Parade ✆ 01493 846346
🖱 visitgreatyarmouth.co.uk
Loddon Library Annexe, Church Plain (leaflets and maps only) ✆ 01508 522020
🖱 loddonpc.org.uk/tic
Norwich 🖱 visitnorwich.co.uk
Wymondham Market Cross, Market Pl ✆ 01953 604721

(🖱 firstbus.co.uk/norfolk-suffolk). There are more local services too, like the Our Bus 85 Norwich to Surlingham service and the 86 Norwich to Beccles route that goes via Loddon and Bergh Apton (🖱 bustimes. org/operators/our-bus).

For **train travel**, the invaluable Wherry Line (✆ 08457 484950 🖱 wherrylines.org.uk) has regular trains between Norwich, Great Yarmouth and Lowestoft that usefully stop at places like Buckenham, Acle, Reedham and Berney Arms, which are ideal starting points for walks. Some of the stations, like Berney Arms, are request stops only, and only a limited number of trains will stop at them, so it is best to study the timetable closely. The Greater Anglia Norwich to Cambridge train service has stops at Wymondham and Attleborough.

WALKING

There's plenty of scope for enjoyable waterside walking, particularly east of Rockland Broad from where a riverside path goes all the way to Breydon Water. There's the same on the opposite bank from Buckenham eastwards and the northern bank has the distinct advantage that there are a couple of useful railway stations along the way that avoid the necessity of doubling back. With a car, circular walks are feasible if you are willing to combine stretches of riverside with paths across marshes and some road walking. The Wherry Line website (🖱 wherrylines.org. uk) also has some good suggestions for walks using its stations.

The area's long-distance trails deserve a look, if only in part, as they lead through some of the most attractive stretches of the river valleys. The **Wherryman's Way** follows the River Yare from Norwich to Great Yarmouth by way of a 37½-mile route that takes in historic sites and wildlife areas. The route – in theory at least – follows the south bank of the River Yare to Hardley, loops around the River Chet to Loddon then, crossing the river at its only ferry point at Reedham, continues along the north bank of the river to Breydon Water and Great Yarmouth. Unfortunately, the section between Loddon and Hardley Flood has been closed for years now because of problems with footpath erosion. Doubly unfortunately, this used to be one of the way's most picturesque sections. Maps and directions for a dozen circular walks along the way can be downloaded from ✎ norfolk.gov.uk/wherrymansway. The website is also worth consulting to check if there have been any further temporary path closures due to improvement work.

The last stretch of the Wherryman's Way between Reedham and Great Yarmouth lies conveniently close to the Wherry Line stations of Reedham and Berney Arms, and so lends itself easily to combined rail and foot outings. A good option is to take the train to the Berney Arms request stop then walk either west to Reedham or east to Great Yarmouth and pick up a return train.

Other long-distance trails are the **Boudicca Way**, a 40-mile route connecting Diss to Norwich that meanders through a number of south Norfolk villages along the way, and the Tas Valley Way, a 25-mile walk from Eaton, just southwest of Norwich to Attleborough. A further route developed in recent years by South Norfolk Council is **Kett's Country**, a 21-mile walk between Cringleford and Wymondham. Details and maps of all of these can be downloaded from Norfolk County Council's Norfolk Trails website (✎ norfolk.gov.uk/out-and-about-in-norfolk/norfolk-trails), which also has plenty of information on other walking routes in the area as well as an interactive map.

CYCLING

As elsewhere in the region, cycling is fine as long as you keep well away from the main roads. Fortunately, there are sufficient minor roads that getting around is reasonable. Some of the narrow lanes close to the river on either bank are a real pleasure, although you need to be ever vigilant of absent-minded locals and Norwich commuters speeding home in their 4x4s.

Sustrans National Cycle Network Route 1 (Harwich to Hull; ✎ sustrans. org.uk) passes through this area, coming up from the Waveney Valley to Loddon and then following minor roads through villages south of the Yare on its way into Norwich. Part of the Wherryman's Way (page 203) is also suitable for cyclists.

1 NORWICH

🏠 **38 St Giles** (page 310), **Maids Head Hotel** (page 310), **The Parson Woodeforde** (page 310) 🏠 **Wellington Apartments** (page 310)

> A fine old city, perhaps the most curious specimen at present extant of the genuine old English town.
>
> George Borrow, *Lavengro*

As the city sign tells you as you drive in, Norwich is a fine city. Former Norwich City goalkeeper Robert Green once dubbed Norwich 'a city the size of a town with a village mentality', which was probably intended as a criticism but could also be interpreted as praise depending on your viewpoint. Despite recent plaudits in 'Best place to live' features by some newspapers, the general image is that of a city out on a limb that is out of step with modern times; a place of gauche, unfashionable attitudes and a football team that seems to perpetually yo-yo between leagues; Alan Partridge, Delia Smith, parochialism, mustard, banking and insurance.

Naturally enough, the reality is somewhat different: Alan Partridge is a fictitious character (although there really is a Radio Norwich these days), Delia Smith lives in Suffolk despite her regular outings to Carrow Road to watch football, and Norwich Union have re-branded as Aviva and outsourced to Sheffield and India. Contrary to expectations, the city is increasingly cosmopolitan, has a thriving university and art school and is one of the fastest growing cities in England. Simply put, Norwich punches well above its weight.

Norwich is a very liveable sort of place. Where I live, close to the city wall, just south of the centre but well outside the fashionable 'Golden Triangle' beloved

"Norwich is just about big enough to forget sometimes that you are living in the middle of a mainly rural region."

of university lecturers and media folk, is a case in point. Within five minutes' walk from my house are two independent cafés and half-a-dozen decent pubs, including a couple of really good ones. It's a five-minute walk to the bus station, and ten minutes to one of the oldest permanent food markets in the country; 15 minutes' walk to a thriving arts centre and 20 to a fantastic independent cinema. There's a 'real meat' butcher's just up the road too, and on Friday mornings a mobile fish van comes from Lowestoft with fish so fresh that it is almost still twitching.

The fishmonger gives me the news from the coast – what the fishing's like at Lowestoft, whether the boats are going out to sea or not. It is good to have this sort of connectedness in an urban environment, as Norwich is just about big enough to forget sometimes that you are living in the middle of a mainly rural region. If this sounds a little smug, then there are a few pitfalls too: traffic noise and fumes, and the perception by metropolitan types that you reside in some dull and decidedly unfashionable backwater.

The story goes that Norwich has a pub for every day of the year and a church for every week. Not quite right – there were actually 700 pubs in the city in medieval times, 363 in 1905 (within the city walls) and around 140 in the whole of Norwich today – but it does give a ball-park figure. As elsewhere in the country, pubs seem to be closing for business almost every week and of the city's surviving 32 medieval churches, two-thirds lie empty or find modern use as puppet theatres, art studios, or even pregnancy crisis centres. That is still a lot of churches for a city of just 145,000... and plenty of pubs.

In recent years Norwich has undoubtedly become a far more fashionable place to live. The Norfolk & Norwich Festival (⊘ nnfestival. org.uk) has been established as an annual event for many years (it can be traced back to 1772) and goes from strength to strength, featuring international names in the classical, folk and jazz world as well as staging a broad range of theatrical, dance and arts events. The festival, which takes place in the second half of May each year, also includes plenty of free events like street theatre and special activities for children.

In 2012 Norwich became England's first **UNESCO City of Literature**, one of only six worldwide joining an elite network along with Edinburgh, Melbourne, Dublin, Reykjavik and Iowa City. Strong associations with the University of East Anglia's MA course in Creative Writing (first student, Ian McEwan, no less) certainly did no harm here. Nor did the fact that the city's literary tradition went back more than 600 years to the time of Julian of Norwich, whose *Revelations of Divine Love* was not only the first book published in English but also the first to be written in English by a woman.

"The story goes that Norwich has a pub for every day of the year and a church for every week."

Around the same time that Norwich earned its UNESCO status, a travel feature about 'Norwich, England' appeared in the *New York Times* that gave the impression of a 'charming medieval town' populated by bookworms and bohemian literary types tapping away at laptops in quaint tea rooms – a somewhat hyperbolic portrait to say the least. On a less cerebral note, the city was also heavily promoted as **Norwich City of Ale** in 2011, an inaugural ten-day beer and brewing event that was successfully followed up in 2012 and has now become an annual occurrence. There are also several smaller beer festivals.

Literature and ale aside, the city has been celebrated more generally in the press in recent years. Norwich was voted 'happiest city to work in the UK' by *The Guardian* in 2016, and in 2018, 2019 and 2020 it was deemed to be one of 'the Best Places to Live' in the UK by *The Sunday Times*, a plaudit that continued into 2022.

So: City of Literature, City of Ale, a desirable place to live and work, and an all-round cultural hotspot (it was runner up to Derry/Londonderry as UK City of Culture in 2013) – if the term 'Slow' were to be applied to cities as well as to market towns then no doubt Norwich would be one of the first to bear the title.

A POTTED HISTORY

Back in the late 11th century, Norwich was England's second largest city. It had existed as a large Saxon town before the conquest but the arrival of the Normans brought the cathedral, castle and a large increase in population. As it was an important weaving centre, Flemish and Walloon migrants came from across the North Sea in the 16th century to join the throng, to be followed later by French Huguenots. Weaving was of sufficient importance in the city for Daniel Defoe to observe in 1723 that 'if a stranger was only to ride through or view the city of Norwich for a day, he would have much more reason to think there was a town without inhabitants... on the contrary, if he was to view the city either on a Sabbath day, or on any public occasion, he would wonder where all these people could dwell'. Norwich's Flemish immigrants brought with them the pet canaries that would later become the emblem of Norwich City Football Club and appear on its crest. It is worth noting that, with the exception of the city's Jews who were persecuted here and elsewhere in England in the 12th century because of blood libel suspicions, Norwich has generally welcomed its newcomers. Indeed, the city has always been demonstrably tolerant of 'strangers' and even sometimes radical in outlook, with a strong working-class tradition.

To see Norwich simply as a quaint cathedral city is misleading; as well as medieval streets and cosy Anglo-Saxon provincialism there are also the usual urban problems. Beyond the centre with its cobbled streets, 12th-century walls and Tudor buildings, lie grids of Victorian terraces, large council estates (some of Britain's very first council estates – Mile Cross and Larkman – were constructed here in the late 1920s) and sprawling suburbs. The city was bombed quite badly during World War II, especially in April 1942 as part of the so-called Baedeker Raids, in which the popular tourist guide was used to select targets of cultural rather than strategic importance.

THE CITY CENTRE

Plenty of guidebooks will give you the nitty-gritty background – the churches, historic buildings, etc. Instead I've picked a few favourite places. All the buildings mentioned below are open throughout the year. If you want to gain access to some of those that are normally closed to the public then a good time to come to the city is during **Norwich Heritage Open Days** (⊘ heritageopendays.org.uk) in September. Sadly The Forum no longer has a tourist information centre to help visitors book accommodation or find their way around the city but there are at least volunteer City Hosts in 'Here to Help' blue tabards scattered around the centre who can help with information and directions.

For self-guided tours of the historic centre, Norwich City Council offers an excellent historic 'Nooks and Crannies' walk that can be downloaded at ⊘ norwich.gov.uk/citywalks. The Norwich Society (⊘ thenorwichsociety.org.uk) also has a selection of heritage walking trails on its website that can be downloaded. A limited number of guided tours of the city centre are offered by The Forum and the Association of Norwich Tourist Guides (⊘ visitnorwich.co.uk/service/norwich-guided-tours.) Other bookable guided tours are available year-round with Paul Dickson Tours (⊘ 07801 103737 ⊘ pauldicksontours.co.uk), who also offer private tours, and Cheryl Cade (⊘ cherylcade.com), who has a range of food and drink tours of the city. There are also regular Norwich Ghost Walks (⊘ 07831 189985 ⊘ ghostwalksnorwich.co.uk) that start outside the Adam & Eve pub on Bishopsgate, near the cathedral.

NORWICH: 1 An aerial view over the city. **2** The interior of the cathedral. **3** The castle, now a museum and art gallery. **4** Elm Hill. ▶

The castle & museums

The first places that most guidebooks mention are the castle and cathedral, both Norman in origin and both worthy of your time. **Norwich Castle** stands on a hill above the city centre, its Norman keep a serious square building that serves as the city's historical museum these days: **Norwich Castle Museum and Art Gallery** (✆ 01603 493625 🖰 museums.norfolk. gov.uk). A sign at the entrance tells the story of Robert Kett, a yeoman farmer who led a peasants' revolt in 1549 and, after camping out on Mousehold Heath with thousands of followers, was finally defeated by government troops. It is probably significant that it took 400 years before he attained local hero status and received a plaque to his memory. As the sign tells you, Kett was hanged at the castle, although it does not mention that he was hanged alive in chains to suffer a slow, cruel death. Norwich Castle once featured in *Monty Python's Flying Circus* as the setting for a particularly silly sketch in which medieval soldiers hurled themselves from battlements, but whenever I see the castle walls, I just think of poor Robert Kett.

Inside the Castle Museum, there's the usual dungeon display to frighten sensitive souls, as well as galleries devoted to archaeology and natural history. An interesting room dedicated to the Iceni-Roman conflict in East Anglia has, as well as displays of Iceni bling – huge gold torcs – from the Snettisham Treasure, a virtual Roman chariot ride to delight children. Probably most distinctive though, is the museum's fine art collection. Several rooms are devoted to works of the Norwich School, with a wealth of paintings by artists such as John Crome, Joseph Stannard and John Sell Cotman. My personal favourites are the watercolours by John Sell Cotman that make use of an exquisite blue and gold palette. St Benet's Abbey (1831) looks as if it is almost floating on the water. Give or take a few Broads cruisers, the scene looks much the same today (page 116).

Contrary to how it might appear, the castle keep was originally built by the Normans as a royal palace rather than a defensive structure. At the time of writing, the museum was undergoing a £15 million 'Royal Palace Reborn' transformation project to reinstate the medieval floors and rooms of the keep and to create a new visitor centre, café and shop. Although it was uncertain when the extensive work would be finally completed – hopefully sometime in 2023 – all other parts of the museum remain open to the public.

On the subject of museums, there are a couple of others that are worth an hour of anyone's time. **Strangers' Hall** (✆ 01603 667229), at Charing Cross in the shadow of St Gregory's Church, is an interesting social history museum in a delightful Tudor building. Just above it, on Colegate, is St John Maddermarket, another recycled medieval church that has long functioned as a tiny independent theatre. There's a good small museum dedicated to Norwich trade and shopping since 1700 at **The Bridewell** (✆ 01603 629127) in Bridewell Alley, a building that once served as a prison and a house of correction. The north wall of The Bridewell is noteworthy for being one of the finest examples of knapped flint work in the country. Built in the late 14th century, around the same time as many of Norwich's flint churches, it was remarked on by the 17th-century equestrian traveller Celia Fiennes, a contemporary of Daniel Defoe, who was hugely impressed by what she found on a visit to the city: 'there is a wall made of flints that is headed very finely and cut so exactly square… there appears to be very little, if any, mortar; it looks well, very smooth shining and black.' St Andrew's Church next door is similarly flinty. Second only to St Peter Mancroft in size, it has a 15th-century window that shows the Devil dancing with a bishop on a chessboard.

The cathedral

Any decent guidebook will tell you that work started on Norwich Cathedral in 1086 at the behest of Bishop Herbert Losinga, so I won't elaborate. It is a magnificent Gothic building, with the second-highest spire and second largest cloisters in Britain, but I like the small details best. Take a peek at the intricately carved wooden bosses in the cloisters and you'll find some that go well beyond the usual themes of the Life of Christ and the Apocalypse, and some which are downright rude. There's an impressive and quite fearsome Green Man too, if you look hard enough. In fact, there are several.

Over the past few years the cathedral's lofty spire has been gazed at for reasons other than its impressive architecture: it has become home to a pair of breeding peregrine falcons. The falcons first appeared at the cathedral in 2009 when a male took up residence to be soon followed by a female. A nesting platform fitted with a webcam was set up by the Hawk and Owl Trust in 2011 and in the following year two healthy chicks were produced, a first for the cathedral. The adults returned in 2013 to produce four chicks this time, one died but three successfully fledged, and peregrines have continued to return to the cathedral to breed every year since and there is now even an annual calendar available that features the birds. The birds are generally quite easy to see – from April and June the Hawk and Owl Trust sometimes have a telescope set up for interested visitors in the cathedral cloister square; there also used to be a live webcam feed to the cathedral's Refectory Restaurant although this was removed when some diners complained – peregrine feeding habits are a little too visceral for those of a delicate disposition.

A city river stroll

❀ OS Landranger 134; start: St Benedict's Street, St Lawrence's Church; ♥ TG227088; 2.5 miles; easy

This walk begins on St Benedict's Street at **St Lawrence's Church**. Descend the steps to cross Westwick Street and pass the apartment block that used to be the Anchor Brewery, before crossing Coslany Bridge to follow the pedestrian access along the River Wensum's north bank. Across the water is a disused warehouse where the entire text of Thomas More's *Utopia* has been scrawled in white across the brickwork as if it were the work of a 16th-century graffiti artist with a taste for political philosophy. It was actually done by local artist Rory Macbeth in 2006 – the building was scheduled for demolition in the following year yet, perhaps as a result of its utopian graffiti, it still stands today.

Crossing Duke Street by means of **Duke's Palace Bridge**, a brief detour along Colegate is necessary to reach **Blackfriars Bridge** by the Norwich School of Art from where a path continues beside the river to reach Fye Bridge and Fishergate. Whitefriars Bridge comes next and the eponymous friary once stood on the site of the large edifice that looms ahead: the Jarrold's Printing Works, built in 1834 and formerly a mill owned by the Norwich Yarn Company.

Beyond the printing works you'll come to a *renga* – a word map created by means of an ancient Japanese tradition of shared writing – stringing a snake of words and phrases along hoardings beside the river. A Renga for St James, which utilises the local Norwich vernacular, was created here on site in 2009.

Continuing east, you soon see **Peter's Bridge**, a footbridge opened in 2012 and named after a former Jarrold's chairman. Most of the Wensum's bridges are so ancient that they are firmly embedded in the city's psyche but there have been three new footbridges so far this millennium: this one, the 2009 Lady Julian Bridge close to the railway station, and the Novi Sad Friendship Bridge, opened in 2001, near Carrow Bridge and Norwich City FC football ground.

From the castle to the river

Another part of the inner city frequently included on city tours, and for good reason, is **King Street**, southeast of the castle mound, which has a number of Tudor buildings, tiny courtyards and, best of all, **Dragon Hall** (✆ 01603 877177 ⌖ nationalcentreforwriting.org.uk), an impressive medieval merchant's hall that is now used as a base for the National Centre for Writing. The centre has an extensive programme of literary events as well as offering a wide variety of tutored courses and workshops for aspiring writers.

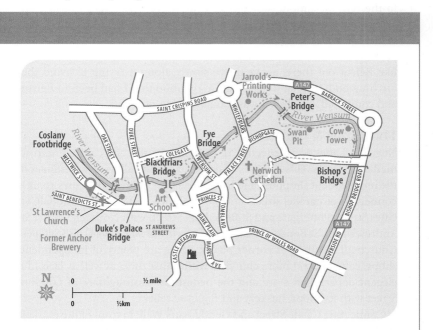

Crossing this graceful, J (for Jarrold's)-shaped footbridge, the riverside walk continues towards **Cow Tower**, a 14th-century defensive tower that was badly damaged in Kett's Rebellion of 1549. Just before Cow Tower you will pass what looks like a sluice leading into the river. This is, in fact, a rare 18th-century example of a swan pit, a pool in which wild cygnets were kept and fattened for the table after having their wings clipped and beaks marked by their owners. From Cow Tower walk a little further on to reach **Bishops Bridge**, then turn right to leave the river behind as you head for Cathedral Close and Tombland.

There are plenty of interesting nooks and crannies around here, so simply delving and wandering at will is probably the best policy. Further on from Dragon Hall there's Wensum Lodge, an adult education centre. The bar that used to operate here, **Jurnet's Bar**, was in the crypt-like basement of a medieval Jewish merchant's house, the oldest dwelling in the city. Sadly, it is now closed because of problems with ventilation and a water leak. Immediately over the river is Riverside, a stretch of new entertainment developments that, to put it mildly, is 'lively' at weekends. Prince of Wales Road, the thoroughfare that leads down across the river to the railway station, sees a great deal of pre-nightclub carousing on Friday and Saturday nights. All cities have similar areas, of course, but Prince of Wales Road is best avoided on weekend nights unless you are under 25 and full of cheap booze. A taxi driver once remarked 'It's like Beirut out there', as we drove slowly along it trying to avoid the lurching bodies. I felt it necessary to mention that I had been to Beirut and compared with this it was actually rather peaceful.

The Lanes & market

Norwich Lanes is an effective re-branding of the city centre's narrow medieval streets. This complex of streets, lanes and alleyways, designated 'the independent shopping and lifestyle quarter' (norwichlanes.co.uk), connect three parallel streets north of Norwich Market and Guildhall: St Giles Street, Pottergate and St Benedict's Street, with Norwich Castle, St Andrew's Hall, St Benedict's Church (just a tower since 1944) and St Giles Church all standing as corner pieces. There are plenty of independent shops, cafés and yet more churches within this zone, as well as Jarrold's elegant department store and the pedestrian thoroughfare of London Street with its shops, buskers and *Big Issue* sellers.

Connecting Castle Street and Gentleman's Walk in front of the market, **Royal Arcade** is the delightful Edwardian passageway with a charming Art Nouveau entrance and lamps. Alongside a decent café and jewellery, toy and fudge shops there is rumoured to also be a 'ghost shop' down here, one that mysteriously appears and disappears from time to time. The arcade was designed in 1899 by George Skipper, a local architect who was also responsible for Jarrold's department store and the Norwich Union headquarters on Surrey Street near the bus station, which has a hugely impressive marble hall inside. John Betjeman, an admirer of Skipper's Art and Craft designs, said that the architect 'is to Norwich rather what Gaudi was to Barcelona'. Skipper also designed many of the grander hotels along the seafront in Cromer.

Norwich Market has operated continuously in the same spot since Norman times (the earlier Saxon market was down at Tombland but was moved when the Normans began to build the cathedral). It's a six-day-a-week affair (closed Sunday) – the largest daily open market in Britain – selling all manner of local food products as well as books, records, clothes, household goods and takeaway meals. There's a place to get keys cut and shoes mended while you wait, and a chip stall that comes highly rated by Norwich residents judging by its never-ending queue. The mushy-pea stall here has been in business for 60 years, with the same family running it all that time. There are also many other take-away outlets that range from Punjabi street food to Sicilian *arancini* to Chinese noodles. The thing to do here, in fine weather at least, is to take your food up to the Memorial Gardens at the top of the marketplace and eat it al fresco while looking across the market to the castle. Beware rapacious herring gulls, however.

The market complex was expensively revamped in 2005 after much deliberation and not a little controversy. The old market had uneven floors and narrow alleyways but the new stalls are a little smaller than those that stood before and haven't gone down too well with some longstanding stallholders and shoppers – a textbook example of a committee coming up with a compromise that, ultimately, nobody really seems to like.

City Hall looms above the market, a long, brick 1930s building with rampant lions at its steps that look decidedly Babylonian. The design was apparently based upon that of Stockholm Town Hall but the large square clock tower, seen from all over the city, always puts me in mind of a Marrakech minaret. I am more taken with the two buildings that stand opposite each other just to the south. **St Peter Mancroft Church** has dominated the marketplace since the mid 15th-century, a wonderful Perpendicular building with a hammerbeam roof that is filled with light – my favourite Norwich church, and I am sure I am not alone in this. The church contains the grave of Sir Thomas Browne (1605–82), a Norwich-based medical man and all-round polymath famous for the books *Urn Burial* and *Religio Medici* (W G Sebald devotes half a chapter to him in *Rings of Saturn*). A statue of him contemplating a piece of urn is just across the way on Hayhill in front of Next. There is also a large modernist 'brain' sculpture – in the spirit of Browne's intellectual pursuits, perhaps, but not without its critics. Browne once lived just across the way on the other side of Gentleman's Walk, where Pret a Manger now stands – there is a blue plaque to commemorate this. St Peter Mancroft really comes into its own during the Norfolk & Norwich Festival in May when the church serves as a medieval backdrop to modern (and often French or Catalan) street theatre. The church interior is made use of too, and candle-lit it is hugely atmospheric. I have fond memories of seeing the great jazz bassist Charlie Haden perform here a few years back – medieval architecture and modern jazz is such a heady mix.

A car park and lacklustre library used to stand opposite St Peter Mancroft but this burned down in 1994 – public records and hardback thrillers are highly combustible. The void has been filled by **The Forum** (⊘ theforumnorwich.co.uk), a bold Millennium Commission project that has been an enormous success. The Forum is a large glass-fronted complex in the shape of a horseshoe that contains the Norfolk and Norwich Millennium Library, one of the most-visited libraries in the country, the regional BBC studios, Fusion – a digital gallery – a café and a pizza restaurant. There's a large internal foyer area for exhibitions and performances, and regular craft and food markets. How a building made of glass, tubular steel and brick can fit so well into such a tight space in a medieval city is remarkable. Part of this may be down to the longer-than-standard handmade bricks used in the horseshoe walls, the same as in the city hall opposite. Between The Forum and St Peter Mancroft is a paved plaza with amphitheatre-like steps that provide a ready venue for street theatre events and for an ice-skating rink in winter. It's always busy and, whether by accident or design, seems to provide what the Italians term 'a convivial space', a natural relaxed focus for the city centre.

In addition to the castle and cathedral, the place most often mentioned on tourist trawls through the city is Elm Hill, a cobbled street that descends down to Wensum Street from behind St Andrew's Hall. There's no longer an elm but I do remember the one that used to stand here and the valiant efforts made to save it once it had become infected with that arboreal plague, Dutch elm disease. Elm Hill has galleries, a café or two and a couple of quirky shops, and by the time you reach the bottom you are very close to Fye Bridge and the River Wensum – once across the bridge you are in the part of Norwich that locals refer to as 'Norwich over the Water'. There are fine walks to be had along the river in either

ROUND TOWER CHURCHES

Norfolk has a total of 124 round tower churches, far more than any other county in England. Although they are found largely in East Anglia – Suffolk also has 38 and Essex six – there are also church towers of similar design in Germany. Most, but not all, round tower churches tend to be of Saxon origin but the reason for their construction is still open to debate. It is likely that they were built because of a lack of suitable building materials for constructing square towers in a region where the only stone available was flint. Corners are hard to build using flint and so round towers may have simply been a pragmatic solution to the problem given the cheap and plentiful supply of building material that was available locally. There are even those who think that round towers may have originally been defensive structures but this seems unlikely. While round tower churches are often associated with churches of pre-Norman, Saxon origin there is plenty of evidence to suggest that they continued to be built concurrently with square tower churches as late as the 14th or even the 15th centuries. While the towers of some round tower churches were replaced over time with square towers, many more were modified to include an octagonal belfry to support the church bells at the top.

direction from here. Head west from Fye Bridge and you'll soon come to Blackfriars Bridge and the impressive Victorian buildings that make up the Norwich University of the Arts to the south of the bridge, with Norwich Playhouse just to the north. Venture east and you'll come to Whitefriars Bridge with the elegantly tall Jarrold's Printing Works building – formerly a mill – a little way beyond on the north bank. The building used to be home to one of the city's lesser-known museums, the John Jarrold Printing Museum, but this, now known as the **Norwich Printing Museum** (⊘ norwichprinting museum.co.uk), has since upped sticks to the Blickling Estate near Aylsham.

Norwich churches

Norwich has so many medieval churches – 32 in fact – that it is easy to overdo it and see too many in too short a time. Ecclesiastical architecture needs plenty of time for digestion. A personal choice would be the aforementioned St Peter Mancroft, Norwich Cathedral, naturally, and perhaps the tiny **shrine church of St Julian**, just off King Street. St Julian's is actually a reconstruction – the original was bombed during World War II – but it still has a story to tell. This was the site where Julian of Norwich, a 14th-century mystic anchoress, built a cell for

UNGODLY NORWICH

Curiously, given so many places of worship, nonconformist or otherwise, Norwich came top in a 2011 survey as the ungodliest city in England, with 42.5% of its citizens saying they have no religion compared to a national average of 25.1%. This is nothing new: Norwich was, in fact, excommunicated by the Pope following anti-clerical riots in the city way back in the late 13th century, the only English city ever having to suffer a spiritual snub of this nature. Norwich has always been true to its motto of 'Do Different': who knows – if a similar survey were to be done on paganism or New Age beliefs rather than orthodox religion then Norwich might actually score rather well?

herself and turned her back on the world to write *Revelations of Divine Love*, the first work to be written by a woman in English. I'm fond too of **St Benedict's Street** with its five decommissioned churches strung along its length like ports of call on a spiritual pub crawl. Closest to Grapes Hill with its flinty scraps of city wall is **St Benedict's Church**, now just a freestanding round tower with an octagonal top thanks to a World War II bombing raid, one of the Baedeker Raids that took place in 1942. A little further on, opposite the Ten Bells pub, is St Swithin's, which has long served as the venue for the **Norwich Arts Centre**, a wonderful institution that puts on a broad range of concerts and events.

A little further still is St Margaret's and then my namesake **St Laurence's**, which in medieval times would have had direct access via steps to the River Wensum below. If you take a close look at its western wall from the delightfully named St Lawrence Little Steps (note the spelling; people get my name wrong too), you should be able to make out a stone carving showing St Laurence's martyrdom on a hot iron grill. Reportedly crying out to his tormentors, 'Turn me over I'm done on this side', he has become the patron saint of both cooks and comedians. Although empty now, the church has served as a craft market in recent years. One of the stallholders told me that some of those who use the place sense a none-too-pleasant atmosphere in the western end of the church. 'There's a very strange feel to it – really quite evil. We all think it. There's a door there and I was thinking of having a look to see what was behind it. Then I just thought to myself, "No, I really don't think so"'. Further on at Charing Cross, the junction of St Benedict's with Westlegate, stands **St Gregory's Church**. All this – five redundant churches – within a five-minute, 400yd walk.

Nonconformist Norwich

Norwich has more than just medieval churches, of course; and the churches built in more recent centuries have not been solely Anglican either. Roman Catholics have their own **pro-cathedral of St John the Baptist**, a massive Victorian Gothic edifice, at the top of Earlham Road, with The Tuns, a genuine (rather than faux) Irish pub, conveniently opposite. As a centre of nonconformity, there have been all sorts of congregations worshipping in the city. The 18th-century **Octagon Chapel** on Colegate, built by Thomas Ivory, the same architect who built the splendid Georgian Assembly Rooms on Rampant Horse Street, is highly unusual and indeed octagonal. Originally built by Presbyterians, it became Unitarian in the 19th century. The chapel with its wonderful wooden acoustic is now occasionally used for musical events.

"This is a delightful place to wander in peace and quiet, listening to birdsong and examining gravestones."

There's also a marvellous curio in the form of the nonconformist **Rosary Road Cemetery** just east of Thorpe railway station, where the same nonconformist worshippers often ended up, as well as quite a few railway workers from the nearby station. This is a delightful place to wander in peace and quiet, listening to birdsong and examining gravestones. Surprisingly, this is the earliest nonconformist cemetery in England, and older than any of the larger London equivalents. In earlier times, resolute nonconformists often met grisly deaths at the hands of the orthodoxy. The site of the Lollards Pit just across Riverside Road from Bishop's Bridge is testament to this, although only a commemorative plate remains today. The site is also remembered in the name of the pub on the corner of Gas Hill and Riverside Road. As George Borrow remarks in *Lavengro*, 'It has had its martyrs, the venerable old town'.

SAINSBURY CENTRE FOR VISUAL ARTS

If modern architecture floats your boat, you might want to make a pilgrimage west of the city to my alma mater, the University of East Anglia, where you'll find the Sainsbury Centre for Visual Arts, an aircraft hangar of a building designed by Sir Norman Foster when he was still relatively unknown. Whatever your view is of the building's aesthetic appeal – I doubt if King Charles III is an admirer – it certainly works well as a gallery for the arts and, as well as the permanent collection,

HELEN HOTSON/S

RICHARD BOWDEN/S

MARY DOGGETT/S

THE NORWICH PRINTING MUSEUM

hosts frequent special exhibitions by prestigious artists. The Sainsbury Centre and 'ziggurats' of the university buildings look down on a tree-lined artificial lake, usually referred to as UEA Broad, which has matured nicely since it was first created out of a gravel pit in the mid 1970s and now has a wealth of wildlife in and around its waters. It's a favourite spot for anglers, local joggers and dog walkers.

"A footpath takes you past a series of meadows filled with rescue horses of all shapes and sizes."

North of UEA Broad, behind woodland and parallel to Bluebell Lane, a footpath takes you past a series of meadows filled with rescue horses of all shapes and sizes: tiny Shetland ponies, standard-size horses, donkeys, even a mule. The kind chap who rescues and nurtures these unfortunate beasts told me: 'We get a lot of them from the continent, Italy especially. It costs a lot to ship them over here but it's worth it.' On regular walks here, it is heartwarming to see what were once sorry animals slowly regain their fettle with time. The place made the local news a while ago when a Shetland pony shared the same field as an old mare. To everyone's surprise, the pair produced a foal together in defiance of the assumption that the stallion was too short and the mare, too old.

GREEN NORWICH

Norwich is by any standards a green city, and I'm not just referring to its many parks and open spaces like Chapelfield Gardens within the city walls and Mousehold Heath, beyond. In 2006, the city was voted England's greenest city, having the highest concentration of eco-friendly businesses in the country. This is probably not unconnected to the fact that the Green Party generally do well here, holding a considerable number of seats in both city and county councils. The first **Norwich and Norfolk Sustainable Living Festival** was held in the city in 2009, with all manner of exhibitions and events taking place at The Forum and the University of East Anglia. The Forum is also the location for regular farmers' markets and One Planet Norwich events.

As you might expect, the city has a number of outlets for local organic produce. **The Green Grocers** (2 Earlham House, Earlham Rd

◄ **1** Colourful houses along the River Wensum. **2** The Cow Tower, a 14th-century defensive structure. **3** Plantation Garden. **4** Norwich Printing Museum.

✐ 01603 250000 ⌂ thegreengrocers.co.uk) sells food and drink that is 90% organic and/or locally produced and also has a carbon-neutral project to offset its emissions. This is also the location for the **Golden Triangle Farmers' Market**, which takes place from 10.00 to 15.00 every second Sunday of the month. For meat eaters, **Harvey's Pure Meat** (63 Grove Rd ✐ 01603 621908 ⌂ puremeat.org. uk) specialises in organic meat and seasonal game. In the city centre, long-established Rainbow Wholefoods (4–6 Davey Pl ✐ 01603 625560 ⌂ rainbowwholefoods. co.uk) has all manner of organic and eco-friendly produce. The best bread in the city can be found at **Dozen Artisan Bakery** (107 Gloucester St ✐ 01603 764798) and also at **Two Magpies Bakery** (27–9 Timberhill ✐ 01603 613172 ⌂ twomagpiesbakery.co.uk) in the city centre, which produces a variety of delicious sourdough loaves as well as cakes and baked savouries. There is also the excellent Bread Source (⌂ bread-source.co.uk), which has several branches around the city as well as a stall in Norwich Market. The market itself should not be overlooked either for its wealth of local produce – cheese, meat, vegetables and fruit – its excellent wet fish stalls and its wide choice of takeaway food.

> *"The market itself should not be overlooked either for its wealth of local produce."*

Returning to the sense of green meaning 'foliage', several city gardens are worth a visit. My first choice would be **The Plantation Garden** (4 Earlham Rd ✐ 07504 545810 ⌂ plantationgarden.co.uk), right beside St John's RC Church. This was created in the mid 19th century in an abandoned chalk quarry but lay completely forgotten until its rediscovery 40 odd years ago. Its Gothic fountain, Italianate terrace and woodland walkways have all been lovingly restored, although it is still very much a work in progress. It is open year-round but there's the bonus of tea and cake on some Sunday afternoons in summer. There are also occasional outdoor film screenings in summer too. **The Bishop's Garden** (⌂ dioceseofnorwich.org), open a dozen or so times in summer, is a delightful swathe of perennial borders hidden away behind 700-year-old walls in the cloistered enclave of Cathedral Close.

¶¶ FOOD & DRINK

Like Aylsham, the 'Slow' market town in north Norfolk (page 131), Norwich has its own Slow Food convivium, which is part of Slow Food Anglia (⌂ slowfoodanglia.org) and works on forging links with local organic producers and promoting Slow Food events in the city and beyond. Pre-Covid, the city used to host an annual Food and Drink Festival weekend as part of the Norfolk Food and Drink Festival but it remains to be seen whether this will return or not. In 2022 the touring Foodies' Festival (foodiesfestival.com) came to Earlham Park in Norwich for the first time. The festival, with its tasty food and drink, live music and demonstrations by top chefs, is set to return in 2023 and subsequent years.

Even without any special events taking place, Norwich is blessed with a large and varied selection of places to eat and drink – from pubs, cafés and tea rooms to gastro pubs and smart restaurants. There's also a lot of talk about good coffee these days – central Norwich has quite a few places where the barista is king or queen. Listed here are some of my favourites.

Cafés & restaurants

Assembly House Theatre St 01603 626402 assemblyhousenorwich.co.uk. Offering elevenses and cake, traditional afternoon tea and pre-theatre dinner (17.00–18.45), this is the place to come for a meal or a snack in elegant Georgian surroundings. The cakes, scones and classic afternoon tea, available noon–16.30, are especially highly rated.

The Bicycle Shop 17 St Benedict's St 01603 625777 thebicycleshopcafe.com. A quirky, cosy café on three floors that, as its name suggests, was formerly a bicycle shop. This place has a bohemian, laid-back atmosphere and decent food made with mostly locally sourced ingredients. Good for breakfasts, tapas and crêpes.

Farmyard 23 St Benedict's St 01603 733188 farmyardrestaurant.com. With a produce-driven menu that sources ingredients from across Norfolk, this modern-style bistro has a short but inspired 'mix and match' menu of starters, mains and extras. Farmyard defines its approach as 'bistronomy' – a bistro atmosphere coupled with no-fuss fine dining.

Frank's Bar 19 Bedford St 01603 618902 franksbar.co.uk. A quirky, relaxed café-bar in the Norwich Lanes serving imaginative food that is free-range, locally sourced, fair trade and organic wherever possible.

Grosvenor Fish Bar 28 Lower Goat Lane 01603 625855 fshshop.com. The Grosvenor is a 90-year-old fish and chip shop that in recent years has been remodelled as a hip fish and chip grotto. Apart from the standard choices there are also sea bass, mackerel, and squid options as well as sandwiches and fish burgers. There's extensive downstairs seating, although many choose to eat their food seated on the benches of the square opposite. Be aware that the Grosvenor closes fairly early in the evening – around 19.30.

Little Red Roaster Norwich Market 01603 624886. An excellent coffee stall in the heart of the market, this has a wide range of coffee beans and associated paraphernalia as well as freshly made coffee by the cup to drink in or take-away. The stall once achieved national fame when its proprietor put up a notice refusing service to anyone ordering while using a mobile phone.

The Merchant's House 7–9 Fye Bridge St ⏣ merchantshousenorwich.co.uk. Formerly known as the King of Hearts and then North, this relaxed café-bar, located in a Tudor merchant's house by the river, has a good choice of coffees, loose-leaf teas and ales, as well as a few cakes and snacks. There's also a lovely hidden courtyard at the back and direct access to the art gallery next door.

Moorish Falafel Bar 17 Lower Goat Lane ☎ 01603 622250 ⏣ moorishfalafel.com. This good-value place has an excellent range of falafels in pitta bread, which are made to order while you wait; delicious homemade lemonade too. Very popular at lunchtime when there is usually a long queue leading out of the door. There's seating available upstairs or you can take away. There is also another branch on Park Lane in the Golden Triangle area of the city.

No 33 33 Exchange St ☎ 01603 626097 ⏣ no33cafe.co.uk. Good value, with tasty sandwiches and huge portions of cake. This often gets so busy that it is hard to find a table.

Sahara 22–24 St Benedict's St ☎ 07417 583667. A friendly and attractively decorated North African-style café serving Arabic coffee and Maghreb dishes like *chakchouka* and couscous. There is another branch on Magdalen St north of the city centre.

Strangers Coffee House 21 Pottergate ⏣ strangerscoffee.com. This small coffee shop in the heart of The Lanes is the base for the Strangers Coffee company and serves excellent fair-trade coffee, paninis, homemade cakes and sausage rolls.

Two Magpies Bakery 27–9 Timberhill ☎ 01603 613172 ⏣ twomagpiesbakery.co.uk. As well as selling all manner of delicious bakery products, this bright modern place at the top of Timberhill is also an excellent café that serves delicious brioches, cakes, light meals and excellent coffee. There's outdoor seating for watching the world go by on Timberhill.

Pubs

Even in the age of the 'eatery' and 'dining pub', Norwich remains one of the best places in the country for good, unadulterated pubs serving good, unadulterated real ale. These are just some of my favourite places for a drink in the city:

Adam and Eve Bishopsgate ☎ 01603 667423. Splendidly ancient and character-laden hostelry, resplendent with floral tubs and hanging baskets. This place is worth visiting if only for the fact that it is the city's oldest pub. It is said that builders working on the nearby cathedral once used it (they were paid in bread and ale) – this may or may not be true but, either way, the Adam and Eve is at least 750 years old. Naturally, the pub is rumoured to be haunted and city ghost tours often set off from here.

Alexandra Tavern 16 Stafford St ☎ 01603 627772 ⏣ alexandratavern.co.uk. West of the city centre, on the edge of the 'Golden Triangle', the 'Alex' is a friendly street-corner pub that has a good choice of locally produced real ales from Woodforde's, Humpty Dumpty, Winters and Norwich's Chalk Hill Brewery, as well as decent, good-value pub food.

Duke of Wellington 91–93 Waterloo Rd ✆ 01603 441182 ⌂ dukeofwellingtonnorwich. co.uk. North of the city centre, this pub has no food other than meat pies and sausage rolls but there are at least 17 real ales to choose from including Wolf. There are also traditional pub games and folk music on Tuesdays.

Fat Cat 49 West End St ✆ 07807 579517 ⌂ fatcatpub.co.uk. A Victorian corner pub that is real ale heaven, with around 30 real ales on offer at any given time. Strictly booze and no food, this traditional pub of the old school, the longest established of Norwich's three Fat Cat pubs, is austere, crowded, noisy and very good fun.

Fat Cat Brewery Tap 98–100 Lawson Rd ✆ 01603 413153 ⌂ fatcattap.co.uk. Better known as 'The Shed' to some, this has all the Fat Cat real ales and many more beers, wines and ciders besides. There are loaded chips and burgers to soak it all up. A lively place that can sometimes get very full, there is live music on some nights.

Kings Arms 22 Hall Rd ✆ 01603 477888 ⌂ kingsarmsnorwich.co.uk. An unpretentious traditional pub just south of the centre. No machines or music to distract; no carpets either, just a good choice of real ales, wines and malts. No food but staff are happy for customers to bring in take-away food, for which they will provide cutlery.

Kings Head 42 Magdalen St ✆ 01603 620468 ⌂ kingsheadnorwich.com. A traditional city pub north of the river, run by the same people who own the Humpty Dumpty Brewery. No frills, just bare floorboards, bar billiards and well-kept real ale.

Trafford Arms 61 Grove Rd ✆ 01603 628466 ⌂ traffordarms.co.uk. This local, which has a strong community feel, lies just south of the centre. Well-kept real ales include Lacons and a steady rotation of guest beers.

Wig and Pen 6 St Martin's Palace Plain ✆ 01603 625891 ⌂ thewigandpen.com. In a 17th-century building opposite Norwich Cathedral, 'The Wig' has good food prepared from locally sourced ingredients, plus a more than reasonable choice of real ales and wines. There's also a nice outdoor seating area for warm summer nights.

ALONG THE YARE – SOUTH BANK

2 WHITLINGHAM COUNTRY PARK

⚑ **Whitlingham Broad Campsite** (page 310)

Across the River Yare a little way southeast of Norwich city centre is Whitlingham Country Park, centred on an artificial body of water that, like UEA Broad west of the city, was once a gravel pit. There's a very active canoeing centre here and a pleasant two-mile track around the lake that is often busy with dog walkers and joggers at weekends. Both lake and woods are a good place for birdwatching, especially in spring. The large converted flint barn at the main car park serves as a popular café.

FINE WINE FROM THE YARE VALLEY

In 2017 Norfolk took an unexpected bow in the heady world of viniculture when a Yare Valley vineyard won an award for the world's best single varietal white wine. This was the first time an English vineyard had won such an award for a still wine. Winbirri Vineyards at Surlingham had already received eight awards in the previous three years, including East Anglian Wine of the Year, for the same wine. The wine in question ('very elegant' with a 'complex, oily nose with spice, elderflower and citrus') was the vineyard's Bacchus 2015, bottles of which became impossible to find in any of the county's supermarkets and wine stores soon after it won the prestigious award. Further plaudits came in 2020 when the website Vivino (⊘ vivino.com) rated Winbirri Bacchus as the number 1 wine in the world in the £10–20 price bracket. The Bacchus grape, according to head winemaker Lee Dyer, was perfectly suited to the Norfolk climate, favouring the dry autumnal conditions found at the Surlingham vineyard.

Not resting on its laurels and looking to the future, Winbirri hopes to broaden its output and aims to be producing sparkling wines and pinot noir vintages of comparable quality in the near future.

3 SURLINGHAM

A few miles east of Norwich, on the south bank of the River Yare, lies the village of Surlingham. The riverside Ferry Boat pub is busy in summer with boat customers but the ferry no longer operates, which is a pity. Most people arriving by boat tend just to call in at the pub, or perhaps moor in the broad further on, but there's plenty to see on foot around the village.

Surlingham parish is a large one that extends east of the village to Surlingham Marsh, Surlingham Wood and **Wheatfen Nature Reserve** (⊘ 01508 538036 ⊘ wheatfen.org), first established by the naturalist Ted Ellis (page 229), who lived in a cottage here for 40 years before his death in 1986. Visitors to the reserve are welcome and there are several trails across marshes and woodland, where you are likely to see (or, more likely, hear) sedge and reed warblers, and perhaps witness marsh harriers gliding overhead. In late May and early June, you might even come across that Broadland speciality, the swallowtail butterfly.

Surlingham is also home to Winbirri Vineyards (⊘ 07595 894841 ⊘ winbirri.com), with a growing reputation for fine wines (see above). Occasional tours and tasting days are hosted throughout the year.

---

1 Whitlingham Country Park. 2 Bitterns can be seen (if you're lucky!) at RSPB Strumpshaw Fen. 3 Rockland Broad. ▶

A walk around Surlingham

✹ OS Explorer map OL40; start: St Mary's Church . ⚲ TG304065; 2 miles; easy

If you have your own transport, St Mary's Church just west of the village is the best place to park up as you can make an interesting two-mile circular walk from here that takes in a good variety of scenery within a relatively short distance.

A footpath leads down past ponds and dykes to the river. There are dragonflies aplenty and all those other things that tend to characterise Norfolk's slow-moving waterways – yellow flag irises, reed-mace, ragged robin, the sweet smell of water mint and the occasional splash of a frog. Arriving at the river, you come to a path that leads to the right, eastwards along the river shaded by willows, that continues past reed beds and a bird hide as far as the Ferry House pub. Blackthorn grows plentifully along the path here, which is one of my favourite places to collect sloes (for making sloe gin) on a bright, late autumn's day when there's a nip in the air.

A concrete road leads inland from the pub through a swampy alder carr, at the end of which is a track to the right next to a house with a dovecote. The path leads along the edge of a field and past a rifle range until it passes beneath the remains of St Saviour's, an evocative ruined church, and continues along a track to St Mary's where you started.

4 ROCKLAND BROAD

This sheltered body of water lies just south of Wheatfen Nature Reserve, and is connected to the Yare by a dyke, or, rather, what is known in these parts as a staithe. The New Inn pub is on the road next to a footpath that leads around the east side of the broad. A bird hide overlooks the broad halfway along but on last inspection this was closed.

From Claxton, the road more or less follows the course of the river through Langley Green and Langley Street to Hardley Street, all tiny hamlets surrounded by vast marshes. The floodplain of the river is very wide, flat and low here and the marshes extensive. The very mention of Hardley Street puts me in mind of a time 25 years or so ago when I found myself out on the marshes here during a violent thunderstorm. In a vast wet area where everything is at sea level and with no trees, a soggy man makes a rather good lightning conductor – or so I thought, as I ran back to my car with jagged shafts of electricity fizzing around me. Fortunately, it did not turn out to be the electrifying experience that it might have been and I escaped unscathed. I tend to listen more closely to weather forecasts these days.

If you make a short detour to the evocative ruins of St Saviour's you'll come across the graves of local naturalist and writer Ted Ellis (1909–86) and his wife, Phyllis. The graves are simple, austere even, but it is undeniably a lovely spot for any lifelong lover of nature to rest their bones.

Continuing up the track towards St Mary's, the house on the left, just before the church, usually has jars of honey for sale and an honesty box at its gate – this is the home of Orchid Apiaries, which produces several tons of honey annually from Surlingham hives.

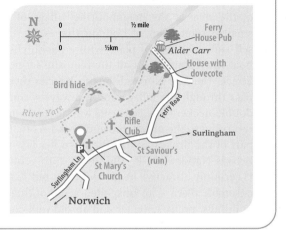

5 BERGH APTON

Bergh Apton – that's *Ber*-apton not *Bergh*-apton – is a large, sprawling village south of Rockland St Mary, just the other side of the A146. The village was originally two separate settlements, Apton to the northwest and Bergh to the southeast, which explains its considerable size. Apton's church disappeared long ago and the two parishes were combined so that Bergh's church of St Peter and St Paul might serve both. There used to be an enjoyable sculpture trail held here every three years in late May and June, which offered the opportunity not only to see works by local sculptors but also to snoop around some rather

"The village was originally two separate settlements, Apton to the northwest and Bergh to the southeast."

wonderful village gardens. Unfortunately, this eventually became a victim of its own success, with several thousand attending the final three events, the last of which was in 2011. The village still stages occasional arts events and has hosted a specially commissioned cycle of mystery plays in recent years.

6 LODDON

🏠 **The Swan Hotel** (page 310)

Continuing southeast along the A146 from the Bergh Apton turn-off, you come to the small market town of Loddon, which lies immediately south of the River Chet, a tributary of the Yare. On the north side of the river is the neighbouring village of **Chedgrave** but it is the small market town of Loddon that is the more interesting – a tidy, self-sufficient sort of place with a parish church, a couple of pubs, a boat-lined staithe and all the requisite services strewn along its High Street. The X22 Norwich bus to Beccles diverts off the main road to pass through the village and it always seems a bit of a squeeze for a double-decker to negotiate its way along the narrow High Street before returning to the unfettered and broad A146. Because the River Chet is part of the Broads system the town lies just within the bounds of the Broads National Park. The town's 15th-century Holy Trinity Church is certainly attractive in its own right but really Loddon is more of an ensemble piece – an unspoiled array of fine Georgian and Victorian buildings, pretty cottages and an old mill complex. The mill complex served as Loddon Mill Arts for several years, organising arts events and even staging a regular comedy club in its converted steam engine room and grain barn. These days, the nearby White Horse pub in Chedgrave hosts similar events from time to time.

A good walk to be had from Chedgrave is to follow the country lane east from the crossroads towards Hardley Street and after about a mile take the footpath that leads off to the right past Hardley Hall down to the edge of the River Chet. The riverbank can then be followed left to reach the River Yare. At the confluence of the two rivers you'll come across Hardley Cross, which dates from 1543. This historic cross marks the boundary between the City of Norwich and the Borough of Great Yarmouth, and also the end of Norwich's jurisdiction over the river and the beginning of Yarmouth's. In past times the mayors of both Norwich and Great Yarmouth would travel here each year by wherry for the annual inquest on river liberties. Coming back, you can either retrace your steps, or better, follow the bank of the River Yare a mile or so west to reach Hardley Staithe near the church. From here, follow the minor lane that leads southwest all the way back to Chedgrave. Please note: the footpath shown on maps that leads along Hardley Flood is no longer open because of flood damage.

🍴 FOOD & DRINK

The Terrace 2 Church Plain, Loddon ✆ 01508 521932 ⌂ theterraceatloddon.co.uk. Located in a former bank, next to the car park on the high street, this bistro-restaurant offers tasty breakfasts and light lunches made using local produce, as well as indulgent afternoon teas and evening meals at weekends. The sunny outdoor terrace at the rear offers fine views over Holy Trinity's peaceful churchyard.

White Horse 5 Norwich Rd, Chedgrave ✆ 01508 520250 ⌂ whitehorsechedgrave.co.uk. Just across the river in Chedgrave, this village pub offers up to five real ales and decent bar meals.

ALONG THE YARE – NORTH BANK

The north bank of the River Yare has the railway line to Great Yarmouth and so is far more accessible if you want to use public transport. A couple of stops along the line are worth heading for if you are looking for a quiet walk or are at all interested in birds and other wildlife.

7 STRUMPSHAW FEN RSPB RESERVE

NR13 4HS ✆ 01603 715191 ⌂ rspb.org.uk/strumpshawfen; free entry for RSPB members

The village of Strumpshaw lies midway between Brundall and Lingwood but Strumpshaw Fen Nature Reserve, an extensive wetland reserve run by the RSPB, is actually closer to Brundall.

The reserve, which lies just across the river from Wheatfen Reserve and Surlingham Marshes, has all the wetland birds that you might expect, plus some others that you might not, with bitterns, various warblers, woodpeckers and numerous waders and ducks all lining up to be seen. Marsh harriers, sometimes in considerable number during the winter, are more or less guaranteed. It is also a reliable place to see swallowtail butterflies, which in my experience are easiest to spot in late May when they are still a tad sluggish.

"It is also a reliable place to see swallowtail butterflies, which in my experience are easiest to spot in late May."

The main entrance and visitor centre are a little over a mile from Buckenham station and so this is a possibility if you are arriving by train. You should bear in mind though that only a limited number of trains stop at Buckenham as it is a request stop – four on Saturdays and Sundays but none during the week.

On a Sunday, you could combine a visit to Strumpshaw with one to Berney Arms and Breydon Water. The rest of the week, you'll have to use Brundall station instead, which requires a slightly longer walk to reach the reserve entrance. Bus 15a (First in Suffolk & Norfolk) also runs hourly between Norwich and Strumpshaw; get off at the stop at the junction of Long Lane and Stone Road, from where it's a ten-minute walk.

8 BUCKENHAM CARRS

A large wooded area just east of Buckenham station, Buckenham Carrs is home to an enormous rook and jackdaw roost mentioned in the Domesday Book. It's thought there may be as many as 80,000 birds. The roost is the central motif of Mark Cocker's *Crow Country*.

A walk from Berney Arms

✳ OS Outdoor Leisure map 40 or Landranger map 134; start: Berney Arms station ♀ TG468052; 6 miles; moderate.

With a limited number of trains running to and from Berney Arms (be sure to check timetables beforehand ♂ greateranglia.co.uk), walking is the only thing to do here, unless you want to spend hours waiting on the platform. Fortunately, the walking is very good: the Wherryman's Way runs nearby and you have the choice of going west to Reedham, northwest along the Weavers' Way to Halvergate or east to Great Yarmouth along the shore of Breydon Water. My preferred choice would be the third.

From the station, follow the footpath, part of the Weavers' Way, to the river, where there is a drainage windmill. Then head east along the Wherryman's Way to reach the **Berney Arms**, which when it was open must surely have been Norfolk's most isolated pub. Unfortunately the pub has been closed for several years now and there seems to be no sign of it reopening for business any time soon. Trade was always sporadic and dependent on walkers, birdwatchers or boaters – there are several moorings here – but in the more distant past this isolated pub would have had a colourful clientele of wherrymen, wildfowlers, poachers and fishermen.

Just after the pub, you arrive at the confluence of the Yare and Waveney and the start of **Breydon Water**. Look south along the Waveney River and you should be able to make out the outline of **Gariannonum/Burgh Castle** (page 240). From here, the Wherryman's Way continues all the way along the north shore of Breydon Water until it reaches **Great Yarmouth,** where it narrows to a channel to flow south into the sea at Gorleston. Great Yarmouth railway station is right by Breydon Bridge at the start of the town.

The Buckenham roost, which takes place in the winter months, roughly between late October and March, is quite a spectacle to behold, a natural phenomenon that has been taking place long before the fields were ploughed here and the church at Buckenham constructed. Ideally, you'll want a crisp winter's evening with a clear sky and a full moon. The best vantage point is to walk up the narrow road from Buckenham station until you reach a copse on the left with a small ruined brick shelter. You'll see it all from here.

The performance – if you can call it that – is a slow burn. Just after sunset, groups of rooks, and some jackdaws, fly in to gather on the large ploughed area immediately to the west; others land in the trees that surround it. Some have come quite a long way to be sociable but

Breydon Water is a large tidal estuary, a wonderful place for birdwatchers and a great place to walk, although it is quite an austere landscape, especially at low tide when glistening grey mud stretches to the skyline. The sky is often grey too, or that is how it seems to me, as whenever I come here it always seems to be overcast as if there were a perpetual cloud hanging over the place.

Winter is peak season here, for birds at least, with tens of thousands of waders, ducks and swans feeding in the mud. With luck you might also catch a glimpse of a peregrine falcon or marsh harrier overhead.

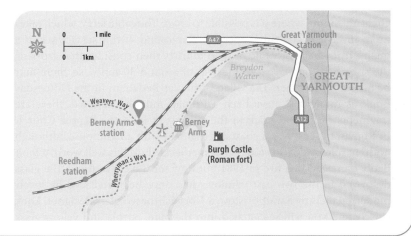

the crow conversation taking place sounds rather tetchy, all guttural complaining caws.

Momentum slowly builds as more and more groups of birds fly in to land in the field. As the light fades, the noise from the congregation builds louder and eerily expectant: something is clearly about to happen. Eventually, when the darkness is almost complete some sort of signal spurs the birds airborne and the sky blackens with rooks that swirl noisily east to settle in the woods of Buckenham Carrs where they will spend the night together.

It's an astonishing, almost primal, event. One that almost laughs in the face of people's perceived dominion over nature. No collective noun can adequately describe it: a building of rooks, a train of jackdaws. It's less a murder of crows, more a mass execution.

9 CANTLEY & 10 REEDHAM

🏠 **The Cockatrice** (page 310) ⛺ **The Old Vicarage** (page 310)

Working eastwards, the next village along the river is Cantley, best known for its **sugar beet factory** that belches out sickly-smelling smoke in the winter months. Cantley's sugar-beet factory, seen from far and wide, is as much an icon of the River Yare as a Norfolk wherry, and is the magnet for all the lumbering lorries that trundle these roads in winter brimful of knobbly roots.

Reedham, further east, has the only surviving **car and passenger ferry** along the river and consequently is the only point between Norwich and Great Yarmouth where it is possible to cross. The cable ferry, which takes up to three cars at a time, operates year-round. If this service seems a quaint throwback of value only to tourists then consider that crossing the river here can save a round-trip of around 30 miles, so there may be queues in summer. The village, listed as Redaham in the Domesday Book, is thought to have been a Roman military station – there are fragments of Roman brick in the village's St John the Baptist Church. In Roman times it was a coastal settlement with a lighthouse, although nothing remains of this today. The medieval church is well worth a look. Badly damaged in a fire in 1981 but now sensitively restored, the glass destroyed in the two east windows has since been replaced by lovely modern panels by Sarah Bristow, a Norwich-based glass designer. Look closely and you will see, etched into the blue, purple and yellow glass, detail from the ordnance survey map of the Yare Valley.

As well as having a popular riverside pub, the village is also home to the **Humpty Dumpty Brewery** (☏ 01493 701818 ⌗ humptydumptybrewery. com), which uses locally produced malt and whose Broadland Surprise has been voted Champion Beer of Norfolk; Little Sharpie, a lower gravity session beer, is another regular prizewinner. Some of the other Humpty Dumpty brews – Reedcutter, Swallowtail, Swingbridge Stout and Railway Sleeper – also take their name from local features. The brewery has an off-sales shop selling beer, glasses and products from other local businesses. It's a 3½ mile walk along the riverbank to Berney Arms from here, a worthwhile outing from which you could return by train if you got your timing right. Otherwise, there are easy circular road walks around the village.

⑪ FOOD & DRINK

Lord Nelson 38 Riverside, Reedham ☏ 01493 700367. Now a little more upmarket than it used to be, with a restaurant and outside dining area and a choice of four real ales, this pub by the water and the swing bridge is a convenient stop.

11 BERNEY ARMS

Berney Arms must be the oddest railway stop in the country. I use the word 'stop' advisedly, rather than station, as that is all there is to it: a sign and small platform to get off or on the few trains that stop here. It takes its name from a local landowner, Thomas Trench Berney, who in 1844 sold land to the railway company on condition that they built a station and kept it open for perpetuity. The station is unstaffed, of course, and as you might imagine, 3½ miles from the nearest road and right in the heart of the vast spread of Halvergate Marshes, rather isolated.

12 GREAT YARMOUTH

Yarmouth is an ancient town, much older than Norwich. And at present, though not standing on so much ground, yet better built, much more complete; for number of inhabitants, not much inferior, and for wealth, trade and advantage of its situation, infinitely superior to Norwich.
Daniel Defoe, *A Tour Thro' The Whole Island of Great Britain, divided into Circuits or Journies*, 1724

Not so great these days, some might say. Great Yarmouth is hardly an obvious Slow destination but it would be wrong to dismiss it completely as it has plenty to offer, especially with regard to historical interest.

Its clean sandy beach is also hard to fault and perfect for families with its safe bathing and opportunities for sandcastle building. There was once a thriving herring fishing industry in the town. This faded out in the early years of the 20th century, by which time the town had found new fortune as a seaside resort. The 1970s heralded an era of cheap Mediterranean holidays and many of the town's former devotees started to look further afield to destinations like the Costa Brava instead. Once again, the town's diminishing fortunes were bailed out by a new source of income; this time, it was North Sea oil and gas.

Great Yarmouth is a town of two halves: an isthmus that shows its seafaring side along South Quay to the west, and its holiday resort face along the promenade to the east. Both will provide a degree of culture shock if you travel here direct from somewhere like Southwold, a very different sort of place although just 20 miles away. Great Yarmouth, the resort, is as you might expect: an East Anglian Blackpool with a pier, sandy beach, deckchairs, buckets and spades – it's traditional in the sense of being a place where you can still buy sticks of rock, promenade in a horse-drawn landau and even have a 'gypsy' woman tell your fortune. The accents are northern, Midlands or Norfolk, although move a few streets in from the promenade and you'll hear plenty of Polish and Portuguese instead.

There's still something quintessentially English about Great Yarmouth seafront, and it's refreshing to discover that not everyone who can afford it has upped sticks to Benidorm or Corfu. Next to the pier, you might see a large extended family of Birmingham Indians, as I did one bright August day: mothers and aunties in glorious saris chatting and devouring chips on the sea wall; teenage girls texting their friends and giggling; boys playing serious cricket on the sand with proper stumps and a hard ball. Observing this heartwarming scene from posters above Britannia Pier are Jim Davidson and Roy 'Chubby' Brown, comedians not known for their love of liberal inclusivity – it all struck a wonderful chord.

Heritage Quarter

The fishiest town in all England
Charles Dickens

Yarmouth's other side can be found in its Heritage Quarter along South Quay, which begins at the bridge and Victorian Town Hall and stretches south along the River Yare. There will also be the 1930 herring boat *Lydia Eva*, the very last of the steam drifters, moored at the top of the quay. **Elizabethan House** (4 South Quay *⌀* 01493 743393 *⌀* museums. norfolk.gov.uk) was the home of a Tudor merchant, while **The Tollhouse** (*⌀* 01493 858900), a little further south and just inland, dates from the 12th century and was used as a gaol. Unique to Yarmouth's South Quay are its extremely narrow alleyways with their so-called 'Row houses', tiny dwellings that originated when larger merchant's residences were subdivided into tenements. Many of these were badly damaged by World War II bombing raids while many more were demolished in the years following the war. Some surviving Row houses (*⌀* 01493 857900; English Heritage) are open to visitors just south of here. Also nearby is Greyfriars' Cloisters, the remains of a 13th-century friary that were later converted into Row dwellings. You'll encounter more Row houses along Nottingham Way near South Quay. Not all Yarmouth's architectural heritage is Victorian or older. The town also has a sprinkling of noteworthy buildings of more recent pedigree too, like the lovely art deco Hippodrome (*⌀* hippodromecircus.co.uk) on St George's Road, dating from 1903, one of only two surviving purpose-built circus buildings in Britain that likes to describe itself as 'East Anglia's mini Albert Hall'. Both Houdini and Chaplin once performed here and shows and summer spectaculars are still staged here today. Regular guided heritage walks are run by the borough council (*⌀* heritage-walks.co.uk). Of special interest is a tour of the town walls, the second most complete medieval walls in Britain (after York), which stretch for over a mile around St Nicholas's Church and through the town before leading back to the river. One of the most interesting and complete sections is that which passes close to the Time and Tide museum (page 239).

If you're not heading straight to the Time and Tide Museum, wander further along South Quay towards the 169ft-high **Nelson Monument** that overlooks the mouth of the river. This is not vintage Norfolk scenery, but interestingly grim, with enormous heaps of metal scrap in yards, closed warehouses and perhaps a few dodgy-looking characters wandering about. There's a semi-abandoned air to the streets here that reminds me a little of Sheffield's Don Valley in the late 1980s – the ghost of unemployment and vanished industry. You can sometimes ascend the Nelson Monument by prior arrangement on Heritage Open Days in September (check with *⌀* visitgreatyarmouth.co.uk), but it is usually

closed to the public. It is quite hard work to climb the 217 steps up the slim spiral staircase to the top, and needless to say, small children and visitors with heart, lung or mobility problems are not allowed to ascend.

The **Time and Tide Museum** (✆ 01493 743930 ⌂ museums.norfolk. gov.uk) on Blackfriars Road, opposite a large chunk of the medieval Town Wall, is rather wonderful and it's worth visiting Yarmouth for this alone. Giving a wonderful account of Great Yarmouth life through the ages, particularly its seafaring tradition, it's a hands-on place that children really enjoy and there's plenty of archive film and taped interviews to make the history come alive. 'We're a bit Tardis-like here,' the guide explained. 'But we manage to pack a lot into a small space. The building used to be a herring curing works and a lot of people ask if we pump the smell in for atmosphere. We don't: it's in the fabric of the building itself.' The building really does smell strongly of herrings, which gives you a clue as to the sort of social stigma that the itinerant Scots fisher girls who came 'tae Yarmooth' must have suffered, given that their working days were spent elbow-deep in briny fish. As well as plenty of great displays and nostalgic newsreels of the joys of the herring fishing life ('There's nothing statelier than a shoal of herring coming

TALL SHIPS IN YARMOUTH

Great Yarmouth's **Maritime Festival,** which used to take place every September, was a fine reminder of East Anglia's once-glorious seafaring tradition. With majestic tall ships moored on South Quay alongside numerous tents and stalls with a general maritime theme, it drew large crowds of local families, old sailors and curious landlubbers. It offered a rare opportunity to poke around a tall ship, talk to experts and hang around with sailors. You could even go on a 2½- or 3½-hour cruise on one of the tall ships if you booked ahead. As well as ships to explore, there were craft stalls, information stands and even displays by Newfoundland rescue dogs, with fried herrings for sale, and salty sea shanties sung by crusty men with pewter tankards in the real ale tent. Unfortunately, the future of the festival is now hanging the balance. It did not take place in 2020 and 2021 because of Covid, nor did the festival go ahead in 2022 as hoped because of lack of funding. As an enjoyable tribute to Yarmouth's once-great maritime tradition, we can only hope the festival makes a comeback in the not too distant future.

◀ 1 Great Yarmouth beach and pier. 2 Time and Tide Museum, Great Yarmouth. 3 Burgh Castle.

over the side'), there's a reconstructed 'row' of cottages with tiny, tidy front rooms and piped voices. It is all rather moving, which is surely what any top-notch museum should aspire to be.

FOOD & DRINK

Mariners Tavern 69 Howard St South ✆ 01493 331164. One of the few real ale pubs in town (it has previously won Norfolk CAMRA Branch Pub of the Year), this has a cosy feel and is reasonably close to the railway station.

Quayside Plaza 9 South Quay ✆ 01493 331777 ⬦ quaysideplaza.com. Convenient for the Rows, this small restaurant is tucked away in the remains of Greyfriars cloisters. Good-value and eclectic Mediterranean-style meals, also cakes, salads and sandwiches, all made using organic locally sourced produce wherever possible.

The Kings Arms 229 Northgate St ✆ 01493 843736 ⬦ thekingsarmsgreatyarmouth. com. This pub with a beer garden, close to St Nicholas's Church, has a choice of real ales that include Humpty Dumpty, as well with bar snacks and well-priced pub standards.

13 BURGH CASTLE

Heading west along the south bank of Breydon Water brings you to the village of Burgh Castle where, as well as a boatyard, a couple of pubs and a small round tower church idyllically set among trees, the impressive Roman ruins of Burgh Castle (originally known as Gariannonum) loom above the confluence of the Yare and Waveney. With massive 3rd-century walls sloping at a precarious angle above the river and reed beds, it's certainly an impressive spot (free access) and well worth the effort of walking to along the estuary bank from Yarmouth. This route is actually the first (or last) section of the Angles Way and so is signposted fairly clearly for the most part. Besides, once you are at the estuary it is impossible to go wrong – just follow the path west until you see the ruins rising to your left. If you are not feeling quite so energetic, you could always catch one of the regular buses to the village from Yarmouth's Market Gates bus station instead, or perhaps take the bus one way and then walk back.

The castle's crucial strategic position is self-evident; these massive brick and flint fortifications were abandoned at the beginning of the 5th century when the Romans finally thought better of occupying such intractable northern territory. It is possible that Burgh Castle also marks the location of Cnobheresburg, a 7th-century monastery founded by Saint Fursa, the first Irish missionary in southern England. Whether or not the monastery's actual site was within these walls or elsewhere on this coast is open to debate; either way, subsequent attacks by Danish raiders soon encouraged Fursa to decamp to the relative safety of France.

AWAY FROM THE YARE

14 VENTA ICENORUM & 15 SHOTESHAM

The River Tas wiggles its way up from south Norfolk to its confluence with the Yare just outside Norwich. There's a Bronze Age henge marked on maps close to this point, beneath pylons next to the railway tracks and the Norwich inner ring road, but I have never been able to make out more than a few vague bumps in a field – evidently it's a job for a photographer with a drone. Having said this, the site – although unprepossessing on the surface – is of considerable importance for understanding the prehistory of the region. A new archaeological investigation of the site began in 2022.

Venture a little further south, past Caistor St Edmund, and there's more impressive archaeology in the form of **Venta Icenorum Roman Town** (sometimes referred to as Caistor Roman Town), a rectangle of raised

TWO HISTORIC TREES

A little way northeast of Wymondham, beside the B1172, the old road to Hethersett and Norwich, stands **Kett's Oak**, the tree that Robert Kett is said to have mustered supporters beneath prior to the 1549 rebellion. Another tale relates that this was actually the tree from which nine of the rebels were hanged. Whether or not this is the original tree in question or a later replacement is open to debate. Either way, the tree is surrounded by railings and much propped-up these days.

There's another historic tree fairly close by. At Hethel, close to Mulbarton to the east of Wymondham, there's an ancient hawthorn. The **Hethel Old Thorn** is a 700-year-old hawthorn, the oldest of its kind in Norfolk and possibly the UK. This once measured 12ft in circumference but is now much reduced. The tree is protected as a Norfolk Wildlife Trust nature reserve, which at just 0.06 acres is the smallest in the country. Not to be outdone by Kett's Oak's historical pedigree, this ancient hawthorn is supposedly where rebels met in the time of King John, while another legend has it that the tree grew from the staff of Joseph of Aramathea brought here by pilgrims from the Holy Land. All Saints' Church that stands nearby is even more ancient, with parts of it, including the tower, nearly a thousand years old and of Saxon origin.

HIGH ASH FARM

Immediately adjacent to the walls of Venta Icenorum are the fields and meadows of High Ash Farm (⊘ highashfarm.com), a holding that welcomes walkers and actively encourages wildlife. The farm, which covers many acres of rolling countryside and includes wildflower meadows and tracts of oak woodland, has a total of five miles of well-maintained permissive tracks passing through it. Some of the routes are designated for sponsors but others are open to the public in general (a map showing these is available at entry points to the farm and also online). In spring, part of the woodland area is also open to the public for a special bluebell weekend. Dogs are welcome throughout but must be on leads.

Biodiversity is encouraged thanks to good farming practices and a number of ongoing conservation projects. Many of the fields are planted with crops specifically to provide an important source of flowers and seeds for insects and birds. Species of bird like owls are also encouraged by the widespread installation of nest boxes in the woodland. Wildlife aside, for walkers many of the routes offer excellent views over the gently rolling south Norfolk countryside. Free parking is available at the Caistor Roman Town car park, although this does get busy.

walls and fortifications with traces of Roman brick that once served as the *Civitas* of the Iceni tribe and the most important Roman centre in northern East Anglia. The Boudicca Way, a long-distance footpath, passes right by it, although the evidence suggests that the streets and buildings of the town were not constructed until well after Boudica's bloody revolt against Roman rule in AD61.

Away from the river, **Shotesham** is an attractive village set among lush bucolic meadows. A good circular walk from here would be to follow the Boudicca Way south to Saxlingham Nethergate, then return to the village via Shotesham Lane and Roger's Lane. On the return leg, you will pass the evocatively ruined church of St Martin alongside its replacement next to Shotesham Old Hall

16 WYMONDHAM

Wedged in between the course of the Yare and Tas rivers southwest of Norwich, just off the A11 dual carriageway, stands the market town of Wymondham, a prosperous sort of place that is just far enough away

---

1 High Ash Farm. **2 & 3** Two historic trees: Hethel Old Thorn (2) and Kett's Oak (3).
4 Wymondham Abbey. ▶

HIGH ASH FARM

RICHARD OSBOURNE

CARMINA_PHOTOGRAPHY/S

CHRIS I WHITE/S

from Norwich to have a life of its own. Wymondham is both well-to-do and well connected, having a major road running past it, a good bus service and regular train connections to Norwich and Cambridge.

The first thing you need to know is that it's pronounced 'Wind-am' – to say 'Wy-mond-ham' will just induce hilarity among the natives. If you take the B1172 via Hethersett to reach the town, as the bus does, you'll pass **Kett's Oak** (page 241) by the roadside a mile short of the town's outskirts. The tree is reputed to be that under which Robert Kett, a Wymondham native, gathered supporters and made a rousing speech that set in motion his uprising against the enclosure of common land in 1549. The tree is partially supported by props these days but it still seems to be flourishing enough to produce acorns.

Like many other market towns, much of medieval Wymondham went up in smoke, and, in 1615, a fire gutted many of the town's buildings. Much of the historic town centre is a 17th-century rebuild, and it is thanks to the town remaining rather a backwater in the Victorian era that so many old buildings still stand today. The prominent 1617 market cross doubles as the tourist information centre and is raised on stilts to protect valuable documents from floodwater and rats. Live rats used to be nailed to it in order to set an example to fellow vermin but the practice was discontinued in 1902 when a child died as the result of a rat bite.

The two towers make **Wymondham Abbey**, or to give it its full name, the Abbey Church of St Mary and St Thomas of Canterbury, a distinctive local landmark. It started life as a Benedictine priory, its monastic buildings being demolished following the Dissolution when the church was partially destroyed. A visit by Elizabeth I in 1573 ensured that some repairs were made. The eastern octagonal tower is the older, part of the original Norman abbey church, while the square western tower dates from 1448 and once had Robert Kett's brother, William, hung in chains from it and left to rot. Looking at the interior, it is hard to imagine such cruel events ever taking place here, as the hammerbeam roof bristles with benign wooden angels beaming goodwill down onto the congregation.

FOOD & DRINK

Bird in Hand Church Rd, Wreningham ✆ 01508 489438 ◌ thebih.co.uk. In Wreningham, close to Hethel Old Thorn, this country freehouse has a relaxed atmosphere, an excellent selection of local ales, good bar meals and Sunday roasts using locally sourced meat.

Green Dragon 6 Church St, Wymondham ✐ 01953 607907. A 14th-century inn serving home-cooked English food with an emphasis on local produce. Cask-conditioned ales, an extensive wine list and choice of over 50 different whiskies.

Station Bistro Wymondham Station ✐ 01953 606433 ♂ stationbistro.co.uk. At Wymondham's 'proper' station, on the main network. All-day breakfasts, snacks and light lunches that use locally supplied meat and vegetables.

17 THE MID-NORFOLK RAILWAY

✐ 01362 851723 ♂ mnr.org.uk ☺ two or three trains a day most days in either direction between Wymondham and East Dereham

Walk towards the River Tiffey from Wymondham Abbey and cross it and you'll arrive at a railway line and the station – well, platform – of the Mid-Norfolk Railway. Enthusiastic volunteers ensure that the trains always run on time and it's a highly enjoyable excursion, especially if you manage to get on one of the steam trains. En route, you'll pass through some forgotten little outposts of central Norfolk like Thuxton and Yaxham, where you can get off if you like and have a walk. East Dereham is the terminus for the time being, but plans are afoot for the line to be restored as far as the former County School station that lies beyond North Elmham.

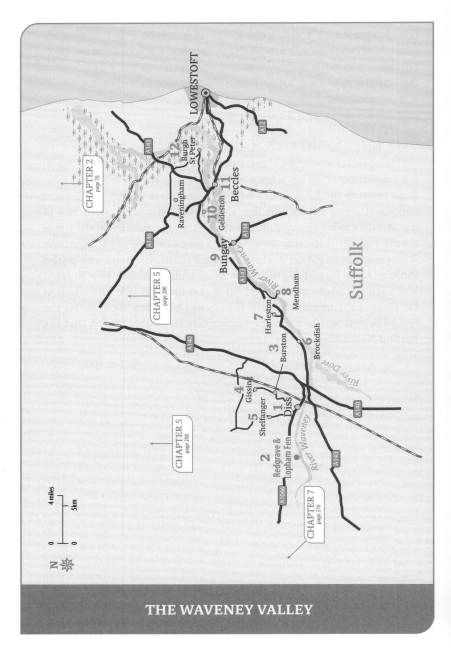

THE WAVENEY VALLEY

6
THE WAVENEY VALLEY

Were I in my castle upon the River Waveney
I wouldne give a button For the King of Cockney.
Hugh 'the Bold' Bigod, 1173

Just as the Little Ouse River forms a natural boundary between Norfolk and Suffolk in the west of the region, the River Waveney performs the same function in the centre and east. The Waveney's source lies between the villages of Redgrave in Suffolk and South Lopham in Norfolk, close to where the Little Ouse also rises. The sources of the two rivers are actually so close that Norfolk is almost an island – a heavy downpour and a flooded road or two and the separation is complete.

From its humble origins in Redgrave Fen, the Waveney flows east through the small towns of Diss (Norfolk), Bungay and Beccles (both Suffolk) before looping north around Lowestoft to join the River Yare at Breydon Water and eventually go to sea at Great Yarmouth. East of Bungay, the river lies within the boundary of the Broads Authority and the river is connected to Oulton Broad just west of Lowestoft by an artificial channel, Oulton Dyke.

All this talk of rivers and county boundaries might suggest that the Waveney forms some sort of impenetrable barrier. Far from it: the river is more of a conduit than anything, a far cry from the situation with the Yare to the north where the river represents a real physical obstacle. The Waveney, in contrast, has plenty of bridges spanning it, especially in its western reaches. The Waveney Valley may not be much of a valley in physical terms – it's hardly Kashmir – but it does have a personality all of its own that seems quite separate from the rest of Norfolk and Suffolk. Teenagers along the Waveney Valley may display keen allegiances to either Norwich City or Ipswich Town but that is about as far as it goes. The birdsong in the hedgerows sounds pretty much the same on either bank. Because of this singular character it will occasionally be necessary to cross the county boundary here and there in this chapter, and so both Bungay and Beccles are included despite belonging to Suffolk.

So what characterises the Waveney Valley? It's a sense of cosy isolation, where south Norfolk eases into the clay country of north Suffolk, where there are fewer big estates, and more commons, ancient hedgerows and moated farmhouses; more meandering tracks that seem to follow every field boundary before ending up nowhere in particular. There has probably been less change over the past half century in this region than anywhere else in southern England. While the attractions of north Norfolk have undoubtedly lured numerous outsiders, downsizers and weekenders over the years, the Waveney Valley has a different kind of draw. Those that have settled here have tended to become more integrated into the existing community. It has long attracted artists, writers and craftspeople and there was a noticeable, if small-scale, invasion of folk escaping the city for something simpler and more wholesome back in the 1970s – they and their children are mostly still here.

THE ARTY SIDE

A surprising number of artists work from the towns and villages of the valley: for two weekends in late May on the annual Harleston and Waveney Art Trail (⊘ hwat. org.uk) you can visit them in their studios. Constable and Gainsborough may have immortalised the Stour Valley on the Suffolk/ Essex border but that just happened to be where they lived. It might just as easily have been the Waveney Valley. To quote author and pioneer of sustainable living John Seymour: 'If John Constable had been born at Harleston, instead of at East Bergholt, we would have processions of motor coaches along the Waveney instead of along the Stour'. As for modern-day local artists, perhaps Mary Newcomb (1922–2008) is the most representative for her innocent, yet evocative, vignettes of country life – not exclusively featuring the Waveney Valley but certainly evoking its spirit.

Several well-known writers are or have been based in the valley too. Roger Deakin, who used to live across the border in Suffolk, just south of Diss, chronicled the changes of the season in *Notes from Walnut Tree Farm* and to a lesser extent in *Wildwood*, while nature writer Richard Mabey moved to the area some years ago and his Waveney Valley home features prominently in his book *Nature Cure*. Louis *'Captain Corelli's Mandolin'* de Bernières has settled near Bungay, and W G Sebald in *The Rings of Saturn*, his meandering introspective walk through a rather sombre , and surprisingly depopulated, Suffolk, spent enough time in the Waveney Valley to be quite spectacularly rude about a small hotel in Harleston.

_i_ TOURIST INFORMATION

Beccles ⌂ visitbeccles.co.uk
Broads Authority ⌂ broads-authority.gov.uk
Bungay Tourist Information Point Bungay Library, Wharton St ✆ 01502 543442
⌂ visitbungay.co.uk
Diss 10 Nicholas St ✆ 01379 652241
Harleston Information Plus 8 Exchange St ✆ 01379 851917 ⌂ harleston-norfolk.org.uk

Like everywhere else, there's an element of reactionary nimbyism here on occasion – the greatest fears seemingly being the provision of caravan sites for travellers and wind-farms – but overall it's pretty welcoming and lacking the self-satisfaction sometimes found in more high-profile parts of the region. The key words here are probably 'self-contained' and 'authentic': real places with real shops serving real people. I begin by looking at Diss, the urban centre for the west of the valley, which exemplifies this outlook perfectly. As Britain's third appointed **Cittaslow** (Slow Town), it is a town that perfectly encapsulates the Waveney Valley's distinctive atmosphere and human pace of life. Diss and Beccles are about as urban as it gets here, which may give you some idea as to what to expect.

GETTING AROUND

Making your way along the Waveney Valley is easy enough. The main towns and villages are linked by the A143 that runs from Bury St Edmunds to Great Yarmouth. From its Suffolk beginning, the road crosses the county boundary at Diss and continues along the Norfolk side of the river as it heads towards the coast, apart from a brief detour into Bungay on the Suffolk bank. For those on four wheels, this makes a convenient way of speeding east or west, but it has to be said that the minor roads that thread through the valley are infinitely more enjoyable. Thankfully – and sensibly – the buses that run along the valley avoid the A143 for the most part, preferring to detour through the villages.

PUBLIC TRANSPORT

This could be better; there again, it could be worse. Diss has a regular train service to Norwich, as it lies on the main Norwich–London line.

Regular trains also run between Norwich and Lowestoft, which has a branch line to Beccles. Bus transport is reasonable enough in daylight hours, with buses running along most of the length of the valley. The Simonds ($\mathscr{O}$ 01379 647300 $\mathscr{O}$ simonds.co.uk) 581 service runs several times a day between Beccles and Diss via Bungay and Harleston during working hours, Monday to Saturday (excluding bank holidays), while the Borderbus 580 between Great Yarmouth and Beccles runs more or less hourly, with two buses a day continuing on to Harleston. The First service 40A/41/41A connects Norwich to Bungay with hourly buses during working hours, Monday to Saturday, while the First X2, X21 and X22 run regularly between Norwich and Beccles. Konectbus services 1 and 2 also connect Norwich and Diss several times a day, but not on Sundays.

RIVER CRAFT & CANOEING

Transport by boat is an option east of Geldeston, which is the limit of navigation for motor boats. Day boats are for hire at Beccles, Burgh St Peter and Oulton Broad and there is scope for canoeing too, although the river is noticeably tidal east of Beccles. A stretch for canoeing

FAMILY CANOEING CAPERS
Poppy Mathews

We are Poppy, John, Jamie (15) and Izzy (12) and we all enjoy canoeing.

The Broads are very busy with cruisers throughout the summer and we were keen to see if it was possible to hire Canadian canoes from the commercial boatyards and still find quiet places to paddle. In early June, John and I caught the train to Wroxham then walked through the moored yachts, gleaming in the early summer sunshine, until we found a little wooden shed that advertised canoe hire.

After paying for three hours, we set off, paddling rather nervously past the shiny hulls towering over us in the marina until we got out into the river. We went under a couple of bridges thronging with shoppers and cars, then upstream into what quickly became an oasis of quiet and calmness. For half of our allotted time we paddled quite steadily, interested in how far we could go without killing ourselves, but also wanting to appreciate the glorious day around us. After a quick stop for lunch, we turned around and headed back, noticing that it was quite a bit harder going back against the wind – or maybe we were just getting tired! In total, we paddled about five miles in three hours.

It was a lovely afternoon and we decided that we should do it again sometime, next time with the kids. Fast forward to the summer hols and, with packed lunch and swimming things, we caught the bus from recommended by the Upper Waveney Valley Project is the 20-mile section of the river between Brockdish, west of Harleston, and Ellingham Weir, east of Bungay. **Canoe hire** is possible at Bungay at Outney Meadow Caravan Park (01986 892338 outneymeadow. co.uk), Geldeston at Rowan Craft (01508 518208 rowancraft. co.uk) and Burgh St Peter at the Waveney River Centre. TheCanoeMan (thecanoeman.co.uk/beccles-hires) based at Beccles Lido also has canoes, kayaks and paddleboards for hire. Contact the Waveney Valley Canoe Club (waveneyvalleycanoeclub.org.uk) for further advice. A helpful guide to canoeing the Waveney is available for download from outneymeadow.co.uk.

WALKING

Some absolutely lovely walking is to be had, particularly by the river. Most villages lie close enough to one another for decent circular walks to be possible and with such quiet back roads even road walking is a pleasure. The Angles Way long-distance route threads its way along the valley between the Brecks and Lowestoft; eastwards from Beccles it

Norwich to Bungay on the River Waveney. We had phoned ahead and booked two canoes, so knew we had a great day ahead of us. After a quick chat about who was going with whom, we were off on our second canoe adventure of the summer. Jamie and Izzy led the way downstream, negotiating a couple of low bridges before we got out into open countryside where the river meandered elegantly through meadows with grazing cows.

The river is quite shallow and we played a game of trying to hit patches of reeds growing in the water with the canoe. Much enjoyment was had with lots of shrieking and laughing; not so good if any of your party was trying to spot water voles as John was.

There was a spot of portaging to do before reaching a mill pool overhung by willows, where we had a sandwich and a swim before heading back.

We paddled upstream past the launching place, with the river becoming much narrower and windy with overhanging branches. This was exciting and we felt as if we were paddling through mangroves. Early morning or evening canoeists have often seen otters in this stretch. We weren't lucky in this respect but were compensated with fine views of kingfishers flashing along the river and diving to catch fish.

Canoeing as a family was less tranquil than being on our own but it was more fun and we will certainly be doing it again.

follows the riverbank – the best option is to walk the nine miles from there to Oulton Broad South station and get the train back to Beccles.

CYCLING

If you want to make use of muscle power alone, there is plenty of potential for cycling in the Waveney Valley, although you will want to avoid the A143 wherever possible. Otherwise, there are lots of quiet country roads and tracks to explore. If needs be, you can hire a bike at Bungay at Outney Meadow Caravan Park and at Burgh St Peter in the Waveney River Centre (✆ 01502 677343 ⌂ waveneyrivercentre.co.uk).

DISS & AROUND

1 DISS

Dear Mary, yes, it will be bliss, to go with you by train to Diss.
John Betjeman in a letter to Mary Wilson

Diss is very much a town of two halves. The modern part of the town, east of the centre close to the A140, with its supermarkets, swimming pool, fitness centre and railway station, is pretty undistinguished and could be almost anywhere: passing through it on the way to the bus station by the park does not prepare you for what is to come. The bus station – just a small bus park with a shelter – lies on Park Road, a busy thoroughfare that has lorries thundering along it shaking the leaves from the trees. But cross the road into the park and walk past a pavilion down to the water and historic Diss will suddenly unveil itself in front of you – a far more appealing prospect.

Old Diss centres around a body of water, The Mere, a six-acre, spring-fed lake that gives the town its name, as *dice* in Anglo-Saxon means 'standing water' or words to that effect. Diss folk claim that this glacial remnant is at least 60ft deep, with about 20ft of water and 40ft of mud, so it is not a place to drop your keys. The common theory is that it was formed when the underlying chalk bedrock collapsed, an altogether more plausible theory than it being the mouth of an extinct volcano, as a few Diss residents still believe. The Mere was badly polluted in the 19th century, with high mercury levels brought about by local hatters and dyers making use of its water. Bizarrely, it was also around this time that The Mere was stocked with eels, which, according to

SLOW DISS

Diss, along with Aylsham, bears the distinction of being one of two Norfolk towns that belong to the **Cittaslow** movement. Diss became a Cittaslow in 2006 and its sense of community is actively promoted by **Diss Community Partnership**. Having helped Diss gain its Cittaslow status, the partnership has gone on to establish a film festival and a local history and art festival in the town, as well as setting up **Taste of Diss**, a festival of local food held in July. Taste of Diss has since been superseded by the **Diss & Harleston Food Festival**, which takes place in Harleston in September.

Fair Green is set apart from the rest of the old town but worth a detour. You can reach it by walking west along Park Road from the bus station and turning left at the roundabout. Once you round the corner, the contrast is extreme. Gone are the noisy lorries thundering along Park Road; you suddenly find yourself next to an idyllic village green with a café, a pub and a restaurant clustered around its eastern end. The trestle tables on the green itself are certainly inviting, the perfect place to sit whilst enjoying an early evening pint at The Cock, but if you keep going, you'll soon reach the bridge across the River Waveney, little more than a weed-strewn stream at this point. The green, which is surrounded by highly attractive 16th- and 17th-century houses, was granted a charter for a fair in 1185 and must have presented quite a sight back in the days when bear baiting and cock fighting were regarded as quite ordinary pursuits. The Cock Inn no doubt gets its name from such activities, as do many other 'Cock' pubs in the region. The fair was finally closed by Parliament in 1872, ostensibly because of its reputation for 'disorderly behaviour'. A fairground elephant is believed to be buried beneath the green.

some accounts, threw themselves from the water at every opportunity such was the level of pollution. Thankfully, it's clean enough to swim in these days, although this is expressly forbidden. Global warming being what it is, it is unlikely that there will ever be a repeat of the winter cricket matches and ice carnivals that were held on its frozen waters in the early 19th century.

A waterside path leads from the southern shore to what is usually referred to as **The Mere's Mouth**, where there is an information centre and the Diss Publishers Bookshop and Café, which as well as a selection of local books has café tables by the water. Quite likely, there will also be someone selling ice creams from the back of a Morris Traveller next to the town sign. It's a place to feed the ducks, lick an ice cream and have a 'mardle' (Norfolk-speak for leisurely chat) on market days. Formerly, this was the only part of The Mere that provided open access

SARA JOHNSON/ HARLESTON AND WAVENEY ART TRAIL

to the public, although now there is access to all of the southern side from the park where Diss's rebellious youth flaunt authority by riding their bikes in a no-cycling area – that's about as lawless as it gets. These days, there's an electric fountain in the middle of The Mere that spouts like a miniature version of Lake Geneva's Jet d'Eau.

Mere Street leads north from The Mere's Mouth up towards the marketplace past a few pubs, cafés and independent shops. There's a good showing of Tudor timber-framed buildings in addition to some fine red-brick Georgian and Victorian houses. Friday – market day – is definitely the day to be here, when the street is filled with locals shopping and socialising, and there is an almost Mediterranean feel of savoured conviviality. The market itself may be small but, unlike in much of clone-town Britain, it's still an important weekly event. It's all very traditional, with stallholders pitching their produce while the market-day chip van does good business, with an ever-lengthening line of hungry locals queuing for a large portion served in recycled squares of the *Daily Express*. As well as the weekly event, there's a farmers' market held here on the second Saturday of each month.

Diss Museum (✆ 01379 673613 ⬧ dissmuseum.co.uk ☉ Mon–Fri), located in a small building right at the top of the marketplace, is a community museum run by enthusiastic volunteers. As well as archive photos of the town and a 19th-century doll's house it has changing exhibitions about Diss and the surrounding villages, which in the past has featured Thomas Paine and John Betjeman, who both had connections with the town. There's a decent selection of secondhand books too: for 50p, I came away clutching a history of Diss Town FC and subsequently discovered that 7 May 1994 was the club's greatest hour: they beat Taunton FC 2–1 in extra time at Wembley to win the FA Vase – real 'Roy of the Rovers' stuff. Chatting with the volunteer on duty, I learned a little about local rivalries in this border town. 'They're a funny lot over there in Suffolk but it's mostly good-natured banter between us,' she said. 'Mind you, there's some old boys at The Cock at Fair Green who'll tell you about how they used to keep a close eye on those that came over the Palgrave bridge. There are all sorts of stories about how some used to lie in wait to attack Suffolk men coming over.'

◀ 1 A Konik pony at Lopham Fen. 2 View across The Mere towards Diss. 3 Kayaking the River Waveney. 4 Artist Sara Johnson's studio on the Harleston and Waveney Art Trail.

BLOOMING BRESSINGHAM

If you're a steam-engine fanatic, you might be interested in the collection at Bressingham Steam and Gardens (✆ 01379 686907 ⏚ bressingham.co.uk) on the road to Diss, which has endless rainbow beds of hardy perennials as well as a large collection of steam engines, a fire museum and a half-mile-long light railway. Alan Bloom, who must have felt a calling given his surname, created the gardens in 1961, and grandson Jason, who manages the nursery over the road, has kept up the family tradition.

We got talking about Fair Green itself – the meadow on the edge of town that was once the setting for medieval fairs and which is still used today for special events. 'If there is one thing that would make Diss people revolt it would be to try to develop Fair Green for new housing. It's an absolute no-no – the people would be up in arms.'

St Mary's Church dominates the marketplace, a fine 13th-century building in the Decorated style with a peaceful churchyard that has benches for market-day chip-eaters, town philosophers and courting couples. The unusual thing about this church is the processional archway through the base of the tower that allows religious processions to remain within the confines of the churchyard. If you have an interest in folklore, you might like to seek out the rather owl-like Green Man grimacing above the south porch. The church's most famous rector was John Skelton, who held the position here from 1504 until his death in 1529. Skelton, who had earlier served as tutor to the young Henry VIII and had been Poet Laureate of both Oxford and Cambridge universities, remains firmly in the number one place of the town's most illustrious citizens. A later Poet Laureate, John Betjeman, another admirer of the town, would become president of the Diss Society, a position of which he was immensely proud. The church puts on free monthly lunchtime concerts in summer and has a few stalls selling local produce at its church hall on Friday mornings.

"You might like to seek out the rather owl-like Green Man grimacing above the south porch."

Opposite the church stands the 16th-century **Dolphin House**, a striking black-and-white timbered building that has seen life as a wool merchant's house and a pub in the past. These days it houses various small businesses. If you continue north along Mount Street from

St Mary's you'll find more handsome Georgian houses lining a quiet street. If, instead, you head west along St Nicholas Street then you'll come to the **Corn Hall**, which like most such buildings in these parts is in the mid 19th-century neoclassical style. The days of cereal wheeling and dealing may be past but it is still an active place, with regular concerts, films and plays.

FOOD & DRINK

Cobb's Yard and **Norfolk House Yard** in St Nicholas Street have a number of tempting independent shops and cafés that include a wholefood shop, **Natural Foodstore**, run as a workers' co-operative (✆ 01379 651832 ⚭ nfs.coop), which is 100% organic and mostly vegan and has a good range of ethically sourced food and environmentally friendly products. There's also **Amandines** (✆ 01379 640449 ⚭ amandines.co.uk), a vegetarian and vegan café with a glass-covered courtyard that occasionally stages live music and theatre nights. If you are just looking for a coffee and a snack, there are several options along Mere Road. **Diss Publishers Bookshop and Café** (✆ 01379 644612 ⚭ disspublishing.co.uk) at number 41 has some tables outside overlooking The Mere, as does **Café Culture** (✆ 07552 330340) at number 11, by the marketplace further up. **The Saracens Head** (75 Mount St ✆ 01379 652853 ⚭ saracensheaddiss.co.uk), just behind the church, has standard pub grub and steaks. The options listed below are at Fair Green a little further away from the centre but really not that far.

Angel Café 1 Fair Green ✆ 01379 641163 ⚭ angelcafediss.co.uk. Rustic, friendly and low-key, the Angel Café serves up organic meals and snacks, with plenty of vegetarian options. It's also good for breakfasts, espresso coffee, homemade cakes and desserts.

Cock Inn Lower Denmark St, Fair Green ✆ 01379 643633 ⚭ cockinndiss.co.uk. With a decent selection of real ales and a great view over the green, this is a sound choice. Live music events on some Saturday nights.

2 REDGRAVE & LOPHAM FEN

West of Diss, the Waveney begins as a tiny trickle at Redgrave and Lopham Fen, very close to where the Little Ouse also rises. Dig a ditch between them and you have an island – Norfolk! The Fen, which covers 300 acres and is the largest surviving area of river valley fen in England, has been managed by the Suffolk Wildlife Trust (⚭ suffolkwildlifetrust. org/redgrave) for the past 50 years (although the reserve straddles both counties and the visitor centre is actually in Norfolk) and has an impressive cluster of designations as a wetland of national and international importance. It is also one of only two sites in the country that has native fen raft spiders, as well as being a prime habitat for dragonflies and butterflies, mammals like otters and pipistrelle bats, and a recorded 96 bird species.

Like the Norfolk Broads, the fen was traditionally used for reed and sedge cutting for thatching, as well as cattle grazing at its drier margins. Part of the Suffolk Wildlife Trust's management strategy is to use Hebridean sheep and Polish Konik ponies to control the vegetation. The black Hebridean sheep look strangely at home grazing here, as do the small grey ponies that thrive in the wet conditions. These all add to its atmosphere as quite a primeval place and the presence of the semi-aquatic raft spiders certainly fits in with this image. Arachnophobes should probably be aware that the fen raft spider is one of Britain's largest, although even here they are pretty scarce. I once spent a long time looking for them to no avail at one of the designated viewing pits but you may be luckier. There's a visitor centre (Low Common Rd, South Lopham ✐ 01379 687618) run by the Suffolk Wildlife Trust, and three dedicated nature trails. Be warned, the mosquitoes can be vicious here in summer, especially in the woodland areas – either lather up with Jungle Formula or similar, or wear long sleeves and trousers.

THE BURSTON STRIKE SCHOOL

The labourer must henceforth take his place industrially, socially and politically with the best and foremost of the land.

Tom Higdon, 1917

In brief, the story goes that Tom and Kitty Higdon were appointed as teachers at Burston School in 1911 after previously working for nine years at Wood Dalling in north Norfolk. The Higdons, who were Christian socialists, had complained about the poor conditions at the Dalling school and the frequent interruption of the children's education when recruited for farm work. Many of the farmers employing the children were also school managers and tensions mounted as a result of this, particularly as the Higdons had also encouraged local farm labourers to join trade unions. When matters came to a head, the Higdons were given the simple choice of dismissal or removal to a different school.

The couple were transferred to Burston, where they found conditions much the same: their complaints to the school managers, the chairman of whom was the local rector, created tensions here too. The pair were dismissed on fabricated charges of pupil abuse on April Fool's Day 1914 and, following their dismissal, 66 of the school's 72 pupils

If you come here, you can take a look at either or both of **South Lopham** and **Redgrave** villages. Both are pleasant places that have exactly what you expect: a pub, a church and (for the time being, anyway) a post office, and a green. Take your pick – Norfolk or Suffolk. Redgrave is slightly closer; South Lopham has the larger, older church with what Simon Jenkins describes as Norfolk's best Norman tower.

3 BURSTON

The village of Burston, a couple of miles north of Diss, is famous for its **Burston Strike School** and its teachers, Tom and Kitty Higdon, who kept the school going from 1914 until just after Tom Higdon's death in 1939 (see below). This was the longest strike in British history and a textbook case of Norfolk's radical tradition. Today, the school is a museum and a rallying point for the old guard of the political Left on the first weekend in September. The strike school **museum** (✆ 01379 677211) on the green has a fascinating photographic display and selection of newspaper cuttings, and an information booklet that has the picture of a Norfolk pig with the words: 'You may push me, You may shuv, But I'm hanged if I'll be druv, From Burston', which says all there is to say.

marched along Burston's 'candlestick' (a circular route around the village) carrying placards that bore messages like 'We Want Our Teachers Back'. Many parents refused to send their children to the official council school and, as a result, a separate 'strike' school was established.

The Burston Strike School began as little more than a tent on the village green but later moved to a carpenter's shop. There was considerable intimidation by local employers against the rebel parents and many workers were sacked or evicted from their tied cottages. The village rector, the Reverend Charles Tucker Eland, who believed that labourers should know their place in the social order, went as far as evicting poor families from church land. Fortunately, the labour shortage created by the onset of World War I worked to the advantage of the labourers. Money was raised by labour organisations such as the Agricultural Labourers' Union and the Railwaymen and, by 1917, there were sufficient funds to build a new schoolhouse. Both Sylvia Pankhurst and George Lansbury attended the opening ceremony in that same year. The school ran until 1939 when Tom Higdon died and the same modest building serves today as a museum of the strike school's history. There has been a rally organised by the TGWU held annually in the village since 1984, the 70th anniversary of the school's founding. It takes place on the first Sunday in September.

The annual rally takes place on the first Sunday in September. It's a colourful, upbeat affair with bunting and trade union banners alongside stalls selling snacks and the collected works of V I Lenin. Proceedings get fully under way after a march 'around the candlestick' that replicates the route taken by the schoolchildren on 1 April 1914. Then there are a few speeches and music. I have been here several times but individual rallies tend to blur into each another. I clearly remember seeing Dennis Skinner with shirt unbuttoned to his waist making a stirring, and very funny, speech on one occasion, and Tony Benn recounting the famous words of Thomas Paine from *Rights of Man*: 'My country is the world, my religion is to do good.' Billy Bragg did a short acoustic set on this occasion too, although I am sure that he has played here several times. After the hiatus of the Covid pandemic, the rally of 2022 seemed better attended than any other I could remember.

> *"It's a colourful, upbeat affair with bunting and trade union banners alongside stalls selling snacks and the collected works of V I Lenin."*

The Higdons lie buried side by side in the churchyard of St Mary's, which lost its tower back in the 18th century and was unceremoniously patched up with red brick. Now the church functions partially as a sort of school hall and is usually kept locked. It would be interesting to know what the Reverend Eland, the Higdons' nemesis, would make of this were he alive.

4 GISSING & 5 SHELFANGER

Heading north from Burston, the next village is **Gissing**, which also has a **St Mary's Church**, this one with a round tower and Norman doorway. There's an old hall with a medieval moat here, now a hotel and events centre, and a modern water tower too – both south Norfolk specialities. To the west, Shelfanger has the square-towered church of All Saint's, which was the site of a holy well in the medieval period. The village also has its **Lammas Meadows**, which stand on the side of the road to Diss forming a tract of land attached to several farms. These are a relic of a medieval open field system of farming and, according to tradition, cannot be cropped, although the various owners are permitted to cut hay after Lammas Day (1 August). I recall seeing them carpeted with wild orchids in early summer 30 or so years ago.

DISS TO BUNGAY

Take the A143 east of Diss and you'll soon end up in Harleston. It's better to take your time though, and explore the villages and footpaths that lead down to the water meadows. Even the local bus has the good sense to avoid the main road where it can and make a tour through the villages along the way.

There's something very ancient about the landscape in this part of the Waveney Valley and, beyond the moated medieval halls, thousand-year-old churches and ancient commons that dot the landscape, there is an underlying sense that the land has been cultivated here for millennia. This is more than an instinct: it has been demonstrated by Professor Tom Williamson from the University of East Anglia that the field system between Scole and Dickleburgh, a few miles north, is older than the Roman road that cuts diagonally across it and probably dates from the late Iron Age.

6 BROCKDISH

The Old Bike Shop (page 310)

Brockdish is a lovely little place in the valley just a few miles shy of Harleston. There's not much here other than a decent pub and a small antiques shop that seems to keep irregular hours. As part of a pattern that seems typical of small regional communities such as this, the village's highly regarded primary school closed down in 2016 due to low pupil numbers. Canoeists might want to note that this is the most upstream point along the Waveney where access to the water can be made. The entry point is at the foot of the common.

There are some good walks hereabouts: you could follow the Angles Way down to the river and cross to the south bank here, or follow it in the opposite direction where it climbs above the village before leading west towards Diss. The valley here, on the East Anglian scale of things at least, is impressive and the briefest of climbs up out of the village is rewarded by a view of the water meadows in the valley bottom that stretch east from here along the Waveney's northern bank. Across the river in Suffolk, there's another short but sharp incline and it's hard to think of anywhere else in the region where you are more aware of actually being in a valley. Granted, it's hardly south Wales but it's impressive after Broadland or the Fens.

7 HARLESTON

⌂ **Grove Barn** (page 310)

Harleston is the urban magnet for this stretch of the valley, although 'urban' is perhaps too big a word for a pleasant little market town. As with many places of this size, medieval fires saw to it that most of the town's earlier thatch and timber frames went up in flames so what remains today is mostly solid Georgian red brick with the odd Tudor survivor. Market day, still important to the town, is on Wednesdays. Although it might seem quite a traditional, old-fashioned sort of place, the town has an arty side too and serves as host to the **Harleston and Waveney Art Trail** (⌀ hwat.org.uk) that takes place over the last two weekends in May and opens up the studios of dozens of local artists to visitors. Most of the studios are within an eight-mile radius of Harleston and can be visited by bike, car or on foot. A guide to the current year's artists and a map can be downloaded from the HWAT website.

Harleston's most conspicuous landmark is the almost minaret-like clock tower on the marketplace that used to belong to St John's Chapel of Ease. The chapel was founded in the 14th century but was in a ruinous state by the 18th. A new church was built on Broad Street to replace it and the old chapel was demolished and replaced with a grocer's shop, which remains there today. Conspicuous by its absence, there is no medieval parish church to be seen in the town. The simple reason for this is that Harleston is part of the combined parish of Redenhall with Harleston and the parish church, St Mary's, a splendid 14th-century edifice with what seems an inordinately tall tower, lies in – or rather, towers over – Redenhall, the neighbouring village.

As with many agricultural towns in the region, there's a conspicuous Victorian corn exchange: a stark white neoclassical building that was opened for commerce in 1849 but which served as a local court in later years. Since its early days, when its walls must have resounded to the bargaining cries of Norfolk farmers, the building has been used as a skating rink, furniture market, dance hall and even a delicatessen and restaurant. In more recent times it has seen service as an antique centre with a 1940s-style tea room and a museum.

The marketplace, which tends to be on the sleepy side apart from Wednesday mornings, has another town landmark: the J D Young Hotel,

1 The market town of Harleston. **2** Outney Common grazing marshes. **3** Bungay town. ▶

originally known as **The Magpie Inn** – the original distinctive sign can still be seen – which has served as a coaching inn for centuries. Churchill and Eisenhower are reputed to have met here during World War II, presumably not over a pint. Just across from the hotel is a large Georgian house with two enormous sequoias that look as if they will burst out of the garden like slow-growing triffids in the next century or two. The town's other coaching inn is **The Swan** in The Thoroughfare, which was built by Robert Green, a conspirator in Kett's Rebellion who may have been rewarded with this property for snitching on his colleague – hardly the noblest of ways to get a start in the pub trade.

The Old Market Place, which no longer has a market, has Harleston's oldest building at number 18, an Elizabethan hall house that originally would have been jettied.

FOOD & DRINK

The Hungry Cat 25 The Thoroughfare ✎ 01379 308971. A vegan café and deli that has good coffee, a great choice of cakes and Mediterranean-influenced snacks and light meals.
Yakety Yak Tea Room 7B Bullock Fair Cl ✎ 01379 855484. A converted furniture shop that now serves as a 40s- and 50s-themed tea room with a choice of 18 different varieties of loose leaf tea and homemade cakes and scones.

8 MENDHAM (SUFFOLK)

Just across the Waveney from Harleston, in Suffolk, is the small village of Mendham. This was the birthplace of Sir Alfred Munnings, the East Anglian painter of horses and rural scenes and one-time president of the Royal Academy, whose father owned the mill just outside the village. Mendham is set in the river's flood valley amid lush water meadows and lines of poplars, and the village feels quite remote despite its proximity to Harleston. It's a quiet, dreamy place, with a church and a single pub that is called, appropriately, The Sir Alfred Munnings. The Angles Way passes through the village as it crosses into Norfolk and there's a footpath that leads across Mendham Marshes past the ruins of a Cluniac priory.

9 BUNGAY (SUFFOLK)

♠ **The Castle Inn** (page 310)

Your school geography lessons may have taught you that the ideal defensive site is either on a hill or in the meander of a river. This is East Anglia, so the first of these requirements is rather wishful thinking;

the second, however, is provided for perfectly at Bungay where the River Waveney coils like a flexing eel. It does have a hill of sorts too, and this is the site Hugh Bigod, the 1st Earl of Norfolk, chose for his castle in 1173, on high ground overlooking a meander. Hugh 'the Bold' Bigod was a fierce rival of Henry II but was forced to surrender his Bungay fortress to the king as a penalty for aligning himself with an insurrection led by Henry's rebellious sons. If it had succeeded he would have gained custody of Norwich Castle; the words at the start of this chapter record his regrets.

I can't quite make my mind up about which Waveney Valley town I like the best – Diss or Bungay (although I'm quite fond of Beccles too). Some days – especially on market days – Diss seems to be firm favourite, but at other times it's the latter that steals the show. Either way, Bungay is certainly a self-contained, likeable place that, with a castle, an independent theatre and a distinctive eccentric character, seems to punch well above its weight for somewhere so small. Over the years, it's been a centre for leather working, boat building and more recently printing, but it has always also been an important market town for the region.

As with most small towns in East Anglia, Bungay's heart is its marketplace. Central to this is the octagonal **Butter Cross** (also written as 'Buttercross') that has a lead figure of Justice with her scales on top of its cupola. Like many other settlements where medieval wood and thatch predominated, a serious fire spread through the old town in the late 17th century and Bungay's plentiful Georgian buildings reflect a post-1688 rebuild. There's a pleasing mix of architecture spread throughout the centre but **Bridge Street**, with its colourfully painted houses sloping steeply down towards the river, is particularly attractive. This is a street that seems to happily harbour some of Bungay's undeniable eccentricities too: take a look at the anarchic bric-a-brac shop with its back-yard chicken coops opposite the Chequers pub for a taste of what indifference to convention can do.

For a sense of Bungay's past it's worth visiting **Bungay Museum** (⊘ bungaymuseum.co.uk ⊘ end May–early Nov Sat & Sun) on the ground floor of the Town Hall on Broad Street. This recently refurbished museum, which is staffed by volunteers, has displays of prehistoric, Roman and Saxon artefacts from the area, as well as information on the history of the town's printing industry. On the other side of the road is

A Bungay loop – Bigod Way & Bath Hills

✳ OS Landranger maps 134 and 156; start: Butter Cross, Bungay ♀ TM336898; 5½ miles; moderate

Although this walk starts and ends in the Suffolk town of Bungay it spends most of its time across the county border in Norfolk. The route follows closely the meander of the River Waveney as it flows around Bungay. Although the river itself is out of view for much of the way, some of the higher sections of this walk offer lovely views over the grazing marshes of Outney Common.

From the Butter Cross, make your way along Earsham Street to follow it out of town, crossing the river over a bridge. Soon reaching a second bridge, take the footpath to the left that leads across fields. Reaching a footbridge, follow the track to the right that leads into Earsham village and, at All Saint's Church, joins the route of the Angles Way: follow the road to arrive at the busy A143 bypass. Cross carefully into Hall Road then, shortly afterwards, turn right along Bath Hills Road.

Follow the lane as it climbs gently above ponds left by old gravel workings. At Valley House, a little less than a mile along the road, continue through the woodland of Bath Hills to reach Wood House bungalow. Bear right here, following the Bigod Way sign through woods and fields until reaching the driveway that leads to Ditchingham Lodge, the former residence of writer Sir Henry Rider Haggard, author of *King Solomon's Mines* and *She*. Cross this and go through a gateway into woods before following the signposted footpath to the left that leads towards Ditchingham village, where Rider Haggard and his daughter Lilias are both buried at St Mary's church.

Arriving at the main road, turn right to reach the roundabout and the A143 bypass. Cross the roundabout to continue in the same direction and, keeping the old malting buildings on your left, follow Ditchingham Dam uphill through the outskirts of the town back into Bungay town centre. It is about a ten-minute walk from the roundabout to the town centre.

the **Fisher Theatre** (⊘ fishertheatre.org), a tiny theatre almost 200 years old that punches well above its weight in terms of the variety of music, film and theatre it stages.

Most of what you see now of **Bungay Castle** was actually constructed by Hugh's ancestor Roger Bigod at the end of the 13th century. Built with 16ft-thick flint walls and standing a lofty 108ft high – taller than the tower of the town's St Mary's church – it was considered impregnable in its time. Largely neglected after Roger Bigod died in the Crusades,

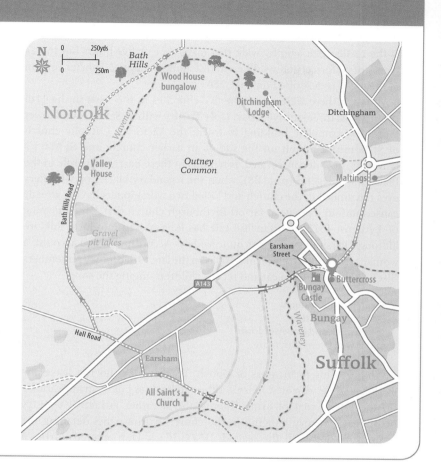

it passed through the hands of several owners before being declared, in a document of 1382, as being 'old, and ruinous, and worth nothing a year'. In 1483 it passed into the hands of the Howards, Dukes of Norfolk, who continued to own it, apart from brief periods, until the end of the 20th century when it came under the auspices of the Castle Trust. Today, there are two crumbling towers of the original gatehouse and some outer walls that you can visit. There's a café, Bigod's Kitchen, at the entrance, which has an interpretive model of the castle in its courtyard.

A good view across to Earsham on the other side of the Waveney Valley can be had from the elevated castle grounds. In celebration of its founder, the Bigod Way is a ten-mile loop around the town that starts and ends at the castle. It's a lengthy walk that takes four or five hours but there's plenty of historical and wildlife interest along the way. A shorter version of this walk is described on page 266.

Although there were said to be five churches in the town in the 11th century, just three survive today: **Holy Trinity** with its Saxon round tower, the oldest complete building in town; the Victorian Catholic church of **St Edmund's**, built on the site of an earlier church; and **St Mary's**. St Mary's, now deconsecrated, is famous in these parts for its role in the Black Shuck legend (page 88), when the legendary black dog with fiery eyes ran amuck in the church and killed two worshippers having already caused untold damage at far-off Blythburgh church that same morning of 4 August 1577. This fanciful tale has long passed into local folklore, although versions of it differ quite widely. According to one account, a woman who went to school in Bungay in the late 19th century remembers Black Shuck as being a cat and recalls children singing the song:

Scratch cat of Bungay
Hanging on the door
Take a stick and knock it down
And it won't come anymore.

Whatever his form, puss or pooch, Black Shuck did not leave any evidence of his visit at St Mary's, although he does put in an appearance on the town's coat of arms. There's also a rather attractive tapestry of Bungay's history hanging in the church with a panel detailing the rampaging dog with the legend, '1577: Black Dog entered during a fearful storm and two men died.'

Bungay is not all about castles and churches. With the River Waveney just a shadow of what it used to be, it is easy to overlook the importance that the river once held for the town. Once the lock at Geldeston was established in the late 17th century, and the river canalised, wherries were able to ship goods up here from the coast. Upper Olland Street in the town centre probably gets its name from a derivation of 'oak lands' and locally plentiful oak would have been used to build wherries in the Staithe area of the town. Indeed, William Brighton, builder of the *Albion* (page 118), used to work here, while the boat itself used to ply its trade between Bungay Staithe and the coast at Lowestoft. These days, Geldeston is as far as navigation goes for anything larger than a canoe.

For cycling, the Godric Way is a 24-mile route around Bungay that starts and ends at Butter Cross and passes through Ellingham, Broome, Ditchingham, Earsham, Denton, Alburgh, Homersfield, Mettingham and The Saints – all places in which a slow cycle through is worth a dozen drive-bys.

¶¶ FOOD & DRINK

Bigod's Kitchen 7 Castle Orchard ✆ **01986 896567** ⌂ bigodskitchen.com. To enter the castle grounds you need to walk through this café, so it's worth stopping for a drink or a bite as you do so. Good for cakes, snacks and lunches.

The Buttercross Tearooms 6 Cross St ✆ 01986 893002 ⌂ thebuttercrosstearooms.com. Just down from the Butter Cross on Cross Street, this is an unfussy but perfectly pleasant place for a snack, coffee or all-day breakfast. There's also a hidden garden with a pond for fine weather.

Earsham Street Café 11–13 Earsham St ✆ 01986 893103 ⌂ earshamstreetcafe.co.uk. Located in an attractive 17th-century building, this popular place is a little more upmarket than The Buttercross Tearooms and has a more adventurous menu. At the back is a courtyard garden where a cock-fighting pit once stood. Good for cakes and light meals as well as brunches at the weekend.

The Old Bank Vintage Tea Rooms 8 Market Pl ✆ 01986 894050 ⌂ theoldbanktearoom. co.uk. As its name suggests, this retro-styled place is located in a former bank building opposite the Butter Cross. A good choice for lunches, scones and three-tier afternoon teas.

BECCLES & THE LOWER WAVENEY VALLEY

10 GELDESTON

Halfway between Bungay and Beccles, just south of the main road on the Norfolk side of the border, Geldeston is a small attractive village with two pubs. One of these, the Wherry Inn, is in the village itself next to the green. The other, **The Locks Inn**, lies at the end of a narrow track right beside the River Waveney. This pub is closely linked to the historic navigation of the river, which was privately owned by coal, grain and malt merchants between the 16th and 18th century. Wherries would pass through here as they hauled goods between Great Yarmouth, Lowestoft and Bungay.

The building that is now the The Locks Inn started life as a mill-keeper's cottage and later served as a dwelling for the lockkeeper before becoming an inn in the 17th century. Given its isolated location on the Norfolk–Suffolk border, the inn became a popular haunt for cross-border smugglers and an ideal setting for illegal prize fights. These days, things are more tranquil. After the pub was put up for auction at short notice in 2020, it was purchased by members of the local community who set themselves up as a Community Benefit Society. With 1,400 shareholders the pub now has the widest ownership of any pub in the country. Geldeston Locks marks the limit of navigation for boats. There is a footbridge across the river to the Suffolk bank here from where the Angles Way may be joined. A footpath runs along the north bank to Geldeston from Beccles – a lovely walk – and there's even a regular boat service from Beccles Lido (page 272).

The river around Geldeston Locks makes for near-perfect canoeing, especially west of the bridge in the Bungay direction – kingfishers and otters are distinctly possible sightings. For details of canoe hire, see page 251. It is a paddle of three hours or more to and from Beccles and one hour or less from Geldeston village to the Locks.

East of Geldeston, the river is wide enough for navigation as it meanders north to merge with the River Yare at Breydon Water, although the low bridge at Beccles deters many hire boats and larger craft from sailing west of the town. This, of course, has considerable effect on the river's character, which morphs from sleepy tranquil backwater to busy thoroughfare – in summer at least – within a matter of miles. The county line itself follows the river faithfully until it branches off to the coast near Herringfleet towards a point more or less midway between Great Yarmouth and Lowestoft.

FOOD & DRINK

The Locks Inn Locks Lane ✆ 01508 518414 🖑 thelocksinn.com. An isolated, traditional pub, now community-owned (page 269), with a sunny garden right by the River Waveney. Decent pub food made with locally sourced ingredients, a good choice of real ales, regular folk music events, and occasional Morris dancing.

Wherry Inn 7 The Street ✆ 01508 518371 🖑 wherryinn.co.uk. A traditional village pub with a range of Adnams beers and a seasonal menu of light bites, burgers and pub grub favourites.

◀ **1** The Locks Inn, Geldeston. **2** Church of St Mary the Virgin, Burgh St Peter. **3** Beccles.

11 BECCLES (SUFFOLK)

The largest town in the valley, Beccles is a pleasant and attractive town but a place that many tend to pass through rather than spend any time in. The town is solidly Georgian as its timbered Tudor core was destroyed by a succession of ravaging fires. The river used to have far more significance to town life than it does now, but this was once a flourishing port with many wherries passing by. Herrings from the coast used to be an important commodity here and, in the medieval period, Beccles annually provided tens of thousands of the fish to the monks at Bury St Edmunds.

Boats still have a part to play, as Beccles is the most southerly point on the Broads system. The river here is not quite as hectic in summer as the Bure and Thurne but it's busy enough. There's some good walking on the Beccles Marshes close to the town and also along the north bank of the River Waveney to Geldeston Locks where there is a pub (page 271). There is also a regular **boat service** to Geldeston Locks, the Big Dog Ferry (𝒶 07532 072761 𝒶 bigdogferry.co.uk), which runs from Beccles Lido between Easter and October. The ferry also drops off at Geldeston Marina with access to the Wherry Inn.

¶¶ FOOD & DRINK

Beccles Farmers' Market Beccles Old Heliport 𝒶 becclesfarmersmarket.co.uk. Has around 30 stalls on the first and third Saturday of the month.

Garden Tea Rooms 4 The Walk 𝒶 01502 712631. Go through a discount shop to arrive at a bright pink dining room and a garden beyond. This small café has the usual cakes, scones, snacks and breakfasts.

Waveney House Hotel Puddingmoor 𝒶 01502 712270 𝒶 waveneyhousehotel.co.uk. With a pleasant terrace right next to the river, the Riverside Bar offers a good varied menu for lunch and dinner.

12 'THE TRIANGLE' & BURGH ST PETER

⚓ Waveney River Centre (page 310)

The Waveney turns back on itself at Oulton Dyke, where there is a channel leading through to Oulton Broad and Lowestoft. To the west of the river, tucked away inland almost equidistant between the Waveney and the Yare, are the somewhat isolated villages of **Wheatacre**, **Aldeby**, where there is a priory, and **Burgh St Peter**, which looks across the river to the Carlton Marshes Nature Reserve on the Suffolk side of the river.

The parishes of these three villages make up an area known locally as '**The Triangle**' – as they are bound on two sides by a bend of the River Waveney and on the third side by the now defunct Beccles to Great Yarmouth railway. This triangle of land has something of the feel of an island about it, with a genuine sense of isolation despite its crow's-flight proximity to Beccles and Lowestoft. There is no through road here nor any bridge across the river, just a single-track road that links the farmsteads that lie on the higher ground above a large area of marshland and the river beyond.

Lovely views extend over the marshes but otherwise there's not so much to see other than the odd-looking **church of St Mary the Virgin** in Burgh St Peter, which has a strange five-section tower shaped like a ziggurat or, as some have fancied, even a collapsible square telescope. The body of the church dates from the 13th century but the tower is a late 18th-century replacement for an earlier one; its curious form is supposed to have been based on a Mesopotamian ziggurat seen by William Boycott, the rector's son, on his travels.

There was, in fact, a whole dynasty of Boycotts serving as rectors at the church for a continuous period of 135 years. It was Captain Charles Cunningham Boycott, the son of the second Boycott rector, who, serving as an Irish estate agent, first introduced the word 'boycott' into the English language when he suffered social ostracism for refusing to reduce rents.

Close to the church is the **Waveney River Centre** (⌀ 01502 677343 ⌀ waveneyrivercentre.co.uk), which, in addition to a variety of accommodation options, a pub, a shop and an indoor swimming pool, has canoes for hire. There's also a regular foot ferry across the river to Carlton Marshes Nature Reserve on the Suffolk bank, where there are plenty of trails to follow as well as access to the Angles Way long-distance path. Lowestoft is really not that far away but you would never guess it given the tranquillity of the marshes here.

13 RAVENINGHAM

Between Beccles and Loddon, just south of the B1136 that leads off the A146 towards Haddiscoe, is the 5,500-acre Raveningham Estate. The main attraction here is **Raveningham Gardens** (⌀ raveningham. com/garden), which contain a walled kitchen garden, late 19th-century glasshouses and an arboretum established in the wake of the 1987 gale.

There's also a herb garden, a rose garden and a 'Time Garden' whose design is influenced by the essays on the passage of time by Sir Francis Bacon. The Bacon family have owned the estate since 1735.

The **Raveningham Centre**, close to Raveningham Park, is a range of converted Victorian farm buildings that contain various craft outlets, secondhand clothes emporia and a café. A number of arts and crafts workshops like pottery, drawing and lino printing take place here throughout the year under the guidance of local artist Sarah Cannell (⌂ sarahcannell.com). In 2017, the centre took over as the base for the annual summer **Waveney Valley Sculpture Trail** organised by Waveney & Blyth Arts. This now takes place under the curatorship of Sarah Cannell and is a Creative Odyssey CIC project that aims to bring creative communities together in various ways, under the name of the **Raveningham Sculpture Trail** (⌂ raveninghamsculpturetrail.com) features site-specific work from a number of established artists and includes bronze sculpture, textiles, ceramics and sound installations. The trail circles through three acres of mixed woodland before returning to the starting point, close to the charmingly rustic Raveningham Centre buildings. For the past few years there has also been a **Woodland Lumiere** held here over three weeks in late winter, a spectacle that guides visitors along the same trail to experience all manner of light and sound installations, which includes fire sculptures and projected images on the wall of the farmhouse.

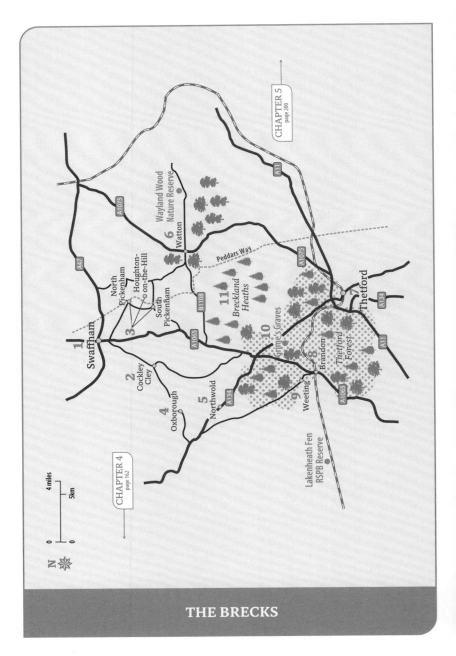

THE BRECKS

7
THE BRECKS

This chapter covers the region known as the Brecks, the western part of Norfolk that lies between Swaffham in the north and Thetford in the south. Both towns have historical interest well beyond what one might expect. Thetford was home to the monarchs of East Anglia and the seat of a bishopric; it was also the birthplace of that staunch anti-monarchist Thomas Paine. Swaffham is an old-fashioned market town in the shadow of a lofty wind turbine. As a discrete region, the Brecks reaches well into Suffolk across the border. Of the five market towns that belong to the Brecks area – Swaffham, Watton, Thetford, Mildenhall and Brandon, the last two are in Suffolk. Although this chapter will deal mostly with the Norfolk part of the Brecks there are occasional detours across the county boundary.

Although the Brecks borders the pancake-flat region of the Fens, it really could not be more different. The Brecks, in contrast to the fertile black soil found in the Fens, has light, sandy soil that is far less ideal for intensive farming. The word 'breck' comes from a word that means land that becomes quickly exhausted. It's the closest thing that Britain has to a desert, as the rainfall is the lowest in the country, summer temperatures can be among the highest, and winter frosts the hardest. The sand that covers the chalk was originally wind-blown, but trees have since been planted to stabilise the soil. Back in the days before such enlightened ideas, when large estates sought to maximise their profits by introducing sheep, the sand blew freely around causing untold damage, depleting thin topsoil in one place and covering up fertile land in another.

"Although the Brecks borders the pancake-flat region of the Fens, it really could not be more different."

Naturally, what is a shortcoming today was actually a boon in the distant past. In Neolithic times, Britain's very first farmers were drawn to the region because its light soil was easy to work with their limited stone tools, and because there was no dense forest needing to be cleared with nothing other than brute strength and a hand axe. The region had a plentiful supply of flint too, the machine steel of the Stone Age.

With careful farming, the Brecks became reasonably prosperous and **Thetford**, its capital, became an important regional capital in the Anglo-Saxon period. It was later, in the medieval period, when the real damage was done. Sheep were introduced to the land in large numbers and allowed to roam freely, overgrazing and damaging the soil with their hooves. In north Norfolk, sheep may have brought fortune to some but here they just heralded disaster. The Brecks became increasingly depopulated as a result – the area is still sparsely populated today – and rabbits and pheasants became the land's only bounty.

The vast **Thetford Forest**, flanking the A11 around Thetford itself, is a recent innovation, planted by the Forestry Commission after World War I to provide a strategic reserve of timber. Much of what is not forest goes to make up the **Stanford Battle Area**, established in 1942, where the Army practise manoeuvres and test ordnance. Vast stands of Scots and Corsican pine may be what most people immediately associate with the Brecks these days but it is a very recent trend. Step back just a hundred years in time and you would see only sandy heath, gorse and rabbits – lots of rabbits. It almost goes without saying that this is a part of East Anglia that many speed through without stopping. Consequently, it is not as well known as perhaps it deserves to be. Outside the few towns, the Brecks' distinctive habitat is a prized haven for wildlife: it is home to several species of plant, insect, bird and mammal that are found almost nowhere else in the country.

GETTING AROUND

PUBLIC TRANSPORT

This is far from wonderful. Swaffham no longer has a functioning railway, but Thetford stands on the Norwich to Cambridge rail line and has a regular **rail service** to both cities – almost hourly during the day. Trains to Ely link with national services north and south.

Bus services run from Norwich to Swaffham and Thetford. There's the useful X1 service run by First in Suffolk & Norfolk, half-hourly through most of the day, which connects Swaffham with King's Lynn and

ℹ TOURIST INFORMATION

Brecks Partnership website ⊘ brecks.org
Swaffham Town Museum, 4 London St ✆ 01760 722255 ⊘ aroundswaffham.co.uk
Thetford Belmont House, 20 King St ✆ 01842 751975 ⊘ leapinghare.org
Watton Wayland Visitor Centre, Wayland House, High St ✆ 01953 880212
⊘ visitwayland.co.uk

Peterborough to the west and Norwich, Great Yarmouth and Lowestoft to the east. Local services also run from all three main towns to outlying villages. Although regular buses run between Thetford and Bury St Edmunds there are none between Thetford and Swaffham; for this, you will need to travel via Norwich, Watton or King's Lynn, a long detour.

WALKING

Most will probably want to rely on their own two legs though, and there's some excellent walking to be had. The obvious choice for long-distance hikers is, of course, the **Peddars Way**, an ancient route that is now a designated National Trail. It begins at Knettishall Heath near the Norfolk–Suffolk border close to Thetford and strides irrepressibly north–northwest until it reaches the Wash at Holme-next-the-Sea. It is perfectly feasible to do short sections of this, and some of its most interesting stretches actually lie within the Brecks. The route is waymarked with acorn motifs and very easy to follow, though its sheer straightness can make the going a tad monotonous at times.

Other **long-distance routes** are **Angles Way** (Thetford to Great Yarmouth via the Waveney valley; 93 miles), **Iceni Way** (Knettishall Heath to Holme-next-the-Sea via Brandon and the Fens; 83 miles), **Hereward Way** (Thetford to Rutland via Peterborough, Ely and Brandon; 110 miles) and the **Little Ouse Path**, a ten-mile meander along the Little Ouse valley.

You can walk anywhere you like on Forestry Commission land and numerous circular walks are waymarked from all the main parking areas. A good choice of short forest trails begin at High Lodge Forestry Centre. Harling Drove between Roudham Heath and Bromehill at Weeting is a good option for a longer, ten-mile walk right through the heart of the forest. Further suggestions for shorter walks are made in the appropriate places in this chapter.

HORSERIDING

Horseriders have free access on all Forestry Commission freehold land. The Peddars Way is bridleway for most of its course, and other possibilities include the Swaffham Bridle Route and the ten-mile-long Hockwold-cum-Wilton Bridle Route.

CYCLING

Given a general lack of traffic and quiet roads, the Brecks have plenty of potential for cycling. Thetford Forest has lots of off-road choices too. For those who want to go further afield, Sustrans National Cycle Route 13 (𝒫 0845 1130065 ⊘ sustrans.org.uk) connects Thetford and Watton with National Cycle Route 1.

The Brecks Cycling Discovery Route is an interesting 20-mile circular route (with a possible ten-mile short cut), centred on Swaffham, that links the wind turbine, Cockley Cley Nature Reserve, Oxburgh Hall, Beachamwell and Gooderstone Water Gardens. There is also a 21-mile Swaffham Bridle Route around the town that makes use of tracks and minor roads.

You can buy a cycling pack that details five easy routes in the Brecks suitable for family cycling from tourist information centres and elsewhere. These routes tend to be theme-based, for instance a Pingoland Explorer Trail and a Flint-Hunters' Explorer Trail.

Thetford Forest Park has three waymarked forest trails of varying difficulty that start from the High Lodge Forest Centre, where bike hire is also available at Bike Art (𝒫 01842 810090 ⊘ bikearthire.cc). Information on these routes can also be found at ⊘ forestryengland.uk. Harling Drove is a fairly long easy route through the heart of Thetford Forest and is suitable for both cyclists and walkers.

For more suggestions in the area, ⊘ cycle.travel/city/swaffham shows several suggested rides of different lengths that start in **Swaffham**: an 11-mile route that loops up to Castle Acre; a 27-mile option to the southeast that passes through North Pickenham, Watton, Thompson, Merton and South Pickering; and a more demanding 43-mile circular route south through Thetford Forest to Brandon. There's scope to abandon two wheels for four legs in the region too and the potential for riding is probably the best in East Anglia.

1 Cycling through Thetford Forest Park. 2 Paddleboarding the River Ouse, Thetford. ▶

FORESTRY ENGLAND

DAWN QUADLING/S

SWAFFHAM & AROUND

1 SWAFFHAM

Swaffham is something of a perfect example of an old-fashioned market town, with all the necessary ingredients: a market square, handsome Georgian houses, a leisurely rhythm and little evidence of the more boorish trappings of modern life. Having said that, Swaffham has its rough edges too and there is certainly more to it than a just a quaint country town frozen in time. Sitting midway between King's Lynn and East Dereham, Fakenham and Thetford, the town has long served as the regional centre for the farming country hereabouts. It lies within the Brecks but only just, located at that region's northern edge. In the 18th and early 19th centuries the town became a fashionable social centre for the gentry and even became known as the 'Montpelier of England', such was its elegance and the reputation of its healthy, dry air. Wealthy farmers would come here with their families in season for dancing and racing. At some stage in its history, hare-coursing was invented here. William E Johns of Biggles fame lived here before World War I.

Swaffham life centres on its **marketplace** where a market is held each Saturday, a tradition that has been going on for over 800 years. Author and self-sufficiency pioneer John Seymour claimed it to be 'one of the excellent surviving old markets where you can buy a secondhand washing machine, a dozen white rabbits, or a goat'. He was writing back in the late 1960s, and things have changed a little, but not that much – it's still thriving, although you might have trouble finding a goat these days. There's a handsome array of Regency buildings neatly arranged around this commercial wedge with its central Butter Cross, a neoclassical dome mounted on pillars, with a statue of the Roman grain goddess Ceres on top, an apposite choice for this arable region. Facing the marketplace, the Italianate red-brick 1858

"Wealthy farmers would come here with their families in season for dancing and racing."

Cornhall – now the location for a well-known coffee chain – has more arable allusions, with a round panel containing a wheat sheaf on its gable. Many of the surrounding buildings are Georgian, the most noteworthy being the 1817 **Assembly Rooms**, home to an indoor market on Fridays with stalls selling all manner of wholesome homemade goods, as well as vintage jewellery and other miscellaneous things.

Among other less grand but cheerfully quirky buildings are the old post office, just off the marketplace on Lynn Street, with its tiny conical tower that serves no obvious useful purpose and handsome Victorian brick lettering above its door.

Swaffham's appeal lies in its detail and mix. Although several of the major supermarkets have a base here there are still an encouraging number of independent shops selling household goods, groceries, hardware and haircuts, while a gent's hairdresser on the square advertises itself with a traditional barber pole and a large wooden sign that takes up half the window stating 'The Town Barber'. Swaffham's more cosmopolitan than first appears and boasts a Lithuanian shop, Indian and Chinese takeaways and even a Russian restaurant called 'Rasputin's' – 'the first in Norfolk' – a strange name for a place to eat perhaps (but then I do recall seeing a 'Lady Di' restaurant in Azerbaijan).

A short distance from the marketplace you'll find the 15th-century **church of St Peter and St Paul** with a splendid hammerbeam roof adorned with 88 carved angels flying in formation. The churchyard itself is a peaceful green haven that seems as if it should belong to a tiny village rather than the centre of a market town. It's worth the teeniest of detours to take a look at the wooden angels inside and perhaps wonder what an untutored medieval peasant might have made of them as they sat there on a Sunday. For a congregation mostly made up of farm workers that rarely travelled far beyond the parish of their birth the local church would almost inevitably be the most remarkable sight they would ever witness. The church's wooden benches have medieval carvings that include the so-called '**Swaffham Pedlar**' – the merchant John Chapman, who also features on the well-known Swaffham town sign. The story behind this is that Chapman, following an impulse to seek his fortune in London, is told by a stranger on London Bridge that he should return home and look under a tree there to find his treasure. Eventually he returns home to find a pot of gold in his own garden. Whatever the truth behind this tale, John Chapman was certainly a generous benefactor of the church, most likely just a wealthy merchant who made his money in the time-honoured way.

'The Pedlar of Swaffham' town sign is the handiwork of Harry Carter, former art teacher at Hammond's High School, who is also the talent behind many other north Norfolk carved village signs. Harry Carter's uncle was Howard Carter, the eminent Egyptologist who discovered the tomb of Tutankhamun and, rather fancifully, is rumoured to have died as the result of the boy-king's 'curse'. Harry Carter's sign is at a corner of the marketplace in a flower bed opposite the old school gates, while an exhibition of Howard Carter's 1922 quest in Egypt's Valley of the Kings can be seen in **Swaffham Museum** (✆ 01760 721230 🖥 swaffhammuseum.co.uk), which also has a gift shop and doubles as the tourist information centre.

Standing outside the door of the museum and looking towards the marketplace you may suddenly become aware of a large white rotor blade slicing up the air above Ceres on the Butter Cross, an astonishing juxtaposition of classical tradition, medieval commerce and the modern green technology of wind-power generation. Modern credibility came to the town with the establishment of this back in 1998, its enormous wind turbine looming next to the A47 giving the impression of blowing speeding King's Lynn-bound motorists further westwards. (There's a local joke that the wind turbines in the Wash do their bit to dissipate global warming by cooling the land with their fanning action.) For many years it was possible to climb 300 steps up a spiral staircase to reach the Norman Foster–designed observation deck at the top and enjoy the panoramic view. Known as the Green Britain Centre, it was, in fact, the only wind turbine in the world that was open to the public. Sadly, a change of ownership in 2018 resulted in the access being suddenly terminated as it was considered to be unprofitable – despite receiving a recorded 22,000 visitors just the year before.

🍴 FOOD & DRINK

A **farmers' market** is held in Swaffham marketplace on the second Saturday of each month (🕐 09.00–14.00), alongside the regular Saturday market that takes place in the town.

Swaffham's marketplace has several cafés and pubs, although most of the latter seem to cater for aficionados of widescreen TV. The **Pedlars Hall Café** (✆ 07387 802587) may well be half-timbered but its interior might best be described as 'down to earth'; certainly, it's unpretentious. By the Butter Cross itself is the **Market Cross Coffee Bar** (✆ 01760 33671) with outdoor tables, while through the arch at the pedestrianised thoroughfare of Plowright Place you'll find the **The Teapot Café** (✆ 07926 952295), again with both inside and outside tables.

Ceres Book and Coffee Shop 20 London St ✆ 01760 722504 🖥 ceresbookshopswaffham. co.uk 🕐 bookshop: Mon–Sat; coffee shop Tue–Sat. This excellent independent bookshop selling new and secondhand books, maps and guides also serves coffee and homemade cakes in its charming three-table backroom café.

The Station Bar Station Rd ✆ 01760 722300 🖥 thestationbar.co.uk. A traditional no-frills pub, popular with locals, that is a good choice for a Sunday lunch roast. There's a beer garden round the back for warmer days and a log fire inside for the winter months.

2 COCKLEY CLEY & AROUND

As you leave Swaffham to the southwest through bungalow-filled outskirts, the Breckland scenery starts quickly to become apparent, with twisted stands of Scots pine shading the verges and large open fields of barley and sugar beet before the forest beyond. The first village you reach is Cockley Cley, a small place that is home to a reconstructed Iceni Village (more low-budget theme park than museum).

Just west of Cockley Cley, **Beachamwell** has the church of St Mary's with its Saxon round tower topped by an octagonal belfry. The church, which has pride of place on a large village green, is the last survivor of four churches that used to serve the area in more populous medieval times when there were two parishes here – Bicham and Wella. 'Last survivor' is perhaps rather ironic as, tragically, the church suffered serious damage in a fire in 2022 and lost its thatched roof. If you take a walk from the village armed with the appropriate OS map (✳ Landranger 143) you can see the visible remains of some of the others. Just south of Beachamwell, All Saints' Church was abandoned in the 17th century and all that remains today are fragments of flint walls. More complete is St John's Church northwest of the village, which still has a standing square tower – an evocative sight in a field full of horses.

When I visited Beachamwell some years ago, I parked my car in the lay-by in front of the village hall. No sooner had I switched the engine off when an elderly woman with a concerned look on her face approached me. 'Excuse me. Are you going to park there? The thing is, the post office van will be coming soon and he'll need to park here as it's the only place in the village he can get a signal.' Sure enough, the post office van arrived a minute or two later and I nudged forwards so it could squeeze in behind me. It turned out that the van was doing the rounds of the north Brecks villages and being pension day a mobile signal was necessary to work the computer so that the villagers could get their allowance. An interesting juxtaposition of modern technology and old-fashioned community spirit, I thought.

GEOGPHOTOS/A

MATT GIBSON/S

WIRESTOCK CREATORS/S

An earthwork just north of Beachamwell – the Devil's Dyke – is believed to be a Saxon territorial boundary. Other earthworks of this type turn up elsewhere in southwest Norfolk, such as west of Garboldisham between Thetford and Diss, as well as in the northeast of the county near Horning. **Barton Bendish**, a little further west, has two churches, St Mary's and St Andrew's. The parish used to have three, but the church of All Saints' was pulled down in the 18th century for material to patch up St Mary's Church and for repairing roads. There seems to be a plethora of St Mary's churches in this part of the county.

FOOD & DRINK

Twenty Churchwardens Cockley Cley ✆ 01760 721439. Close to All Saints' Church in the village; the name refers to a type of clay pipe rather than the pub's clientele. This used to be a school and it has only been a pub since 1968. Adnams and other real ales are served alongside straightforward, homemade food that includes some tasty pies.

3 THE PICKENHAMS & HOUGHTON-ON-THE-HILL
Å Spring Farm (page 310)

Just east of Swaffham, on the route of the Peddars Way and next to the banks of the River Wissey, are North and South Pickenham. **South Pickenham** has All Saints, a lovely little round tower church with a very rural feel to it. You can find five round towers within a nine-mile radius of here: at South Pickenham, Merton, Watton, Threxton and Rockland. Pickenham Hall is central to the village, a large turn-of-the-century edifice that stands out very much as the local squire's abode.

The restored **St Mary's Church** (⌂ houghtonstmarys.co.uk ⊙ late Mar–late Oct 14.00–16.00 daily; late Oct–late March 14.00–16.00 Sat & Sun) at nearby **Houghton-on-the-Hill** is little more than a five-minute detour for Peddars Way walkers and a worthy expedition in its own right too. The church has become quite well known for its wall murals but is equally famous for its remarkable restoration story, the work for the most part of just one man. The church has been painstakingly restored thanks to the efforts of Bob Davey, a retired engineer from North Pickenham. He first began work on what was an ivy-covered, semi-derelict ruin back in 1987, when it had been abandoned since the 1930s.

◀ 1 Cockley Cley is home to a reconstructed Iceni Village. 2 Oxburgh Hall. 3 The 'Swaffham Pedlar' in the church of St Peter and St Paul.

By 1993, thanks to Bob's interest and hard work, it had attained Grade I listed status. This involved far more than simply physical renovation. When he first discovered the church, it was being used for black magic rituals and the Satanist congregation were none too keen on Bob's renewed interest in their ceremonial centre (Satanists had been reported here back in 1968 by a frightened walker who had accidentally stumbled upon them). Almost single-handedly, Bob stood up to what he considered a desecration of the church and continually tried to bar the Satanists' entry, despite death threats and curses that were hurled his way. Pragmatically, he did go on to recruit a burly Territorial Army unit to lie in wait for the Satanists one night, and this surprise ambush seemed to drive them away for good, although the threats continued for a while. Since then, the church has been re-blessed and used for occasional non-denominational services – it had never actually been deconsecrated. There's no doubt that St Mary's has had

A VISIT TO ST MARY'S, HOUGHTON-ON-THE-HILL

Some years ago I walked up here on a hot summer's afternoon to be greeted by Pam, one of Bob Davey's enthusiastic helpers, who showed me around and explained the murals using an artist's impression of what they may have looked like in their original, complete form. Pam pointed out the details on *The Last Judgement*, in which the virtuous rose to heaven while sinners had to undergo torment by little red devils.

'The idea was to scare the locals into leading good lives.' The drawings are cartoon-like, not especially skilled but endearing, with figures that have the moonish faces and big eyes of Byzantine frescoes. *Adam and Eve in the Garden of Eden* portrays Eve as a much larger figure than Adam, which leads me to mutter something about this being a pre-Renaissance lack of understanding about perspective. 'Yes possibly, but Bob thinks this

just may be the way that women were revered back in those times. Most men got killed one way or another when they were still young. Women generally lived longer and were more important than we might give credit for.'

Bob himself came over to speak, a twinkle-eyed octogenarian in a bright yellow shirt with a flowing snowy beard. He handed me some leaflets on the church before telling me, 'We haven't had a chance to print it yet but this all needs updating a bit I'm afraid. We've got some new dates now and everything's a bit earlier than it says in the booklet.' He went on: 'Originally there was a Roman spa up here – it's a natural aquifer – and there's quite a lot of recycled Roman brick in the nave. There was a wooden church here first that was dedicated to St Felix and we've found some evidence of that. Then they added a flint chancel in the 7th century and a round tower in the 13th century more than its fair share of problems over the years. During World War I, a returning Zeppelin dumped its bombs in the churchyard damaging the building and in the 1930s it lost all of its parishioners when the neighbouring village of Houghton was finally deserted. The indignity of Satanistic worship came with the second half of the 20th century, and to cap all of this, thieves stole lead from the newly replaced roof in 2007. For good measure, it is also supposed to be haunted by a couple of Carmelite monks.

Bob – later to become Bob Davey MBE – passed away in 2021 aged 91. A dedicated support group, the Friends of St Mary's, is now responsible for the work and activities here. There is now also a beautiful garden in what was once an overgrown churchyard. The hamlet that once stood near here was known as **Houghton Town**, but the church and a few farm buildings are all that now remain. The last villagers left in 1936, evicted by a squire who wanted to turn his arable land over to the more

but that fell down, so they put up one of those fashionable square towers instead.'

Since interest in St Mary's, and especially the wall paintings, has taken off, there has been a constant stream of experts coming to offer their opinions about the church's history. With so many axes to grind, it is hardly surprising that sparks have flown on occasions. Opinions vary but the nave that stands today may be anything between late Saxon to early Norman in origin. As for the murals, estimates favour the 11th century or, as Bob himself thought, perhaps even earlier. It is undoubtedly a complex sequence, but a church in some form or other has stood here since Anglo-Saxon times. The murals are faded and partial but, having been buried beneath later medieval wall paintings and Victorian plaster for centuries, it is quite remarkable that they have survived at all,

especially as they were exposed without a roof for many years. Spend a little time contemplating the paintings and savouring the atmosphere of this remote place and you may feel that you are getting some rare insight into what the world would have looked like to Anglo-Saxons at the dawn of the second millennium. It is certainly a special place. After being ticked off by Pam for standing too long, and being told to sit down, Bob went on to tell me something of his television appearances – he has become quite a celebrity in the world of church restoration. The BBC had wanted to do a re-enactment of the time when a Satanist tried to run him over with a car. 'They had to do about six takes for that one,' he tells me, chuckling mischievously. 'I had to keep jumping out of the way of this car until they got the camera angles right.'

profitable use of shooting for game. The last of the surviving cottages were bulldozed in 1994. Look carefully and you may be able to make out a few bumps in the fields to the north – the ghostly remnants of what was once a community.

North Pickenham, the village to the north, has St Andrew's as its parish church, a much grander affair than little St Mary's. Just west of the village is an old airfield that used to be RAF North Pickenham, which served as an American B-24 Liberator bomber base during World War II. This became a base for nuclear missiles in the late 1950s and 60s and a focus for early CND (Campaign for Nuclear Disarmament) protests. The planes and missiles are long gone now and these days the airbase provides the site for a karting circuit, a wind farm and a Bernard Matthews turkey farm, which according to the *Guinness Book of Records* is the world's largest, producing one million birds annually.

4 OXBOROUGH

🏠 **Bedingfeld Arms** (page 310) 🏠 **Honey Pots** (page 310)

Oxborough is only a tiny village but it is also the location of **Oxburgh Hall** – note the different spelling – a splendid Tudor country house. Even without the Tudor hall, the village is interesting for the **church of St John the Evangelist**, with its adjoining Tudor Bedingfeld Chapel, endowed by Sir Edmund Bedingfeld and containing the terracotta tombs of Sir Edmund and his wife. This was no exercise in humility: terracotta may be commonplace today but it was considered ultra chic in Tudor times. The main church building, just outside the walls of the house, has a ruinous demeanour thanks to its spire collapsing in 1948. The nave was ruined by the incident but the chancel, south chapel and north aisle managed to escape damage.

Oxburgh Hall

Oxborough PE33 9PS ✐ 01366 328258 ⊙ April–Oct daily; Nov–Mar Sat & Sun; National Trust

This is an undeniably lovely building. Its location is very special too, in fertile farmland on the edge of both the Fens and the Brecks. With turrets and crenellations, intricate brickwork, tall chimneypots and a surrounding moat, it is pretty much the ideal of the perfect stately home. The Bedingfelds built the place in 1482, obtaining a charter for a fortified building from Edward IV, but despite its turrets and crenellations, it has always served as an ancestral home and never as a castle. As both Catholics and Royalists in Protestant East Anglia, the Bedingfelds tended to find themselves caught between two stones: Rome and the English crown. Their position was precarious, but they managed to survive and even became prosperous once more during the Restoration. The hall passed into the hands of the National Trust in 1952.

Just up the road from Oxborough is the neighbouring village of **Gooderstone** with its Gooderstone Water Gardens ($\mathscr{O}$ 01603 712913 $\mathscr{\partial}$ gooderstonewatergardens.co.uk), with six acres of ponds, waterways and nature trails connected by footbridges.

¶¶ FOOD & DRINK

Bedingfeld Arms Oxborough $\mathscr{O}$ 01366 328300 $\mathscr{\partial}$ bedingfeldarms.co.uk. Originally an estate coach house, this pub with rooms close to the entrance and car park for Oxburgh Hall has a beer garden for summer drinking and a log fire for cold winter days. The emphasis is on seasonal, locally sourced food with their own herd of Aberdeen Angus providing the beef, plus lamb and venison from nearby Foulden Latimer Estates, and fish from Coles of King's Lynn. There's also a choice of cask ales and a comprehensive wine list.

THE BRECK–FEN BORDER COUNTRY, & INTO THE BRECKS PROPER

Continuing due south from Oxborough you enter a borderland where the Brecks meets the Fens. Some have gone so far as to describe this as a coastline, which is not so fanciful when you ponder that not so very long ago most of the Fens were underwater. It's a marvellous area, explored by few outsiders, that has all the wide horizons and enormous skies you might expect. Although it's a long way from the traditional notion of 'hilly', it can almost seem as if you can see halfway across England as the land dips down west into Fenland and lays out a tapestry of fields filled with corn, barley and beet. Among a clutch of notable villages here, Northwold is one of the finest.

5 NORTHWOLD

🏠 **Garden House** (page 310)

This long linear village comes as an unexpected delight when you first stumble across it after a long, confusing meander south from Oxborough. With bee-buzzing gardens of hollyhocks and roses lining the road, and walls sporting a diverse array of brick, carrstone, chalk and flint, it's a place that might genuinely fit into the clichéd category of 'best-kept secret'. If this were on the north coast it would be full of holiday homes, with a delicatessen and a stream of motorists passing by. Thankfully, it's refreshingly ungentrified – there's just an active pub and a post office/shop – and the road is mercifully quiet.

There's a lovely church here too. St Andrew's Church is best known for its Easter Sepulchre in the chancel, largely made from chalk, which has a relief of Roman soldiers skulking in an olive grove. Being chalk, it's soft and was easily damaged by marauding Puritans who came this way in the mid 17th century; nevertheless, it's easy enough to make out the detail. The hammerbeam roof is likely to draw your eyes upwards before you even reach the chancel as it's painted sky blue, as are the pipes of the

"This long linear village comes as an unexpected delight when you first stumble across it."

organ – the same colour as the bunches of delphiniums that filled the church when I visited. There had just been a flower festival to celebrate 900 years of the Ely diocese and the air was redolent with the cloying scent of lilies. 'That'll be quite a job clearing up that lot,' the cheery churchwarden told me. 'There's a wedding coming up so we'll be getting in some fresh blooms.' They do like their flowers in Northwold.

Methwold, the neighbouring Breck–Fen border village, is quite a bit bigger, almost a small town, and has a church with a steeple that can be seen from afar. Head west from here to Methwold Hythe and then climb up the road south towards Feltwell and you really get off the beaten track with vast views west across the Methwold Dens and south to the giant satellite-tracking 'golf-ball' domes at RAF Feltwell.

6 WAYLAND WOOD & WATTON

Just south of the workaday market town of Watton, Wayland Wood is where the nursery tale of Babes in the Wood has its origins, based upon a 16th-century legend in which a pair of orphaned children were taken to the wood to be killed by two men in the pay of a wicked uncle who lived at Griston Hall. With a twinge of conscience, one of the hired men decided to kill his accomplice instead and, instead of killing them, left the children to their fate in the wood. The legend has it that the brother and sister perished and that they still haunt the wood to this day.

ENGLISH WHISKY FROM ST GEORGE'S

St George's Distillery, Harling Rd, Roudham, nr East Harling NR16 2QW ✆ 01953 717939
⌨ englishwhisky.co.uk

'English Whisky' might sound almost oxymoronic to some ears, particularly Scottish ones, but in the distant past whisky was widely distilled on both sides of Hadrian's Wall. Although the practice lapsed south of the border a long time ago, St George's Distillery at Roudham near East Harling has turned history on its head by becoming the first place to brew whisky in England for over a century.

The location, a little way east of Thetford on the edge of the Brecks, might at first seem an odd choice, but it does makes sense geographically. Whisky requires two principal ingredients – barley and water – and the first of these is available in profusion in grain-growing south Norfolk. The second ingredient is perhaps less plentiful – this is, after all, one of the driest parts of Great Britain.

Fortunately there is a ready supply of pure, clean water available from deep below the ground in an underground aquifer.

At St George's the operation is small enough in scale for both cask-filling and bottling to be done individually by hand. Small-scale or not, since the original distillation back in 2006 many thousands of casks have been produced, and many more are still maturing. The first release, limited to 2,694 bottles, was made in 2009, and several different peated and non-peated bottles have been released since then. In addition to fine single malts, fruit-flavoured liqueurs like Norfolk Bramble, Norfolk Quince, Sloe Liqueur and Norfolk Nog are also made.

St George's has an on-site shop and tours (£20) of the distillery are available at 11.00, 12.30 and 14.00 daily.

Fortunately, the printed version, first published as the ballad *The Norfolk Tragedy* by Thomas Millington in Norwich in 1595, has an altogether happier ending in which the siblings find their way home. The village signs of both Watton and nearby Griston contain representations of the 'babes'.

The wood's name seemingly refers to the 'Babes in the Wood' legend, as Wayland is most likely a corruption of 'wailing'. However, rather than the ghostly moans of abandoned children, you are far more likely to be soothed by the contented buzzing of bees and chirruping of birds. Wayland Wood is in the hands of the Norfolk Wildlife Trust these days and is a gorgeous place in late spring when the bird cherry is in bloom and the ground is carpeted with bluebells and early purple orchids.

This is a real live chunk of rare ancient woodland and the spirit of the wildwood looms large here. Wayland Wood has probably stood since the

SOME HISTORY

As a strategic crossing point where the Icknield Way crosses the Little Ouse River, Thetford takes its name from the Anglo-Saxon *Theod* ford – people's ford. Whether or not it was the royal seat of Boudica, the Iceni queen, is highly uncertain but it was certainly an important centre during the late Iron Age and early Roman period. In Anglo-Saxon times, when it was sacked on several occasions by invading Danes, Thetford became the home of the East Anglian monarchs and seat of a bishopric. A more peaceful Dane, Canute, made the town his capital too in 1015, half a century before the Norman Conquest, when Bishop Herbert de Losinga's building of a cathedral in Norwich brought about a slight downsizing of what had become the sixth largest city in England. Despite the religious focus being transferred to Norwich, a Cluniac priory was established here in the 12th century that lasted until the Reformation.

Like much of the Brecks, Thetford saw a decline in its fortunes in the medieval period when the bulk of the wool trade shifted to north Norfolk where there was better land and closer ports. The town came back into favour in the 1960s when an influx of people from London moved here to work in the newly opened factories. These days, Thetford has a surprisingly large Portuguese population, which in 2011 was estimated to constitute around 30% of the town's total. Not surprisingly this has declined markedly since Brexit, although current figures are unavailable. There had been a slow trickle of foreign workers here since the late 1990s when Portuguese migrants started to come to the town to take up low-paid jobs in the agricultural and food-processing sector. Many Portuguese have chosen to settle here long-term, hence the number of Portuguese-language signs on shops, cafés and even hairdressers.

It is a similar situation in nearby Brandon, in King's Lynn, Great Yarmouth and, to a lesser extent, East Dereham. Polish is another language you will hear widely spoken around town and keen linguists might detect Russian, Lithuanian, Slovakian and Spanish too.

last Ice Age; it's a dappled, mysterious place but, unlike some woods that have a slightly dark and foreboding atmosphere, this one feels light and benevolent. Nevertheless, there used to be a large oak tree here, struck by lightning in 1879, that was rumoured to have been the place where the abandoned children died. The wood is far from completely wild but has been carefully managed since time immemorial to yield hazel rods by coppicing. Indeed, it is the long-term practice of coppicing that has enabled such wonderful ground flora to thrive.

As well as Griston Hall, where the wicked uncle is said to have resided, the nearby village of **Griston** is home to Wayland Prison, a category-C establishment that has included Jeffrey Archer and Reggie Kray among its inmates, although not at the same time.

Nearby **Watton** was host to a large RAF base for many years, which both stimulated the local economy and created a distinct atmosphere in the town. These days it seems somewhat gloomy and the constant parade of thundering goods lorries along the High Street make the town a little hard to love. Nevertheless, its traffic-ravaged main thoroughfare is home to a really good antiquarian bookshop – J C Books (✆ 01953 883488) at number 55 – and the friendliest of cafés – Adem's (✆ 01953 884838) at number 37. The town's most prominent 17th-century clock tower, also on the High Street, was put up in 1679 to house a fire warning bell (there had been a serious fire here a few years earlier). The lower part of the clock tower was also once used as a lock-up for prisoners, which gives new meaning to the expression 'doing time'. The Wednesday market has been taking place in the same spot since the 13th century.

7 THETFORD

Raced past by motorists on their way up the A11 to Norwich and the coast, and long dismissed as little more than a 'London overspill town', Thetford tends to get overlooked. Like King's Lynn and Great Yarmouth, it can seem a bit run down compared with the rest of the county and, true, it does have some large and unlovely housing and industrial estates that were built for an influx of workers from the south in the 1960s. This is just part of the picture though. Thetford was hugely important before the Norman invasion and even held the bishopric of East Anglia before Norwich did. In historical terms, Norwich is still the young pretender. Ignore the lacklustre outskirts and head straight to the centre and you will find some lovely medieval architecture and absorbing history.

Beyond the humdrum shopping precinct just across the river from Thetford Grammar School, the town centre has a good assortment of medieval and Georgian buildings in timber and flint. The best of these is the **Ancient House**, now the **Museum of Thetford Life** (✆ 01842 752599 ⬧ museums.norfolk.gov.uk), in a 15th-century timber-framed building on White Hart Street. As well as exhibitions on Thomas Paine and Maharajah Duleep Singh, the museum has 4th-century gold and silver jewellery from the so-called Thetford Treasure hoard discovered in 1979: an object lesson to those who think that putting in long hours with a metal detector is inevitably a waste of time.

Further down White Hart Street is the **Church of St Peter's**, the so-called 'Black Church' because of the dark knapped flint used in the

DAD'S ARMY
MUSEUM

chequerboard patterning on its tower. One of three surviving medieval churches in the town, it has been empty since 2008 but has been earmarked for refurbishment and future use as an educational centre.

The stonework of the town's Norman castle is long gone but the motte remains to provide a satisfying mound to climb up and get a view over the town. There is rather more to see at the site of the **Cluniac priory** west of the centre by the river. This was founded in 1103–04 by Richard Bigod to become one of the largest and richest priories in East Anglia. The priory was torn down after the Dissolution but there are still some impressive flinty remains and even bits of original tile flooring in places. The towering remains of the arch of the massive Presbytery window are particularly striking and give a real sense of the scale of the original building.

"The towering remains of the arch of the massive Presbytery window are particularly striking."

Nearby, **Thetford Grammar School** dates back to Saxon times, was re-founded in 1566 and is still active today. Its most famous ex-pupil is Thomas Paine (1737–1809), who had the distinction of being involved in both the French Revolution (where he only escaped execution by a whisker) and the American War of Independence; he was one of the original signatories to the Declaration of Independence and invented the term 'United States of America'. Born in the town, he attended the school between 1744 and 1749 before going on to be apprenticed to his father as a corset maker. The part of the school that Paine would have attended serves as the school library today and, although you cannot enter, you can get a look at this through its wrought-iron gate on Bridge Street.

Adjoining St Peter's church, just around the corner on King Street, are the council offices at **King's House**. Paine's gilt **statue** by Sir Charles Wheeler, President of the Royal Academy, stands outside, with the radical thinker clutching a copy of his revolutionary book *Rights of Man* upside down. Why he holds the book upside down is open to some speculation, although it is generally believed that Wheeler did this as a means of stimulating debate. The statue was erected by an American benefactor, Joseph Lewis, who was shocked to discover that

◀ **1** Wayland Wood. **2** Cluniac Priory, Thetford. **3** The Little Ouse River running through Thetford. **4** Dad's Army Museum, Thetford.

THOMAS PAINE:
CORSET MAKER & REVOLUTIONARY

My country is the world, my religion is to do good.

Rights of Man

Chad Goodwin of the Thomas Paine Society, a font of knowledge regarding all things relating to the man, led walking tours of Paine's Thetford during the bicentennial celebrations of 2009. Standing by the statue in front of the Town Council building, he filled us in on details of his early life before we moved around the corner to White Hart Street where the Ancient House is. 'This used to be the main London to Norwich road and anyone and everyone who came through Thetford would pass this way. Thetford assizes used to be held here each year and this was the next best thing to a public holiday, with all sorts of entertainment going on and, naturally, public hangings. They used to hang somebody for simply stealing a sheep in those days and it was probably partly from seeing the goings on here that Paine started to develop his social conscience and sense of injustice. Thetford was a classic rotten borough and I am sure that later on when Paine wrote about the corruption of the political class he was probably thinking of Thetford. Reading between the lines, I get the impression that he couldn't wait to leave.'

We walked uphill to the Thomas Paine Hotel, where a plaque commemorates Paine. 'This used to be a private residence known as Grey Gables. There are those who think that it is where Paine was born but there's nothing certain about this. It could have been here, or perhaps it was a place called the Wilderness next to St Andrew's Church. Unfortunately, there is no record of his birth at all.' Paine spent just a fraction of his early life in Thetford, and returned to the town only on rare occasions to see his mother once he moved south. 'It's worth noting that Paine left Thetford with its River Ouse, Cluniac monastery and round tower church to go and settle in Lewes in Sussex, which coincidentally also has a River Ouse, a Cluniac monastery and a round tower church. You could say this was just coincidence but Paine must have felt quite at home there.'

After receiving an invitation from Benjamin Franklin, Paine crossed the sea to America but he was rarely still for long, frequently flitting across the Channel to France and even crossing the Atlantic a total of five times in his lifetime. He died and was buried at New Rochelle in New York State in 1809. One of his former adversaries, William Cobbett, who had been gradually converted, partially at least, to Paine's cause, turned up ten years later to dig up his bones and bring them back to Britain for a heroic burial that never happened. 'Cobbett carried the bones around with him when he was fighting a by-election at Coventry. This may not have been considered bizarre in those days, but it was certainly unusual.' By all accounts, Cobbett kept Paine's mortal remains in a box underneath his bed but following his death they disappeared completely, never to be found again.

the birthplace of one of the great supporters of American independence did not have a monument to his memory. Naturally, there was some controversy regarding the erection of the statue as Paine was a freethinker and deeply republican. To their credit though, most natives of Thetford have since taken Paine to their hearts and seem happy to celebrate their connection with this extraordinary man. The statue, which may not be to everyone's taste, stands on a plinth that bears the legend: *World Citizen – Englishman by Birth, French Citizen by Decree, American by Adoption*. The Leaping Hare (🖰 leapinghare.org) shop at Belmont House on King Street can provide leaflets for a self-guided **Thomas Paine Trail** through the town. There are also occasional guided tours that can be booked at the shop.

Tom Paine aside, Thetford's other associations include the TV series *Dad's Army*, much of which was recorded in and around the town. A Dad's Army tourist trail highlights spots that became the fictitious Sussex town of Walmington-on-Sea. In 2010 the Thetford Society erected a bronze statue of Captain Mainwaring (the Arthur Lowe character) seated on a bench next to the River Ouse by the bus station. There's a Dad's Army museum (🖉 07470 165795 🖰 dadsarmythetford. org.uk ⊙ 10.00–15.00 Sat, plus Aug 10.00–13.00 Sun) at the back of the Guildhall on Cage Lane, and you can see Jones's butcher's van from the series at the nearby **Charles Burrell Museum** (🖉 01842 751166 🖰 charlesburrellmuseum.org.uk ⊙ closed in winter) on Minstergate. *Dad's Army* connections aside, the museum houses a collection of machinery built by Charles Burrell & Son, who were builders of steam traction engines and agricultural machinery, and were Thetford's main employer until the business closed in 1928.

Nearby, and reached by means of a footbridge, **Maharajah Duleep Singh**, the former squire of the nearby Elveden Estate a little further down the A11 in Suffolk, has a very fine equestrian statue set among the shady willows of Butten Island in the midst of the Little Ouse River. This memorial statue is a popular pilgrimage place for Sikhs from all over Britain and beyond and you may well find yourself becoming involved in a friendly photo session here. The town's three statues – 18th-century revolutionary pamphleteer, 19th-century Anglophile maharajah and 20th-century pompous sitcom character – make for a strange juxtaposition: one cannot help but wonder what the characters would have made of each other.

A Little Ouse walk

Outside the town, some good walks are to be had around Thetford. The most obvious route is along the **Little Ouse Path** that links Thetford with Brandon, most of which follows an old towpath. It's about ten miles of easy walking in total and if you are up to this you could walk all the way then catch a bus or train back from Brandon. A slightly shorter, circular option is to walk west and north along the Little Ouse from Thetford, past a tempting picnic spot at Abbey Heath Weir, and through waterside woodland as far as a large factory. Soon after a footbridge over the river you can zigzag south through forest until you reach a waymarked path to the left, leading you back to the river and a footbridge at Abbey Heath Weir from where you can retrace your steps to Thetford.

Even if you walk just a short distance along the river path past the abbey ruins you get a sense of being in open countryside despite the proximity of the town's council estates. A group of otters caused quite a stir down here a few years ago when they displayed themselves freely to visitors and even posed for photographs in a most un-otter-like way.

FOOD & DRINK

Bell Hotel King St ✆ 01842 754455. This 15th-century inn, right in the heart of town, was where the *Dad's Army* cast and crew used to stay. The hotel, now part of a national chain, tends to make the most of this association as well as its reputation for being haunted but serves decent enough pub food and Greene King ales.

The Mulberry 11 Raymond St ✆ 01842 824122 ⌂ mulberrythetford.co.uk. A cut — actually, several cuts — above all of the town's other dining options, this tastefully decorated restaurant offers a sumptuous Mediterranean and English menu that makes excellent use of locally sourced ingredients.

Tall Orders 22–24 King St ✆ 01842 766435. This conveniently located café in the town centre has seating on several levels including tables outside — a decent enough choice for coffee, cakes, breakfasts and sandwiches.

8 BRANDON (SUFFOLK)

Just over the border into Suffolk, and west of Thetford on the southern bank of the Little Ouse, is Brandon. If the presence of nearby Grimes Graves is not enough to attest that the town was once central to an important flint industry, then just take a look at the buildings. Many of the Victorian houses down Thetford Road are built of the black flint typical to the area, and many of the town's modern buildings also feature flint in their construction. The flint trade was big business in this area as far back as the Neolithic period and returned to prominence with the invention of the musket and the need for gun flints. It is interesting to reflect that, given the area's USAF and RAF bases, the war industry has long played a part in the region.

Brandon's flintknappers had their work cut out back in Napoleonic times when the town grew quite prosperous through supplying the essential parts for the British Army's muzzle-loaders. Virtually all the shots fired at Waterloo would have involved Brandon flint to spark them off. Apparently far superior to any that the French troops had at their disposal, it is said that a single Brandon flint was good for dozens of shots, in contrast to the few a French flint would last for. The invention of the percussion cap saw the demise of this trade but, according to John Seymour, flintknappers were still active in the town in the 1960s, when he witnessed men in leather aprons chipping away in the back yard of the Flintknappers Arms pub – where else indeed? The 1960s would, in fact, have been at the very tail end of the industry, when the only demand would have been from replica gun aficionados. The very last of the Brandon flintknappers hung up their hammer for good in 1975.

You can get a good idea of the town's flintknapping past by visiting the **Brandon Heritage Centre** (✆ 07882 891022) in George Street, which has several displays on the industry as well as the original deeds of the Brandon Flint Company, written on scrolled vellum and kept in a wooden box, and a lengthy list of all the flintknappers that lived and worked in the town from the 19th century onwards.

The town's other main industry was the production of rabbit furs for the hat trade, a lucrative business in the late 18th and 19th centuries and an industry that gave the town a notorious and unenviable aroma back in the day. Initially the pelts were obtained from the extensive rabbit warrens that used to characterise this part of the Brecks but the demand for fur eventually became so great that rabbit skins had to be imported from Australia and New Zealand in order to provide an adequate supply for the Brandon factories.

The Little Ouse River used to be of far more importance here back in the days when Brandon served as the port for nearby Thetford. These days, forestry rules supreme and it is articulated lorries and the A11, not boats and water, that provide the means of transportation and distribution for Brandon's produce.

Brandon Country Park, a mile or so south of the town, has forest walks, a tree and history trail, an orienteering course and a visitor centre with a café (✆ 01284 757088). About the same distance to the east, along the B1107 to Thetford, is the **Thetford Forest and High Lodge Forest Centre** (✆ 03000 674401 ⬚ forestryengland.uk/high-lodge), which has a café, toilets, a children's play area and an information point. Four waymarked walks of varying length explore the forest area from the car park, and the four cycling routes include a family route as well as more challenging mountain-bike rides. Cycle hire is available from Bike Art (page 280). Activities such as archery lessons, adventure golf and bushcraft courses can be pre-booked on the website.

9 WEETING

Weeting is a village just north of Brandon back over the Norfolk border. A Norfolk Wildlife Trust **nature reserve** here, just west of the village, is home to a summer population of stone curlews, which might be described as the signature bird of the Brecks – a stocky wader that doesn't wade, with thick strong legs and a large, yellow gimlet eye. It looks the kind of exotic thing that you might expect to come across on parched African plains and, indeed, the Senegal thicknee is a very close relation. The Brecks are, after all, the closest thing we have to African savanna, and birds like stone curlews just emphasise this exoticism. The NWT reserve has a visitor centre (✆ 01842 827615) and hides with wheelchair access open between April and September, the breeding season of the stone curlew. You might also see woodlarks here, another Breckland speciality, as well as wheatears, hobbies and plenty of butterflies. Interestingly rabbits, often vilified for the damage they do to crops, are actually encouraged here to keep the heathland habitat in check and accordingly are fenced in. The prisoners seem content enough – more *Watership Down* than *Colditz*.

The village itself has a round tower church, **St Mary's**, alongside an evocatively ruined Norman **castle**. It is also home to what is considered to be the longest terrace of **thatched-roof cottages** in England – I counted eight chimney pots in total. Unfortunately, many of the roofs

1 Brandon Country Park. 2 The dimpled landscape of Grime's Graves. 3 A stone curlew, the signature bird of the Brecks. 4 The longest row of thatched-roof cottages in England can be found in Weeting. ▶

were damaged in a fire in 2007 but they seem to have been neatly repaired to their former reedy glory now. The castle, owned by English Heritage and with free access, is not, in fact, a castle at all but a 12th-century fortified **manor house** with a 14th-century moat. On one corner of the moat stands a domed ice-house, previously used to store ice broken from the frozen moat in winter.

10 GRIME'S GRAVES

Near Lynford IP26 5DE ✆ 01842 810656 ⊙ Apr–Oct 10.00–17.00 daily; English Heritage
🏠 **Acer Lodge** Mundford (page 310)

If the Peddars Way can be described as being a Roman period M1, then Grime's Graves might be seen as being the equivalent of a Neolithic Sheffield. The 'graves' referred to are actually mine shafts and they belong not to Grime but to Grim, a pagan god. Anglo-Saxons probably knew the site as 'the Devil's holes' because any earlier human working of the landscape was usually viewed to be the work of dark forces.

The product here was that Neolithic equivalent of steel – flint – the hard, sharp-edge fracturing stone that litters the fields of the area. The black flint extracted from the pits here was of much higher quality than frost-damaged field flint and, generally speaking, the deeper down it was mined the better the quality. The site consists of a large complex of flint mineshafts that were worked between about 2600 and 2200BC, and also during a later period between about 2000 and 1500BC as flint was always more plentiful and easier to extract in comparison to metal, and continued to be used to make tools well into the Bronze Age. Even after hand axes had long disappeared from the craftspeople's and farmer's toolkit, good-quality flint was still in demand for building, and later for the firing mechanism for muskets.

"The complex is certainly impressive on the ground but aerial photographs give an even more compelling view."

Grime's Graves can be found a little way east of Weeting, down a long track off the Mundford road. The complex is certainly impressive on the ground but aerial photographs give an even more compelling view of this dimpled landscape of over 400 filled-in shafts covering an area of over 90 acres. Contrary to what you might think on seeing such a large expanse of pits, what went on here was never industrial scale in the modern sense: it is probable that only one or two pits were worked at any given time and throughout the site's active life probably no more than a few dozen individuals were involved in the labour together.

Thirty or so pits have been excavated to date and you can actually go down one of them, the only place in the country where you can do this. By descending the ladder and peering into the extremely low-roofed galleries you really get a feel for what life must have been like working on the Neolithic flint-face. Bear in mind that Neolithic miners had only red-deer antlers available for picks and had to work in cramped and extremely low light conditions. Excavation has revealed that, for each pit examined to date, an average of 142 antler picks has been found. Interestingly, about 10% of these were left-handed. A herd of at least a hundred red deer would have been necessary to provide an adequate supply of antlers for excavation.

11 THE BRECKLAND HEATHS

Just north of Thetford is the vast expanse of heathland occupied by the **Stanford Military Training Area** marked on OS maps somewhat alarmingly as 'Danger Area'. For obvious reasons, you are not allowed to go here, although limited access is permitted for walkers passing through on the Peddars Way that runs across its eastern edge. It is a shame in a

TURNING THE STONE AT GREAT HOCKHAM

Lying just east of the A1075, close to the expanse of Breckland heaths north of Thetford, is Great Hockham, a pleasant village with little to recommend it other than the unusual stone that has pride of place on its village green. The large sandstone boulder, an erratic mass from the Lower Cretaceous that was deposited in the Brecks during the last glacial period, was actually discovered in a pit close to the village in the 1800s before it was dragged by horses to its current resting place.

It soon became village practice to turn the stone over on special occasions – no mean feat given its bulk and weight, an estimated 2 tons. The first recorded turning was to celebrate Queen Victoria's Golden Jubilee in 1887. In more recent times it was turned over for Queen Elizabeth's Silver Jubilee in 1977, and again in 1995 to celebrate the half-century anniversary of the end of World War II. The millennium was another occasion that was celebrated appropriately with some community heavy lifting, as was Queen Elizabeth II's Golden Jubilee in 2002, the Diamond Jubilee in 2012 and the Platinum Jubilee in 2022. The stone has been turned to celebrate more local events too: in 2008 it was turned to celebrate the saving of nearby Holkham Woods from quarrying.

way because, apart from the odd tank and artillery unit, this is mostly unspoiled heathland with all its usual attendant wildlife. Naturally, the very fact that the public are not permitted to trample across the area means that it is pretty good for wildlife anyway, at least those species that are able to tolerate the odd exploding shell and spurt of mortar fire.

In my capacity as a surveyor of historic farm buildings 35 years or so ago, I did manage to visit the area once with a military escort. There used to be a number of farms dotting the area and we were interested in taking a look. Unfortunately, the army had used most of the buildings for target practice and so there wasn't very much to see, but it was good at least to witness what a wild and unspoiled area this was. The area continues to be used for military training of all sorts; during the time of the British Army's deployment in Afghanistan, a facsimile Afghan village was constructed here for training purposes. This came complete with flat-roofed adobe houses, a mosque and a street market. The roles of Afghan villagers, friend and foe alike, were played by injured Gurkhas. How much useful preparation this gave for subsequent operations in Helmand Province is uncertain. As civilians, we will never get to know just how authentic this faux Afghan enclave was but it's certainly a surreal notion to think that the equivalent of a one-time Taliban theme park once lay hidden out here in the Brecks.

With all this talk of where you cannot go, it is important to identify where you can. A couple of places on the fringes of the battle area give an authentic flavour of true Breckland heath. **East Wretham Heath**, off the A1075 and belonging to the Norfolk Wildlife Trust, has old pine woodland and grass heathland on what used to be an airfield. It also has a couple of meres (small lakes) that fluctuate depending on groundwater levels and recent rainfall. **Brettenham Heath**, nearby, has acid heath but no public access although you can view it from the Peddars Way. Of more interest to most and a great place for walking is **Thompson Common** on the eastern fringe of the battle area.

This NWT wetland area is best known for its three hundred or so pingo ponds that were created during the last glacial period. Pingos are mounds of earth-covered ice that collapse to form shallow depressions when the ice eventually melts. The pingo ponds, which provide habitat for rare water plants, dragonflies and damselflies, were formed here around 10,000 years ago. At least, that is the theory: I know of one geologist who maintains that they are more probably the result of ordnance testing on the battle area. For walkers, the **Great Eastern Pingo Trail** is a circular route that follows the route of a disused railway as well as part of the Peddars Way. It runs for around eight miles in total, taking in both Thompson and Stow Bedon commons and heathland at Great Hockham and Breckles. With luck, you'll see roe deer in the woodland rides. The route also passes through wet woodland at Cranberry Rough, which was once a large lake, the product of retreating glaciers of the last Ice Age. The former lake, known as Hockham Mere, was an important source of fish and wildfowl as recently as Tudor times but it eventually silted up to create the large swampy area that remains today. Now it is a designated Site of Special Scientific Interest with many species of plant, bird and insect – there are certainly plenty of mosquitoes here in summer. Access to the trail is from a car park on the A1075 Watton to Great Hockham road. There's a shorter alternative route too that cuts through woodland at Stow Heath and a short 'access for all' trail from the car park. The Peddars Way stretch of the trail goes right past Thompson Water, a shallow artificial lake created by damming the River Wissey in the 19th century, which is an excellent place to see grebes and reed warblers in summer and wildfowl in winter. As it's the only sizeable piece of water for miles around, even ospreys sometimes turn up here on passage.

¶¶ FOOD & DRINK

Chequers Inn Griston Rd, Thompson ✆ 01953 483360 ♦ thompsonchequers.co.uk. This attractive 17th-century thatched inn opposite the village cricket pitch has seen service as a manor court, doctor's surgery and meeting room in the past. Today it's a village pub convenient for the Great Eastern Pingo Trail. There's decent pub grub, cooked using ingredients from local Norfolk suppliers, and a reasonable range of real ales.

ACCOMMODATION

The places to stay listed below have been selected for their location and because they embrace the Slow mindset, either in terms of their overall feel or because they embody a 'green' approach. Prices for hotels vary, but two people sharing a room in a B&B can expect to spend around £80–100 per night. Holiday cottage prices also cover a wide range, depending on capacity, season and location. Of course, school holidays mean peak prices. There is plenty to be said for visiting out of season in order to save money. Campsites run the gamut from no-frills to luxurious 'glamping' options.

The hotels and B&Bs featured in this section are indicated by 🏠 under the heading for the town or village in which they are located. Self-catering options are indicated by 🏡 and campsites by ⛺. For complete listings, go to ◈ bradtguides.com/norfolksleeps.

1 THE NORTH NORFOLK COAST

Hotels
Gunton Arms Cromer Rd, Thorpe Market NR11 8TZ ◈ 01263 832101 ◈ theguntonarms.co.uk
Titchwell Manor Titchwell, near Brancaster PE31 8BB ◈ 01485 472027 ◈ titchwellmanor.com
The White Horse Brancaster Staithe PE31 8BY ◈ 01485 210262 ◈ whitehorsebrancaster.co.uk

B&Bs
Cley Windmill The Quay, Cley-next-the-Sea NR25 7RP ◈ 01263 740209 ◈ cleywindmill.co.uk. Self-catering is also available in the converted stable building.

Self-catering
Albert's Cottage Wells-next-the-Sea ◈ cottage-choice.co.uk
Bagthorpe Treehouse Bagthorpe Hall near Burnham Market ◈ 0117 2047830 ◈ canopyandstars.co.uk
Cliff Cottage Sheringham ◈ 07791 870948 ◈ sheringhamsalt.com
Little Orchard Cley-next-the-Sea ◈ glavenvalley.co.uk
The Maltings Brancaster Staithe ◈ norfolkhideaways.co.uk
The Music Room Thornham ◈ holidaycottage.com
Sea View Barn Titchwell ◈ norfolkhideaways.co.uk

Camping
Bumblebarn Sheringham ◈ 07500 003612 ◈ bumblebarn.co.uk
Deepdale Camping & Rooms Deepdale Farm, Burnham Deepdale PE31 8DD ◈ 01485 210256 ◈ deepdalebackpackers.co.uk; page 67.
Kelling Heath Holiday Park Weybourne, Holt NR25 7HW ◈ 01263 588181 ◈ kellingheath.co.uk
Scaldbeck Cottage Campsite Stiffkey Rd, Morston NR25 7BJ ◈ 01263 740188 ◈ scaldbeckcottagecampsite.co.uk
Wild Luxury Thornham Bay ◈ 01485 750850 ◈ wildluxury.co.uk

2 THE NORTHEAST NORFOLK COAST & THE BROADS

Hotel
Norfolk Mead Hotel Coltishall NR12 7DJ ✆ 01603 737531 ⌂ norfolkmead.co.uk

B&Bs
The Green House Cromer Rd, Thorpe Market ✆ 01263 834701 ⌂ thegreenhousenorfolk.co.uk
Lawson Cottage Stubb Rd, Hickling NR12 0YS ✆ 01692 597016 ⌂ lawsoncottage.com

Camping
Clippesby Hall Touring & Camping Park Clippesby NR29 3BL ✆ 01493 367800 ⌂ clippesbyhall.com
Lanterns Shepherds Huts & Glamping Lantern Ln, Happisburgh NR12 0QD ✆ 07900 201101 ⌂ lanterns-shepherds-huts-and-glamping.co.uk

3 NORTH CENTRAL NORFOLK

Hotel
The Dial House Reepham NR10 4JJ ✆ 01603 879900 ⌂ thedialhouse.org.uk
Greenbanks Hotel Main Rd, Great Fransham NR19 2DA ✆ 01362 687742 ⌂ greenbankshotel.co.uk

B&Bs
Byfords Posh B&B 1–3 Shirehall Plain, Holt NR25 6BG ✆ 01263 711400 ⌂ byfords.org.uk/posh-bb
Carrick's at Castle Farm Swanton Morley, Dereham NR20 4JT ✆ 01362 638302 ⌂ carricksatcastlefarm.co.uk
The Old Bakehouse 33 High St, Little Walsingham NR22 6BZ ✆ 01328 820377 ⌂ walsinghambakehouse.com
White Horse Barn Sharrington Rd, Holt NR24 2PB ✆ 01263 860693 ⌂ white-horse-farm.co.uk

Self-catering
Fox Cottage South Creake ⌂ norfolkhideaways.com
Garden Cottage Manor House Farm, Wellingham, King's Lynn PE32 2TH ✆ 01328 838348 ⌂ manor-house-farm.co.uk
Norfolk Courtyard Westfield Fram, Foxley Rd, Foulsham NR20 5RH ✆ 07969 611510 ⌂ norfolkcourtyard.co.uk

Camping
Deer's Glade Caravan & Camping Park Whitepost Rd, Hanworth NR11 7HN ✆ 01263 768633 ⌂ deersglade.co.uk

USEFUL BOOKING WEBSITES

B&Bs
Norfolk Bed and Breakfasts ⌂ norfolk-bed-and-breakfast.co.uk. More than 250 properties that can be searched for online according to location and facilities.
Self-catering
Glaven Valley ⌂ glavenvalley.co.uk. A large range of cottages in north Norfolk.

Norfolk Cottages ✆ 01263 715779 ⌂ norfolkcottages.co.uk. Hundreds of Norfolk cottages.
Norfolk Hideaways ✆ 01485 558547 ⌂ norfolkhideaways.co.uk. Over 500 cottages to rent throughout the county.
Sowerby's Holiday Cottages ✆ 01328 730880 ⌂ sowerbysholidaycottages.co.uk. A large selection in north Norfolk.

4 NORTHWEST NORFOLK & THE WASH

Hotels

Congham Hall Hotel Lynn Rd, Grimston PE32 1AH ✆ 01485 600250 ⊘ conghamhallhotel.co.uk
The Lodge Old Hunstanton Rd, Old Hunstanton PE36 6HX ✆ 01485 532896 ⊘ thelodgehunstanton.co.uk
Rose and Crown Old Church Rd, Snettisham PE31 7LX ✆ 01485 543172 ⊘ roseandcrownsnettisham.co.uk

Self-catering

The Summerhouse Heacham ⊘ big-cottages.com

5 NORWICH & THE YARE VALLEY

Hotels

Maids Head Hotel Tombland, Norwich NR3 1LB ✆ 01603 209955 ⊘ maidsheadhotel.co.uk
The Swan Hotel Church Plain, Loddon NR14 6LX ✆ 01508 528039 ⊘ theloddonswan.co.uk

B&B

38 St Giles St Giles St, Norwich NR2 1LL ✆ 01603 662944 ⊘ 38stgiles.co.uk
The Cockatrice Ferry Rd, Norton Subcourse, Reedham NR14 6SF ⊘ booking.com
The Parson Woodforde Church St, Weston Longville NR9 5JU ✆ 01603 881675 ⊘ theparsonwoodforde.com

Self-catering

Wellington Apartments 60 St Faiths Ln, Norwich NR1 1NN ✆ 01603 551655 ⊘ wellingtonapartments.co.uk

Camping

The Old Vicarage Moulton St Mary NR13 3NH ⊘ oldvicaragecamping.co.uk
Whitlingham Broad Campsite Whitlingham Ln, Trowse NR14 8TR ✆ 07794 401952 ⊘ whitlinghambroadcampsite.com

6 THE WAVENEY VALLEY

Hotel

The Castle Inn 35 Earsham St, Bungay NR35 1AF ✆ 01986 892283 ⊘ the-castle-inn.co.uk

B&B

Grove Barn Middle Rd, Denton, Harleston IP20 0AH ✆ 01986 788015 ⊘ grovebarnbedandbreakfast.com

Self-catering

The Old Bike Shop Brockdish, near Harleston ⊘ cottages.com

Camping

Waveney River Centre Burgh St Peter NR34 0BT ✆ 01502 677343 ⊘ waveneyrivercentre.co.uk

7 THE BRECKS

Hotel

Bedingfeld Arms The Green, Oxborough PE33 9PS ✆ 01366 328300 ⊘ bedingfeldarms.co.uk

B&B

Acer Lodge Ashburton Rd, Mundford, IP26 5JA ✆ 01842 878026 ⊘ acerlodgenorfolk.co.uk

Self-catering

Garden House Northwold IP26 5NF ⊘ sykescottages.co.uk
Honey Pots Foulden, near Oxborough, IP26 5AR ⊘ cottages.com

Camping

Spring Farm Little Hale, Shipdham IP25 7PL ✆ 01362 822109 ⊘ springfarmcampsite.co.uk

INDEX

Page numbers in **bold** refer to main entries; *italics* refer to walk maps.

Z

INDEX OF ADVERTISERS

In the beginning

It all began in 1974 on an Amazon river barge. During an 18-month trip through South America, two adventurous young backpackers – Hilary Bradt and her then husband, George – decided to write about the hiking trails they had discovered through the Andes. *Backpacking Along Ancient Ways in Peru and Bolivia* included the very first descriptions of the Inca Trail. It was the start of a colourful journey to becoming one of the best-loved travel publishers in the world; you can read the full story on our website (www. bradtguides.com/ourstory).

Getting there first

Hilary quickly gained a reputation for being a true travel pioneer, and in the 1980s she started to focus on guides to places overlooked by other publishers. The Bradt Guides list became a roll call of guidebook 'firsts'. We published the first guide to Madagascar, followed by Mauritius, Czechoslovakia, and Vietnam. The 1990s saw the beginning of our extensive coverage of Africa: Tanzania, Uganda, South Africa, and Eritrea. Later, post-conflict guides became a feature: Rwanda, Mozambique, Angola, Sierra Leone, Bosnia and Kosovo.

Comprehensive – and with a conscience

Today, we are the world's largest independently owned travel publisher, with more than 200 titles, from full-country and wildlife guides to Slow Travel guides like this one. However, our ethos remains unchanged. Hilary is still keenly involved, and we still get there first: two-thirds of Bradt guides have no direct competition.

But we don't just get there first. Our guides are also known for being more comprehensive than any other series. We avoid templates and tick-lists. Each guide is a one-of-a-kind expression of an expert author's interests, knowledge and enthusiasm for telling it how it really is.

And a commitment to wildlife, conservation and respect for local communities has always been at the heart of our books. Bradt Guides was championing sustainable travel before any other guidebook publisher.

Thank you!

We can only do what we do because of the support of readers like you – people who value less-obvious experiences, less-visited places and a more thoughtful approach to travel. Those who, like us, take travel seriously.

Bradt GUIDES
TRAVEL TAKEN SERIOUSLY